AF606019

CHINESE SCIENCE FICTION DURING THE POST-MAO CULTURAL THAW

HUA LI

Chinese Science Fiction during the Post-Mao Cultural Thaw

UNIVERSITY OF TORONTO PRESS
Toronto Buffalo London

© University of Toronto Press 2021
Toronto Buffalo London
utorontopress.com
Printed in the U.S.A.

ISBN 978-1-4875-0823-4 (cloth) ISBN 978-1-4875-3781-4 (EPUB)
ISBN 978-1-4875-3780-7 (PDF)

Library and Archives Canada Cataloguing in Publication

Title: Chinese science fiction during the post-Mao cultural thaw / Hua Li.
Names: Li, Hua, 1969–, author.
Description: Includes bibliographical references and index.
Identifiers: Canadiana (print) 20210154942 | Canadiana (ebook) 20210154977 | ISBN 9781487508234 (cloth) | ISBN 9781487537814 (EPUB) | ISBN 9781487537807 (PDF)
Subjects: LCSH: Science fiction, Chinese – 20th century – History and criticism.
Classification: LCC PL2275.S34 L53 2021 | DDC 895.13/0876209 – dc23

This book has been published with the assistance of the Dean's Office of the College of Letters and Science, Montana State University.

University of Toronto Press acknowledges the financial assistance to its publishing program of the Canada Council for the Arts and the Ontario Arts Council, an agency of the Government of Ontario.

Canada Council for the Arts Conseil des Arts du Canada

Funded by the Government of Canada | Financé par le gouvernement du Canada | Canada

Contents

Figures

Acknowledgments

Writing an academic book can be a lonely journey. Along that road, I have nonetheless encountered many writers and scholars who share my passion about the world beyond our immediate reality. They have helped me in various ways: reading and providing feedback on my manuscript at various stages of this project, letting me interview them, sharing precious primary source materials and photos, and offering comments on my research presentations at various conferences. They are: Ye Yonglie, Philip F. Williams, Wu Yan, Yao Haijun, Liu Xingshi, Zhang Feng, Liu Jian, Jiang Zhenyu, Veronica Hollinger, Allan Barr, Mingwei Song, Nathaniel Isaacson, Xinmin Liu, Cara Healey, Zhan Ling, and Wang Yao. I would also like to thank the two anonymous external reviewers who have given me insightful and constructive criticism and suggestions to greatly improve the quality of this book. Moreover, I wish to thank my editors at University of Toronto Press, Mark Thompson, Janice Evans, and Ian MacKenzie, whose professionalism and efficiency have guided this project forward.

My thanks also go to Montana State University (MSU), where I have worked since 2009. I am grateful that the MSU and College of Letters and Sciences have provided research support in the form of a Scholarship & Creativity Grant, Faculty Enhancement Grant, sabbatical leave, and research and conference travel grants. I would like to thank the MSU Library for having facilitated numerous inter-library loans. I also want to thank *Science Fiction Studies* and *The Association for Chinese Animation Studies* for having granted me permission to reprint some excerpts from articles I published in these two academic journals. My thanks also go to Chen Wei for having granted me permission to use his art work on the front cover of this book.

CHINESE SCIENCE FICTION DURING THE POST-MAO CULTURAL THAW

1 The Field of Chinese Science Fiction, 1976–1983

Chinese science fiction has gained increased visibility among both academic specialists and general readers in the West as more English translations of Chinese science fiction works have become available and Chinese writers have won prestigious prizes worldwide. Academic research on Chinese science fiction (hereafter SF) in the West has also tried to catch up with the achievements of SF writers themselves in recent years with the publication of monographs, translations, special issues of journals, and journal articles. For example, Mingwei Song edited a special issue of *Renditions: Chinese Science Fiction: Late Qing and Contemporary* in 2012 to introduce Western readers to several Chinese SF narratives written between 1900 and 2010. In 2013, Wu Yan and Veronica Hollinger co-edited a special issue of *Science Fiction Studies,* which includes ten critical essays on Chinese SF. In 2017, Nicolai Volland published *Socialist Cosmopolitanism: The Chinese Literary Universe, 1945–1965,* which contains sections on Chinese SF during the Mao era. In the same year, Nathaniel Isaacson published *Celestial Empire: The Emergence of Chinese Science Fiction,* which traces the origins and early development of Chinese SF from the late Qing dynasty to the New Culture Movement (1890s–1919). These works have been limited primarily to the three "SF boom" periods of the first couple of decades of the twentieth century, the 1950s to 1960s, and from the 1990s to the present. Though some researchers such as Dingbo Wu, Rui Kunze, Rudolph Wagner, and Paola Lovene have published essays and book chapters on Chinese SF from the late 1970s to the early 1980s, many questions remain to be explored about Chinese SF during this important moment in the history of Chinese SF. It is a bridge between the SF of the 1950s and 1960s that popularized science and what Mingwei Song has called New Wave Chinese SF from the late twentieth century to the early twenty-first century.[1]

This chapter provides a comprehensive introduction to Chinese SF during the post-Mao cultural thaw. It describes how the field works and how we can make sense of it, while attending to its logics and practices in the context of the time. It will also help us gain a more nuanced understanding of Chinese literature during this period. In general, the post-Mao thaw begins with the death of Mao in 1976 and ends in 1983 with the Chinese government's "Campaign to Eliminate Spiritual Pollution."[2] But in order to clarify a few issues, some of the phenomena to be discussed in this book will extend as far back as the 1950s and as far forward as the 1990s.

Chinese SF is cultural, political, and commercial. In *Popular Fiction: The Logics and Practices of a Literary Field*, Ken Gelder indicates that academic articles on popular fiction have mainly conformed with the approach of "form and ideology" interpretation, but he finds the method inadequate for analysing popular fiction. Gelder criticizes the way academics have often engaged in "reading out of or from the novels themselves in order to say something about their relationship to their genres, or in order to deduce something about their specific social or ideological function."[3] He advocates a kind of "quasi-academic or para-academic reading" of popular fiction: an interpretive approach "involving publishers and bookstores, organizations committed to genre fiction, fanzines and prozines (professional genre magazines), and an extraordinarily wide range of fans and readers."[4] On the one hand, "much of this activity is in fact academic in its own way, often concentrating on the finer details of the fiction and even working at the level of literary scholarship"; on the other hand, this approach provides "detailed attention to a literary field outside of the university,"[5] which is an appealing alternative to conventional form-and-ideology interpretations of popular fiction.

In this chapter, I adopt Gelder's method of "para-academic reading" to approach Chinese SF as a type of cultural product, and try to provide a relatively comprehensive picture of the field by examining the production, distribution, and consumption of Chinese SF from 1976 to 1983. I shall also draw upon Pierre Bourdieu's theories about cultural production. Bourdieu describes types of capital that cultural producers accumulate in what he calls the "field of cultural production."[6] Bourdieu points out that a cultural field is "structured by the distribution of available positions (e.g., consecrated artist vs. striving artist, novel vs. poetry, art for art's sake vs. socially engaged art) and by the objective characteristics of the agents occupying them."[7] Bourdieu refers to positions within a cultural field as the "space of creative works" and argues that a field of cultural production results from interactions among different cultural-social positions.[8]

I am aware that both scholars' methodologies and theories are based on Western literary works and their cultural fields in a Western cultural context. In contrast, Chinese SF during the post-Mao thaw era was situated in a transitional period between the Party leadership of Hua Guofeng's "whateverist" faction (meaning that whatever Mao Zedong said was absolutely "correct") to the leadership of Deng Xiaoping's "reform and opening" faction, and from an old-style state socialist planned economy to a diversified mixed economy. My practical solution is to analyse the socio-political and cultural factors that have coloured Chinese SF, and reveal how it has been shaped by socio-political and cultural circumstances that are largely peculiar to China. I shall examine the political approval or disapproval that a given work of Chinese SF received at a particular time, along with the production, distribution, and consumption of Chinese SF works from 1976 to 1983. Upon that basis, I shall argue that Chinese SF of the post-Mao cultural thaw had striven to overcome the limitations of both *kexue wenyi* (literature and art about science) and children's literature, and thereby took its rightful place in Chinese literature as an independent subgenre of popular fiction.

Chinese Literary Fiction and Political Approval of Chinese Science Fiction

In his research on Russian SF written during the former Soviet post-Stalin thaw (1953–72), Istvan Csicsery-Ronay proposes that the new scientific intelligentsia and the centrality of literature in people's daily lives provided a foundation upon which SF could thrive in Russia. He further argues that none of the SF from other countries or during other historical periods "has had as much immediate impact on the public sphere, the political culture, and the currents of mainstream literature" as that of the Soviet post-Stalin thaw.[9] Moreover, SF literature was viewed as "a potent threat by the ruling order."[10] His depiction of the status of SF during the Soviet thaw resembles the milieu of Chinese SF written during the post-Mao thaw.

During the post-Mao cultural thaw, Chinese literary fiction experienced two major phases: a "warming" period of more relaxed political controls from 1976 to 1979 during which "scar" literary exposés such as Liu Xinwu's (b. 1942) "The Homeroom Teacher" ("Ban zhuren," 1977) and Lu Xinhua's (b. 1954) "Scar" ("Shanghen," 1978) were published; and a "cooling" period of tighter political controls from 1980 to 1983 during which the influential "contemplative" (*fansi*) literary works such as Yu Luojin's (b. 1946) *A Winter Fairy Tale* (*Yige dongtian de tonghua*, 1980) and Dai Houying's (1938–96) *Ah! Humanity* (*Ren a, ren!* 1980) were published.[11]

The period in the late 1970s became known to Chinese as "scar literature" (*shanghen wenxue*). Perry Link compares this post-Mao Chinese "scar literature" to the "thaw literature" that followed the death of Stalin in the former Soviet Union because of similarities between the two periods. First, the historical situations were similar. The literary scenes of both countries had just endured a literary deep freeze (1946–53 in the Soviet Union, and 1966–76 in China) when outlets for literary and artistic creativity were mostly suppressed or even nonexistent. There was no prospect that the literary deep freeze would come to an end prior to the deaths of the countries' all-powerful heads of state: the USSR's Stalin in 1953 and the PRC's Mao Zedong in 1976. New leadership in both countries "sought a return to a more normal [state] socialist situation."[12] Both PRC leader Deng Xiaoping and Soviet leader Nikita Khrushchev cited literary critiques of the recent past to rally support for their new policies. The fluctuating literary warm and cool spells reflected changes in the countries' political weather. Meanwhile, intellectuals and especially writers stepped into the limelight as the "conscience of society," not only exposing "previous forbidden truths," but also to "speak out against corrupt and incompetent authority."[13] In addition, love interests and humanist thought became prominent literary features in the literature of both countries. Publication of Lu Xinhua's "Scar" in 1978 was as significant as that of Ilya Ehrenburg's novel *The Thaw* in Russia in 1954. The terms "scar" and "thaw" were used to refer to literature written during the thaw in each country. Popular response to the scar and thaw literature was mostly enthusiastic in both countries. It was reflected in a broadening readership, a rapid increase in the number and circulation of literary periodicals, and the launch of unofficial journals. The "scar" or "thaw" phenomena eventually subsided after a few years, whereupon literature entered a stage of greater pluralism, which included "roots-seeking literature" (*xungen wenxue*), modernism, avant-garde experimentation, and reportage fiction.[14]

Just as in the former Soviet Union, literature played a central role in the lives of many educated Chinese during the thaw. According to Link, "In life within the system, Chinese writers, readers, critics, and political authorities – though sometimes holding very different or even opposing views on various matters – agreed almost unanimously in the assumption that literature is relevant, or even essential, to morality, social life, and politics at every level from the policymaking of the highest leadership to the daily life of the average reader."[15] The importance of literature to many facets of contemporary life provided an impetus for the revival and flourishing of SF in China.

In his study of cultural production, Bourdieu claims that "the field of cultural production is structured, in the broadest sense, by an opposition between two sub-fields: the field of restricted production and the field of large-scale production."[16] "Restricted production" normally refers to high art, such as "classical music, the plastic arts, and 'serious' literature."[17] It is located at the autonomous pole in the field because it is based on symbolic capital and influenced mostly by internal or intrinsic factors. The sub-field of large-scale production involves mass or popular culture, such as television, most cinematic productions, radio programs, and mass-produced literature. This sub-field is located at "the heteronomous pole" because it is based mainly on economic capital and influenced mostly by external or extrinsic factors.[18] If we adapt Bourdieu's paradigm in our examination of Chinese literature, Chinese literary fiction belongs in the realm of high culture, which is characterized as autonomous and influenced mostly by intrinsic factors; in contrast, popular fiction belongs in low or middlebrow culture, which is heteronomous and influenced mostly by extrinsic factors.

Chinese literary fiction produced by such writers as Liu Xinwu, Bai Hua, and Dai Houying has typically been categorized as *chun wenxue* (pure literature) or *yansu wenxue* (serious literature). In contrast, popular literature and popular fiction have generally been categorized as *tongsu wenxue* or *tongsu xiaoshuo* and include such genres as detective thrillers, romance novels, martial arts fiction, and SF. Chinese literary fiction has often been somewhat elitist. Its elitism is evident not only in how it is typically considered "pure" or "serious" literature, but also in its themes, publication venues, and readership, along with the identity of its writers as serious artists. Though some serious literary works such as Liu Xinwu's "The Homeroom Teacher" and Dai Houying's *Ah! Humanity* became extremely popular soon after their publication, these authors identify themselves and are recognized as creators of serious literature, not purveyors of popular fiction. Their writings are not associated with any specific genre; instead, their works are identified by theme and typically labelled as "scar literature" or "contemplative literature." Furthermore, many writers of literary fiction made great effort to distinguish their works from popular fiction and express their concern about the artistic and imaginative features of their fiction. This emphasis on the artistic merit of literature comes across clearly in two literary conferences held in 1980. Xia Yan, the vice minister of culture at the time, asserted that "a narrowly dogmatic interpretation of the slogans 'the arts serve politics' and 'the arts are subordinate to politics' resulted in a decline or even complete disappearance of artistic standards in China since 1949."[19] Xia's remarks garnered an enthusiastic reception from the writers in attendance. For example, the novelist Bai Hua emphasized the importance of characterization in a literary work: "The strength of literature resides in the forcefulness of its characterization; the writer's skilled characterization conjures forth the typicality of everyday people.... A serious and responsible writer ... will always create his characters in accordance with the canons of realism."[20] Moreover, these mainstream writers usually have a sense of mission. The critic Feng Mu addressed this issue, arguing that high-quality literature aims to raise the level of the reader's consciousness and to make the reader's thought processes purer and more focused; in this way, the reader could cultivate a more profound sensibility and more lofty ideals.[21] Bai Hua also insisted that "a writer must stand on the high ground of history and bear responsibility to the people."[22]

Literary fiction has usually been published in major literary magazines. Li Jingze points out that in the 1980s, literary magazines were almost the sole publication venues for literary writers and the only mechanism for selecting literary works of high quality and discovering new talent.[23] Aside from the prestigious *People's Literature* (*Renmin wenxue*) launched in 1949, four major literary magazines were established in the country. *October* (*Shiyue*) was launched in August 1978 by the Beijing Press; after a long hiatus during the late Mao era, *Harvest* (*Shouhuo*) resumed publication in 1979 through the Shanghai Writers Association; the first issue of *Flower City* (*Hua cheng*) was published in May 1979 by the Guangdong People's Press; and *Contemporary* (*Dangdai*) was inaugurated at the end of 1979.[24] In addition to these major literary magazines, many regional literary periodicals were sponsored by provincial and municipal writers' associations. Pure literary magazines comprised approximately one-eighth of all magazines published in the 1980s.[25]

Though these Chinese writers aim to write for the masses and emphasize the social function of their works, the readership of literary fiction has been relatively small in comparison with that of popular fiction. In Perry Link's discussion of the readership of Chinese literature in the 1980s, he argues that "the masses in socialist China generally did not read" because of factors such as widespread illiteracy and the cost of books and magazines.[26] An overwhelming majority of Chinese readers of literature were urbanites, and fewer than 40 per cent of even these urbanites read literature. Link divides this urban readership into popular readership, a socially engaged readership, and an elite readership. The popular readership, composed mainly of young workers in the cities, preferred reading popular fiction and found "literary works [here referring to serious literature] too difficult, and perhaps too political, for their tastes."[27] Therefore, the readership of serious literature consisted mainly of socially engaged readers and elite readers "who were drawn to literature for its critiques of society and politics," or "whose purposes were less time-bound, more literary, and often more academic."[28] The urban population ranged between17.9 and 22.9 per cent of the total Chinese population between 1978 and 1985.[29] Therefore, the maximum readership of literary fiction was much less than 10 per cent of China's population during the first half of the 1980s.

Chinese fiction writers during this time did not care greatly about how well their books sold; their key concern was to cater to the political sensibilities of their readership. Most PRC writers of this period held salaried positions in governmental work units in the cultural realm, or at least were members of the Chinese Writers Association. Gaining profits or large sales from their books was not a major concern. However, an enthusiastic reception from their largely elite readership would help them gain symbolic and political capital. Though these writers criticized the way that "political interference ruined literature and made it impossible for many good writers to write," they were almost always careful to avoid crossing any red lines of ideological correctness.[30] The widespread popularity of a literary work meant that it probably exerted positive social effects on society and catered to the needs of the masses.

The above discussion shows that serious Chinese fiction during the post-Mao era was generally "self-contained, enclosed, and completed by the author's apparent uniqueness."[31] It was underwritten by a sense of creativity and originality, and used relatively artistic language. Its authors emphasized its social function by self-identifying as serious writers of literature. The readership of serious literature was relatively small, and its publication venues were confined mainly to literary magazines of limited popularity. These authors of serious literature thus situated themselves in Bourdieu's "field of restricted production" at the autonomous end of the spectrum of Chinese literature.[32]

Chinese SF contrasts with the elitism and autonomous traits of Chinese serious fiction. The following section examines the ways in which Chinese SF was produced and consumed: its political and social milieu, its publication venues and readership, its professional and fan organizations, its prozines and fanzines, and its critical evaluations and awards. An understanding of these factors will help reveal how Chinese SF of the post-Mao thaw strove to overcome its former categorization as a mere subgenre of *kexue wenyi* or mere children's literature, to rise to the level of popular fiction and bona fide Chinese literature.

Though SF is a subgenre of popular fiction, it has been very different from other popular fiction in China, such as the romance, the detective thriller, and martial arts fiction, which are designed mainly for entertainment and commercial purposes. Ever since the emergence of Chinese SF during the late Qing dynasty, it has been always a utilitarian subgenre and closely related to politics. During the first half of the twentieth century, Chinese SF commonly advocated modernization and promoted modern science. During the Mao era, it became a vehicle for moulding new socialist man by popularization of modern science and technology, among young people in particular. During the post-Mao thaw, Chinese SF responded to the Party's imperative to achieve the Four Modernizations. However, the post-Mao era also witnessed a new tendency in Chinese SF of making itself more appealing as popular fiction, and avoiding its earlier straitjacket of being merely a politicized utilitarian genre. Chinese SF increasingly accumulated symbolic, cultural, and economic capital and took its position at the heteronomous pole in the spectrum of Chinese literature.

In the PRC since the 1950s, Chinese SF has often been categorized as children's literature. Educating the younger generation became an even higher priority after Mao Zedong declared in 1957 that the future belongs to young people. Equipping the younger generation with a basic knowledge of modern science and technology became a major part of the country's educational agenda. In the 1950s and 1960s, Chinese SF works were written mainly for juvenile readers, and were published in children's magazines or by presses catering to juvenile readers in Shanghai and Beijing.[33] Sometimes SF writers benefited from the label of children's literature because it provided them with a relatively relaxed space in which to explore controversial and forward-looking ideas that would be difficult to articulate effectively in most genres of serious or realist literature.[34]

Chinese SF has also been a sub-branch of *kexue wenyi*. The Russian version of the term *kexue wenyi* was coined by the former USSR writer Maxim Gorky (1868–1936) in his essay "On Theme," in which he encouraged scientists to delve into the literature and urged fiction writers to explore the world of science. In this way, science and literature could possibly form an alliance. The popular science writer Mikhail Il'in (1896–1953) put Gorky's advocacy into practice by writing science primers and essays about science during the 1930s and 1950s. Many of his works were translated into Chinese and exerted a profound influence upon Chinese intellectuals and readers during the 1950s and 1960s.[35] In Zheng Wenguang's (1929–2003) essay "A Miscellany on Literature and Art about Science," he divided the works of *kexue wenyi* into two categories: popular science writing (*wenyi xing de kexue duwu*) and literary works with scientific themes (*yi kexue wei zhuti de wenyi zuopin*). Popular science writing uses literary language to make scientific knowledge more accessible to readers, especially juvenile readers. This body of writing includes science primers, science essays, scientific accounts, descriptions of scientific research, and science travelogues. Literary works with scientific themes are defined as genuine imaginative literature and typically emphasize literary qualities such as characterization, plot development, flights of imagination, and narrative techniques. These works include SF, science fairy tales (including science fairy tale films), science poetry, and comedic dialogues with scientific themes. Within the broad spectrum of *kexue wenyi*, with non-fiction narratives about science at one end and literature at the other, science primers, science essays, science travelogues, and descriptions of scientific research are closer to the pole of science; science stories, comedic dialogues about science, and science fairy tales are in the middle of the spectrum; and SF is closest to the pole of literature.[36]

During the post-Mao era, though many SF narratives were still published by children's literature presses and juvenile magazines, and played the practical role of popularizing modern science and technology, this genre vigorously went beyond the categorical confines of *kexue wenyi* and children's literature, having manifested characteristics of popular fiction such as a burgeoning readership, a large circulation, a variety of publication venues, fanzines and fan clubs, writers' increased remuneration, multimedia adaptions, and awards.

Similar to literary fiction, Chinese SF also experienced a warming period from 1976 to 1978, during which the central government affirmed the importance of science and technology as a part of the Four Modernizations, and many SF writers resumed their creative writing. Two especially clear political signs of a literary thaw occurred soon after Mao's death in 1976. One was the gradual reappearance of pre–Cultural Revolution literary figures such as Zhou Yang, Xia Yan, Mao Dun, and Zhou Libo, all of whom had fallen into obscurity or had been denounced during the Cultural Revolution. Another was the gradual return of the Soviet-style literary administration that had been in place in the 1950s and early 1960s. For example, provincial branches of the state-run Chinese Writers Association announced their reopening and launched their own literary magazines.[37] In a similar way, the SF field also witnessed the return of veteran SF writers and the re-establishment of its own associations. More importantly, popular science writing received a special endorsement from the central government.

On 18–21 March 1978, the National Science Conference was convened in the Great Hall of the People in Beijing. Deng Xiaoping gave a speech at the opening ceremony, which emphasized three points. First, he affirmed that science and technology were productive forces. He also claimed that among the Four Modernizations, the modernization of science and technology was key. Highly educated professionals such as intellectuals, scientists, and technicians would henceforth be considered part of the working class – implying that they would no longer fall under suspicion as "bourgeois elements," as was common during the Mao era. Second, Deng called for the building of a science and technology community whose members would be politically sound at the same time they were professionally competent – scientists would no longer be judged by the Mao-era dichotomy of red versus expert. Third, he laid down guidelines for the sub-branches of Party committees in research institutes and science and technology units to collaborate with the intelligentsia.[38] Many scientists and other intellectuals were moved to tears upon hearing Deng affirm the central importance of science and technology in the Four Modernizations and insist that intellectuals would now be considered an integral part of the working class.[39]

Responding to Deng's talk, the first National Conference of Popular Science Creative Writing was convened in Shanghai on 23 May 1978. More than 300 renowned scientists, editors, and popular science writers attended this conference, and they celebrated the arrival of a new springtime for science in China. The China Popular Science Creative Writing Association was subsequently founded in 1979, and nearly all PRC SF writers joined. In August of that year, the association launched the first issue of *Popular Science Creative Writing* (*Kepu chuangzuo*), which included physicist Zhou Peiyuan's (1902–93) "Embrace the Springtime for Popular Science Creative Writing," the physicist Qian Sanqiang's (1913–92) "Contribute to the Improvement of the Scientific and Cultural Level of the Chinese Nation," and the SF writer Zheng Wenguang's "On the Prosperity of Popular Science Creative Writing."[40] Amidst this warm and optimistic environment, many veteran SF writers returned to popular science writing. Inevitably associated with its most prominent authors were Tong Enzheng (1935–97), Zheng Wenguang, Ye Yonglie (1940–2020), Liu Xingshi (b. 1931), and Xiao Jianheng (b. 1930). Most of them had been prolific writers prior to the outbreak of the Cultural Revolution in 1966. This large creative community also included mainstream literary writers such as Yan Jiaqi (b. 1942) and Meng Weizai (1933–2015). Most SF writers were faithful Marxists and Communists who took Deng Xiaoping and his Party at their word when the central government promised to reform socialism and emancipate science for the good of China and humankind alike.

The year 1976 witnessed the publication of the first SF work since the Cultural Revolution – Ye Yonglie's "Petroleum Protein" ("Shiyou danbai"). During the following year, Ye Yonglie, Xiao Jianheng, and Wang Yafa (b. 1947) published three more SF works. The year 1978 saw an even greater increase of SF writing. *A Compendium of Chinese Science Fiction* includes forty-two stories published in literary magazines during 1978.[41] The SF scene was permeated with a resurgence of creative vitality. The successful reception of Tong Enzheng's "Death Ray on a Coral Island" ("Shanhu dao shang de siguang") heralded the boom in SF that lasted from 1979 through 1982. Meanwhile, the political climate had also become more favourable for writing SF than at any time in the PRC since 1949.

The Fourth National Congress of Writers and Artists was convened in Beijing from 30 October to 16 November 1979. Deng Xiaoping gave a talk on 30 October to promise writers and artists a new era of creative freedom: "Literature and art involve complicated mental work. This work requires writers and artists to develop their individual creativity. Writers and artists should explore and find solutions through practice, and decide what to write and how to write. There should be no arbitrary interference in this process [from Party committees]."[42] In his speech, Deng also encouraged the publication of more SF works. On 26 July 1980, the Party leadership unveiled its "long-awaited" and "carefully wrought" slogan: "Literature in service of the people and of socialism" to replace Mao's "Literature in the service of politics," which had dominated mainland Chinese literature and arts in the wake of Mao's prescriptive "Yan'an Talks" of 1942.[43] Taking advantage of the unusually relaxed political atmosphere, popular science journals, SF magazines, mainstream literary magazines, and even influential newspapers all provided publication venues for SF.

Meanwhile, the translation of foreign SF works helped stimulate the growth of Chinese SF writing. The years between 1979 and 1982 witnessed the PRC's largest increase since 1949 in the dissemination of imported literature, movies, and TV shows. Besides reprinting classic SF narratives by Western authors such as Jules Verne (1828–1905) and H.G. Wells (1866–1946), the works of more recent Western writers were also translated and introduced to Chinese readers, such as the works of Arthur C. Clarke (1917–2008), George Lucas (b. 1944), and Isaac Asimov (1920–92). During these years of the cultural thaw, a large number of Soviet SF works were also translated into Chinese, such as A. Kazantsev's (1906–2002) *Strong Times*, and Alexander Belyaev's (1884–1962) novels *Glittering Man* and *Master of the World*. The works of Japanese writers such as Sakyo Komatsu (1931–2011) and Takashi Ishikawa (b. 1953) were also translated into Chinese.[44] These foreign SF works introduced Chinese readers and writers to an even broader range of subject matter and techniques, and inspired Chinese writers to experiment with this unprecedented, wide variety of subject matter and techniques. It was during this period that many Chinese SF narratives transcended the limitations of juvenile literature and achieved breakthroughs in form, content, and technique. There were as many as 150 SF authors active in China during the post-Mao thaw.[45]

However, this favourable political climate for SF did not last long. A "Campaign to Eliminate Spiritual Pollution" was launched by the Communist Party with Deng Xiaoping's speech at the Second Plenum of the Twelfth Central Committee on 11–12 October 1983. The campaign aimed to root out Western-inspired liberal ideas among the Chinese populace. Deng defined the substance of spiritual pollution as "disseminating all varieties of corrupt and decadent ideologies of the bourgeoisie and other exploiting classes and disseminating sentiments of distrust towards the socialist and communist cause and to the Communist Party leadership."[46] This crackdown on PRC cultural circles started out as a denunciation of pornography and certain trends in philosophical, literary, and art circles, expanding swiftly into an attack by hardline apparatchiks in the Party against a broad range of cultural phenomena and social forces. On the literary and artistic front, Party Central's Propaganda Bureau singled out specific types of works and genres to attack and suppress. Popular literary magazines and newspaper became one of the main targets. For example, Guangdong province began closing down popular broadsheets (literally "small newspapers," a generic PRC term for unlicensed newspapers that suffered little or no Communist Party supervision or control) because "some of these newspapers published bizarre and uncanny stories in order to increase their circulation and hanker after stimulation of the senses."[47] "Science fiction works that contain ghost stories, violence, sex, anti-scientific assumptions, and veiled criticism of socialism" were among the genres and subgenres castigated as spiritual pollution.[48] For example, Ye Yonglie's short story "The Miracle on the Summit of Mount Everest" ("Shijie zuigaofeng shang de qiji," 1976) was criticized as advocating "fake science" because it recounts the discovery of fossilized dinosaur eggs on top of Mount Everest. Similarly, Wei Yahua's SF story "I Decided to Divorce My Robot Wife" ("Wo jueding he jiqiren qizi lihun," 1981) was labelled "pornographic literature."[49]

This campaign of cultural suppression reached its climax in mid-November 1983, and faded into obscurity in the spring of 1984 after intervention from Deng Xiaoping himself, who finally realized that many individuals in and outside the Party were taking advantage of this campaign to "attack people, policies, and behavior they disliked, with potentially severe consequences for social stability and the Four Modernizations."[50] Although this political crackdown was "so short-lived as to last only a few months, it hurt the authors so badly that the small contingent of SF writers quickly shrank and gradually dispersed."[51] As a result, many PRC SF writers left the field in 1983 and 1984. Chinese SF remained at a low ebb from the mid-1980s to the mid-1990s. The publication of PRC SF works slowed to nearly a standstill, and the translation of foreign works of SF also fell sharply in comparison to some previous periods.

SF Publication Venues, Organizations, Fandom, and Fanzines

From 1976 to October 1983, political endorsements from the central government and high-ranking Party officials helped the field of Chinese SF to accumulate political capital, and stimulated the increase of culture capital of both the field and individual authors. Bourdieu "defines cultural capital as a form of knowledge, an internalized code or a cognitive acquisition which equips the social agent with empathy towards appreciation for or competence in deciphering cultural relations and cultural artefacts."[52] In other words, cultural capital is the amount of knowledge a person has about an aspect of the cultural field. Gelder describes the importance of accumulating cultural capital for popular writers: "The more cultural capital one is able to claim on behalf of the genre, the better genre novels one writes."[53] Bookstores, genre magazines, professional and fan organizations, and writers all play an important role in demonstrating their understanding and knowledge of the field. Genre magazines sift, select, and evaluate new works. Besides writing, writers also involve themselves heavily in promoting genre fiction, such as book-signing at genre bookstores, participating in writer forums, and meeting readers at gatherings arranged by bookstores or publishers. They also write features and review articles for genre magazines, and sometimes even edit magazines.[54]

Publication of SF works during the post-Mao thaw was mainly through SF and popular science magazines, publishing houses, mainstream literary magazines, and popular genre magazines. SF, popular science, and popular fiction magazines published the latest SF stories; publishing houses published SF novels and SF criticism, and arranged for the translation of notable foreign SF works; and mainstream literary magazines published the works of prominent SF writers.

The period from 1978 to 1983 witnessed a boom in SF magazines, which was greatly influenced by the central government's shift to a relatively relaxed policy on magazine publications. In 1978–80, the power to review and approve publication of new magazines was devolved to local governments. This led to large increases in the publication of magazines by 48, 58, and 49 per cent respectively during these three years. According to a survey conducted by *Literary Gazette* (*Wenyi bao*) in 1981, the PRC had already amassed 634 literary periodicals produced at the provincial, regional, or municipal level. Among them, 320 belonged to either the provincial level or above.[55] These periodicals became venues to publish not only mainstream literature, but also popular fiction in such subgenres as romance, SF, crime fiction, detective thrillers, martial arts fiction, and folk tales.[56]

SF magazines and newspapers prospered within the relatively relaxed regime of political control during the cultural thaw. Various articles and books provide a chronology of PRC SF magazines of the 1980s. For example, in his *Science Fiction Rebels: The Story of the Science Fiction Magazines from 1981 to 1990*, Mike Ashley provides a brief history of major Chinese SF magazines of the 1980s.[57] In *The Odyssey of Chinese Science Fiction*, Zheng Jun offers a more detailed introduction to PRC SF magazines during this period. Though many new popular science magazines were launched in every province, beginning in 1978, "the true science fiction magazines proved more popular … and began to blossom from 1979 onward."[58] Both Ashley and Zheng Jun indicate that there were five major publishing venues for SF writers, in addition to magazines that specialized in mainstream literature or popular fiction. These five venues are summarized as "the four magazines and one newspaper": *Science, Literature and Art* (*Kexue wenyi*, first quarterly then bimonthly, 1979–89) in Chengdu; *Age of Science* (*Kexue shidai*, bimonthly, 1979–84) in Heilongjiang; *Wisdom Tree* (*Zhihui shu*, bimonthly, 1981–5) in Tianjin; *Science Fiction Ocean* (*Kehuan haiyang*, anthology series, 1981–2001) in Beijing; and the newspaper *Chinese Science Fiction Gazette* (*Zhongguo kehuan xiaoshuo bao*, biweekly, 1981) in Heilongjiang.[59] These magazines and newspaper published not only speculative fiction, but also popular science articles, interviews, reviews, and essays about the genre. "The balance was towards speculative fiction and science."[60] Among these "four magazines and one newspaper," the *Chinese Science Fiction Gazette* was the most short-lived.[61] *Science, Literature and Art* is the only periodical from this period that continues to be published, but it has gone through several name changes, from *Science, Literature and Art* to *Amazing Stories* (*Qi tan*) in 1989, and subsequently to *Science Fiction World* (*Kehuan shijie*) in 1991 (see figures 1.1 and 1.2).[62]

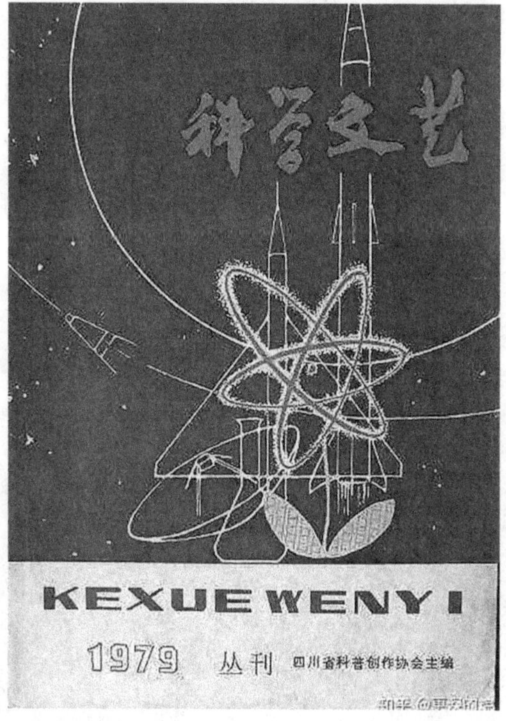

Figure 1.1. Front cover of the first issue of *Science, Literature and Art* (*Kexue wenyi*, 1979) (courtesy of *Science Fiction World*).

The above-mentioned SF magazines and newspaper published works written by both prominent veterans and obscure new writers. They published short SF stories, novellas, and full-length novels in serialized format. The primary role of these SF magazines was to feature new works in the field. They also published critical essays and review articles in order to evaluate and discover new talent. Some essays provided specialized information on the history of SF in China and overseas. The magazines also regularly hosted meetings and forums for writers and editors, and tried to expand the roster of the magazines' own regular contributors. In addition to SF magazines, many literary magazines and newspapers also added supplements to publish SF works. Some publishing houses printed collections of SF stories, edited volumes of SF reviews and essays, and translated volumes of foreign SF works. For example, in 1980 the Jiangsu Science and Technology Press launched

Figure 1.2. Front cover of the first issue of *Science Fiction World* (*Kehuan shijie*, 1991) (courtesy of *Science Fiction World*).

the Translation Series of Literature and Art about Science, which published seven volumes from 1980 to 1983, including translated SF narratives, popular science articles, scientific news, and SF film reviews.

Many SF writers wrote review articles to introduce the works of other writers and discuss important issues related to the genre. Some even produced edited volumes. For example, Ye Yonglie edited *On Literature and Art about Science* (*Lun kexue wenyi*), published by Popular Science Press in 1980, and *An Anthology of Chinese Science Fiction* (*Zhongguo kexue huanxiang xiaoshuo xuan*), published by Liaoning People's Press in 1982. This practice was very different from that of mainstream serious novelists, who focused on writing literary works and rarely wrote reviews or edited collections of essays.

These Chinese SF publications have the "para-academic" trait that Gelder attributes to genre magazines, because they typically deploy their scholarship outside the university and other educational institutions.[63] Shanghai Foreign Language Institute (later renamed Shanghai International Studies University in 1994) began to offer a small-scale course in SF as early as 1979. It was not until 1990 that a second PRC university offered a SF course, which was taught as an elective by the renowned SF scholar Wu Yan at Beijing Normal University.[64] In the 1980s, SF scholarship was conducted mainly by writers, editors, and critics of SF through SF magazines and edited volumes.

Moreover, these SF writers, editors, and critics often engaged in lively theoretical debates. Dingbo Wu has discussed what he pinpoints as the six major foci of debate in SF during the 1980s: the nature of SF; its mission; its definition; its connection to fantasy; detective SF; and issues of style and form. These debates benefited development of the genre and demonstrate "the health and vitality of science fiction in China."[65] Edited volumes served as the vehicle for many of these debates and discussions. For example, the most comprehensive theoretical discussions of the genre during the early 1980s were Huang Yi's two edited volumes: *Writers on Literature and Art about Science* (*Zuojia lun kexue wenyi*, 1980) and *On Science Fiction* (*Lun kexue huanxiang xiaoshuo*, 1981). *Modest Discussions of Popular Science Writing* (*Kepu xiaoyi*, 1981) was another important volume of short critical essays on SF and popular science writing during this period.

Aside from discovering and publicizing talented new SF writers and composing critical essays and reviews, SF editors and scholars engaged in research and wrote literary history, often reviving interest in long-forgotten Chinese SF writers and their works. "Their cultural capital is demonstrated every time they recover a now-forgotten writer or fill in the blanks in a writer's bibliography."[66] For example, in 1982 Rao Zhonghua edited a three-volume compilation entitled *A Compendium of Chinese Science Fiction* (*Zhongguo kehuan xiaoshuo daquan*), which not only provides a chronology of the vast majority of Chinese SF works from 1905 to 1982, but also includes traditional myths and prototypical Chinese science fantasies from pre-modern Chinese collections such as "A Flying Wooden Bird" ("Nengfei de muyuan") from Duan Chengshi's (b.?–863) *Miscellaneous Morsels from Youyang* (*Youyang zazu*) and "Lower Jaw Transplantation" ("Xiahe yizhi shu") from Hong Mai's (1123–1202) *Records of Yijian* (*Yijian Zhi*).[67]

In addition, the publishers often aimed for a full record of a writer's works and published anthologies of prominent SF authors. For example, in 1983 the Guangdong People's Press published *An Anthology of*

Zheng Wenguang (*Zheng Wenguang zuopin xuan*); in 1978, the Children's Press published a collection of Tong Enzheng's SF stories entitled *Dense Fog over the Old Gorge* (*Guxia miwu*); and in 1979, the People's Press published Tong's *Magic Flute on the Snowy Mountain* (*Xueshan mudi*). According to Gelder, any type of genre fiction "is all about knowledge and competence."[68] Knowledge about SF is precisely what readers acquired from these Chinese SF magazines, literary anthologies, and edited volumes. These publications have also served as archives of Chinese SF works and key sources for SF researchers.

In addition to SF publishers, SF organizations and fan clubs also helped the genre accumulate cultural capital. In the 1980s, the boundary between fan clubs and professional organizations was blurry. Most SF fans in the 1980s were college students or professionals working in universities or other cultural organizations. Many were writers, professors, translators, cultural officials, or literary critics. Some local fan organizations acted as SF research associations, publishing SF works, critical articles, and translations of foreign SF works. Some fan clubs and organizations were affiliated with local governments or universities. The relatively high educational level of most SF fans endowed their clubs with some of the aura of a professional or even academic milieu.

According to Dingbo Wu, the first Chinese SF fandom club was established in July 1980 in Shanghai. In 1979, Philip Smith, a professor of English from the University of Pittsburgh, taught a course in SF while a visiting faculty member at Shanghai Foreign Language Institute. Shortly afterward in July 1980, fifteen faculty members from this institute's English Department founded a SF fandom club, whose president was Professor Qin Xiaomeng. In February 1981, a student fandom club was founded in the same institute, with Chen Yu, an SF translator and commentator, serving as club president. In 1988, Chen Yu published a volume of translated U.S. SF entitled *An Anthology of Contemporary American Science Fiction*, and Zheng Wenguang wrote a foreword for this book, which includes works by Ray Bradbury, Robert Heinlein, Isaac Asimov, and other American SF writers. During the 1980s, SF fan clubs spread throughout the PRC in such provinces as Sichuan, Guangdong, Heilongjiang, and Liaoning.[69]

The first Chinese SF fanzine, *Nebula* (*Xingyun*) was published by an avid and dedicated reader named Yao Haijun. Originally a worker at the Yichun Forestry Centre, Yao wrote a letter to the editors of *Science, Literature and Art* proposing that he establish an SF fan organization with its own fanzine. The chief editor enthusiastically responded to Yao Haijun's proposal with strong support. Yao thereupon got in touch with SF writers and fans across the country with the assistance of editors at

Figure 1.3. Mimeographed front cover of issue 9 of *Nebula* (courtesy of Yao Haijun).

Science, Literature and Art. Yao Haijun mimeographed the first issue of *Nebula* at his own expense in October 1988.[70] His fanzine consisted SF news, reviews, criticism, readers' correspondence, and brief announcements of activities of SF fans throughout the country. A new issue of Yao's fanzine came out every two or three months (see figure 1.3). The fanzine received manuscripts provided by writers and essayists without any requests for remuneration. Yao himself mailed off each issue to his subscribers, who numbered approximately 1,200 at the peak of this fanzine's run.[71] *Nebula* was heralded as the PRC's only SF fanzine at the 1993 World Science Fiction Convention. The magazine finally adopted offset printing in 1995 after publishing thirteen issues in stencil printing. From then on, *Nebula* regularly published three issues per year. Zheng Jun argues that the significance of this pioneering PRC SF fanzine was to connect SF writers, readers, researchers, editors, and publishers with one another[72] and continued to function as a liaison between SF fans and writers until 1997 when Yao Haijun joined the editorial staff of *King of Science Fiction* (*Kehuan dawang*). At that point, *Nebula* rebranded itself as the newsletter of the Research Association of Chinese Science Popularization and Science Fiction. This change was reflected in the contents of the volume 21 (1997, issues 3 and 4), which consisted solely of scholarly articles and reviews. Having undergone this major overhaul, the first Chinese fan magazine successfully rebranded itself as a relatively serious literary magazine. The magazine had published forty-four issues by 2007, when it was converted into an academic journal.[73]

Several other fanzines were published in the mid-1990s, such as Beijing's *Cube Light Year* (*Lifang guangnian*, 1995–6), Tianjin's *Supernova* (*Chao xinxing*, 1996–7), Zhengzhou's *Milky Way* (*Yinhe*, 1996), and Chengdu's *Ladder to the Sky* (*Shang tianti*, 1996). However, none of these fanzines lasted as long or exerted as much influence on SF circles as *Nebula*.[74]

Chinese SF critic Zhang Feng has pointed out that most Chinese SF fanzines functioned as mere newsletters for fan clubs and organizations. The scope of fan organizations can be categorized as campus-based, region-specific, or nationwide. For example, *Nebula*, *Milky Way*, and *Ladder to the Sky* were the newsletters of their own fan clubs, and reached their members across the nation through the postal service. *Cube Light Year* and *Supernova* were regional newsletters of the Beijing SF Fan Sodality and Tianjin SF Fan Sodality, respectively. *Critical Point* (*Jidian*) was the campus-based newsletter of the local fan club at Sichuan University with a modest circulation of 300 subscribers.[75]

From this summary of the evolution and significance of Yao Haijun's *Nebula*, we can see links among genre magazines, fan organizations, and fanzines, which reveal the connections and shared interests between SF writers, editors, and fans (see figure 1.4). The fan readership knows a great deal about the SF field and stays in contact with it. In fact, among popular fiction genres in China, SF has the longest history of organized fandom and fanzines. Chinese SF readers and fans participate in the SF cultural world and have helped compile histories of the genre. My analysis of these issues has shown that professional organizations, fan clubs, professional magazines and books, and fanzines and fan books have helped the field of Chinese SF accumulate cultural capital. They have published new works, provided information and knowledge about the genre, compiled and archived sources, and formed a community for writers, readers, editors, critics, and publishers. In sharp contrast with mainstream literary writers, who have focused mainly

Figure 1.4. SF fans meeting in the late 1980s. *Left to right*: Zheng Jun (later an SF editor, writer, and SF historian), Xu Jiulong (an avid SF fan and founder of the fanzine *Ladder to the Sky*), Liu Wenyang (later a prominent SF writer in the New Wave era), and Yao Haijun (courtesy of Yao Haijun).

on their own writings, SF writers have also promoted the SF genre as a whole: They have reviewed other SF writers' works, discussed major issues in the field, become members of professional or fan organizations, and frequently interacted with editors, commentators, and fans.

SF Evaluation, Awards, and Canonization

According to Bourdieu's conceptualization of a cultural field, "Competition often concerns the authority inherent in recognition, consecration and prestige," and the "authority based on consecration or prestige is purely symbolic and may or may not imply possession of increased economic capital."[76] He points out that "symbolic capital refers to the degree of accumulated prestige, celebrity, consecration or honor, and is found on a dialectic of knowledge (*connaissance*) and recognition (*reconnaissance*)."[77] Symbolic capital involves peer recognition and prestige through winning awards or government incentives. Symbolic capital can also be "endowed by those already holding prestigious positions in the cultural field," such as "a university appointment, state support, a literary award, an article written about [an author] in a prestigious journal," or even through appearance or mention on TV or in newspapers.[78]

As discussed earlier in this chapter, Chinese SF magazines, anthologies, and edited volumes not only process new works and rediscover long-forgotten writers, but also evaluate SF works. Publishers, writers' associations, and fan organizations often evaluate an SF writer on the basis of awards the writer received, and whether the writer's fiction has been published in prestigious venues. Gelder indicates that the evaluation of genre fiction often proceeds in one of two possible directions. One is "towards the essence of the genre," with a focus on the "pace, precision, plot, detail, a sense of wonder, and no superfluous internal thoughts," while the other is "towards something akin to 'literary values'" with a focus on humanity, theme, style, and mode.[79] Sometimes an evaluation proceeds in both directions at the same time. The evaluation of Chinese SF works also reveals one or both of these tendencies, depending on the evaluator. When SF works are published in prestigious literary magazines beside mainstream literary works, they are usually evaluated to the same standard used for mainstream literary fiction. That is akin to the literary value of the work. In contrast, if SF works are evaluated by SF magazines or organizations, the evaluation criteria tend to be far more genre-based.

Tong Enzheng's "Death Ray on a Coral Island" may be the best example of a thaw-era PRC SF work that was evaluated for its literary value. The story was published in *People's Literature* in August 1978, and won a Best Short Story Award in the PRC that same year. As Dingbo Wu has pointed out, this was a truly ground-breaking honour, for it was the first PRC SF story to receive such a prestigious nationwide literary award.[80] This particular award was based on a tabulation of readers' ballots. The votes that Tong's story received ranked it at the very top of the list. However, the awards committee downgraded Tong and his story to the bottom of the winners' list because they were influenced by their establishmentarian prejudice against the genre of SF.[81] In spite of the awards committee's bias, Tong's story still won the prize on the basis of its literary merits.

Among other early thaw-era SF awardees, Zheng Wenguang wrote *Flying toward Sagittarius* (*Fei xiang renmazuo*, 1978), which won first place in the National Children's Literature & Arts Award competition in 1978. In 1986, Zheng's *Magic Wings* (*Shen yi*, 1982) was given first place for the Children's Literature & Arts Award, which was bestowed by the Chinese Writers' Association. The evaluation criteria for judges for such an award combine literary achievement and genre mastery. When selecting prize-winning SF works for juvenile readers, judges not only expected an interesting plot and lively characterization, but also scrutinized how well an SF work communicates scientific knowledge to a youthful readership.

The first PRC SF award was the Galaxy Award, which was established by the magazine *Science, Literature and Art* in 1986. In order to locate new literary talent and solicit manuscripts, *Science, Literature and Art* and its sister magazine *Wisdom Tree* jointly initiated the first Galaxy Science Fiction Competition in 1985. Even though *Wisdom Tree* closed down before the award ceremony in 1986, the first Galaxy Award still divided the prize winners into two categories, depending on which magazine first published a given work. In other words, one prize went to an SF work in *Science, Literature and Art*, while the other went to an SF work in *Wisdom Tree*. Each award was further split into the categories of winner and runner-up. Winners included prominent writers such as Wei Yahua and Liu Xingshi, and relatively obscure writers such as Xiao Jian, Li Zhen, and Hong Mei. The subjects of the prize-winning works ranged from a surrogate birth, to a sound wave, a typhoon, a robot, and cryonics. Since then, *Science, Literature and Art* has single-handedly hosted the annual Galaxy Award competition.[82] Because all the works participating in the competition of the Galaxy Awards have been confined to those published in *Science, Literature and Art*, the award has become an important means for the magazine to build its team of writers and establish its status and authority in the field, thereby accumulating symbolic capital.

While bestowing literary awards through state-run organizations such as the Chinese Writers' Association, the PRC government provided other incentives also to encourage SF writers to be productive and accumulate symbolic capital: granting the title of model worker or advanced worker on a given writer, awarding a cash prize, offering the invitation to attend an important conference, or promoting the writer to an official post.

Ye Yonglie's autobiography *Pursuing Historical Truth: My Writing Career* contains an entire chapter about the literary awards and honours he received during the thaw era. In 1979, Ye was presented with one thousand Chinese yuan at the Planning Session for Science Education Films. For Ye, that meant more as symbolic capital than as mere economic capital, in large part because the award came with the honorific title "Advanced Worker in Science Popularization." The Xinhua News Agency and China News Press both broadcasted the news; *People's*

Daily, *Wenhui Daily*, and the magazine *Popular Cinema* also published reports of the award ceremony and praised Ye as a role model for workers in science popularization.[83]

After the success of Ye's novel *Xiao Linglong Travels to the Future* (*Xiao Lingtong manyou weilai*, 1978), reporters Xu Mingshou and Xie Jun interviewed Ye and published two articles in *Guangming Daily* about his life and writing career in 1978 and 1979, respectively. The latter article by Xie Jun attracted the attention of Deputy Premier Fang Yi (1916–1997). Fang read the report when it was first published in an "internal reference" for circulation only among high-ranking CCP officials, prior to its formal publication in the *Guangming Daily* on 15 February 1979. At that time, the deputy premier was in charge of the country's system of science education and was impressed by Ye's achievements in SF and popular science writings. Fang's praise for his writings boosted Ye's career and standard of living alike. Ye made headlines in such newspapers as *People's Daily*, *Liberation Daily*, *Tianjin Daily*, and *People's Education*. Officials in the Shanghai municipal government soon invited Ye in for a chat. He was also introduced to prominent scientists such as Qian Xuesen (1911–2009). As Ye remarked in his autobiography, "As the result of Deputy Premier Fang's support, all sorts of prominent people in society have shown me favour, and honors and titles flowed my way."[84]

Ye was soon promoted to deputy chairman of the Shanghai Association of Popular Science Writing while still retaining his post at the Shanghai Science Education Film Studio. He also became a committee member in national organizations such as the Chinese Science and Technology Association and the Chinese Youth League. His standard of living also rose as his fame grew. In addition to a cash reward, the Shanghai municipal government also allocated Ye's family a two-bedroom apartment, which was considered quite spacious at that time.[85] Ye's case illustrates that as an increasingly renowned writer in the realm of PRC popular culture, he not only made money from his work, but also gained symbolic and political capital from it, through the approval of individuals holding prestigious positions in the cultural or political fields. The most significant perks came in the form of government subsidies, literary prizes, news media features of his achievements, and broadening range of contacts with high-ranking PRC officials, prominent cultural figures, and famous scientists. Later, Ye went on to use his symbolic and political capital to full advantage when he undertook a change in occupation from popular science writer to biographer.

In addition to bestowing prizes and awarding government incentives, society can also enhance the prestige and authority of favoured writers through canonization. According to Bourdieu, "A canonical vision of a literary school, movement, or writer represents a structure of authority in the field."[86] Around 1980, the field of Chinese SF started to canonize works by inclusion in anthologies of prominent writers and their fiction, along with critical analysis in volumes of literary interpretation. These anthologies and volumes of literary criticism often focused on the works of prominent writers. For example, Huang Yi and Ye Yonglie edited anthologies of Chinese SF in 1980 and 1982. Their collections tended to include fiction by the same group of SF writers, such as Zheng Wenguang, Ye Yonglie, Tong Enzheng, Liu Xingshi, Xiaojianheng, Wang Xiaoda, and Chi Shuchang. Other editors published somewhat different collections of fiction by the same writers. For example, a WorldCat author search of anthologies of Chinese SF writers published between 1978 and 1983 reveals twelve anthologies edited by Zheng Wenguang, eighteen by Ye Yonglie, and five by Tong Enzheng. In addition, many of their works were also adapted into films, radio dramas, TV dramas, and comic books, confirming the enduring value of their SF and canonizing it.

As I mentioned earlier in this chapter, many prominent writers also wrote critical essays about the works of other writers and discussed important issues in the field. By writing critical essays, they "declare[d] not only their judgment of the work but also their claim to the right to talk about it and judge it."[87] With their focus on specific writers, these articles of literary criticism helped establish the authority of a given author and a sort of hierarchy within the field of Chinese SF. As a result of his canonization in the early 1980s, Zheng Wenguang has often been called "the father of Chinese science fiction."[88] Meanwhile, Zheng and the four other writers Tong Enzheng, Ye Yonglie, Xiao Jianheng, and Liu Xingshi, have collectively been anointed the "Five Big Names" in 1980s PRC SF.

Readership, Remuneration, and Economic Capital

Compared with political, symbolic, and cultural capital, economic capital had been comparatively unimportant for Chinese SF writers during the post-Mao thaw. A writer or artist gains economic capital when producing cultural goods in large-scale circulation for the mass market; in short, it is the money an artist or writer makes.[89] Though many PRC SF writers did not set out to make money from the SF they wrote, they did benefit economically from their creative writing through royalties and other remuneration. Thaw-era SF writers lived in a transitional phase, as China moved from an old-style socialist planned economy to a more diversified and complex mixed economy. These writers of the 1980s began to receive substantial remuneration while the income of most Chinese white-collar employees was still modest.

The accumulation of economic capital is inseparable from the popularity of a given type of genre fiction. The popularity of SF has been affected by the quality of the writing, the reputation of the publication venue, the size of the readership, and marketing and promotion. The following section will discuss how such factors affected the accumulation of economic capital in Chinese SF during the 1980s.

In contrast to the largely juvenile readership of Chinese SF during the 1950s and 1960s, the profile of SF readership age rose substantially during the post-Mao cultural thaw, for three major reasons. The first was the Party's confirmation of the important role of science and technology in the country's gradual achievement of Four Modernizations. SF emerged as a significant tool for the government to promote science and technology. PRC SF writers now needed to write for a much broader and more mature readership. As Zheng Wenguang remarked, "In recent years, many of my SF works have not been written for juvenile readers any more. This is not my personal choice, but the general tendency of Chinese SF. This literary genre has matured, and it calls for writings that depict people's life and society in a more profound way than before. Therefore, I have had to focus more of my energy on my writing [of SF]."[90]

The second reason was improvement in the literary quality of SF works. For example, Dingbo Wu points out that the "clear-cut portrayal of characters and the intriguing plot" of Tong Enzheng's "Death Ray on a Coral Island" marked "a break from the bondage of its classification as juvenile literature."[91] The third reason was the growth of a relatively well-educated readership. The PRC's resumption of rigorous university entrance examinations in 1978 encouraged many school dropouts to return school or even study for the college entrance exam. Loosened restrictions on nearly all post-Mao PRC business enterprises also encouraged growth in the publishing industry and new opportunities for an increasing number of writers, critics, and editors.

In the view of Hugo award winner and veteran SF novelist Liu Cixin, during the 1980s there was no clear distinction between SF fans and general readers in the PRC. SF readers were scattered among all walks of life. A well-crafted SF narrative such as "Death Ray on a Coral Island" had considerable influence on society as a whole, instead of on a narrow fan base. That was totally different from the present situation in which SF has become a type of "fan literature."[92] In contrast with the relatively small readership of literary fiction at that time, the readership of PRC SF amounted to a much higher proportion of the population.

According to Link, the popular readership comprised approximately 40 per cent of the urban population. They preferred popular fiction to serious literature. As for the socially engaged readers and elites, they read not only serious literature, but also SF and other genre fiction – the latter primarily for entertainment.

Link points out that while hardly any rural Chinese read fiction because few were literate, they often listened to radio broadcasts, which included dramatizations of fiction. Around 1980, many SF stories were adapted for radio. For example, "Death Ray on a Coral Island" was transformed into a radio drama in 1978 by the Shanghai Film Dubbing Studio. And adaptations of Ye Yonglie's *Veiled Strife* (*An dou*, 1981) and *Secret Column* (*Mimi zongdui*, 1981) were broadcast by the Central People's Broadcasting Network and the Hunan and Sichuan People's Broadcasting Network in 1981.[93] In this way, a large cross-section of the mass audience in rural areas also became consumers of PRC SF. Therefore, the consumers of Chinese SF during this period included not only juveniles, college students, researchers, scientists, technicians, and educators, but also a mass audience of radio listeners in both rural and urban areas. Chinese SF also found expression in other media such as film, television, and comic books. PRC SF's multimedia practice will be discussed in detail in chapter 7.

Naturally, PRC SF writers benefited from the popularity of their works. Most Chinese writers in the 1980s held a stable professional day job, which was not necessarily related to creative writing. This means that remuneration for SF writers typically amounted to extra money they earned in addition to their regular salary. Therefore, economic capital for these SF writers tended to be less important than the symbolic or cultural capital they had accrued.

The remuneration rate for SF magazines during the 1980s was within the range of three to twenty yuan.[94] Some especially prominent writers such as Zheng Wenguang, Tong Enzheng, and Liu Xingshi sometimes received more from particularly prestigious literary magazines or prominent publishers. SF writers sometimes received cash awards from the government for their contributions to the cause of science popularization. Ye Yonglie recounted how the resumption of authorial remuneration after the Cultural Revolution lifted him out of long-term economic hardship. He recalled that on 20 December 1977 he received his first payment since the outbreak of the Cultural Revolution: ¥320. When he deposited this rather hefty sum in his account, it caused something of a sensation in the bank. Fifteen months later, the Ministry of Culture and the Association of Science Popularization jointly awarded him ¥1,000 for his distinguished contribution to science popularization and his creative writing.[95] One thousand Chinese yuan was a sizeable sum in 1980, when the average income of a middle-aged white-collar professional was ¥77.5 per month.[96] Ye's friend Wang Defeng recalled that Ye was envied by some of his colleagues and friends for his unusually high income. Wang added that Ye paid little attention to what he earned, and sometimes returned part or all of a payment to the publisher. Ye also once donated more than ¥4,000 to the Shanghai Science Popularization and Creative Writing Association.[97] Many memoirs about the SF writers in 1980s include anecdotes about money. For example, the SF writer Wang Yafa recalled that he and several SF fans visited Tong Enzheng in Chengdu in 1983, where Tong treated them to lunch with the funds he had just received from his publisher.[98] Liu Xingshi recalled that the university where he taught demanded that he share his payments with the university. The university even requested that the Shanghai Children's Press send Liu's remuneration directly to the university.[99] These anecdotes show that virtually all of these thaw-era SF writers had regular income from their day job and did not depend on authorial remuneration for a living. However, the money they received did enable them to accumulate symbolic capital by providing them with spare funds to facilitate socializing with other writers or donations to their employers or other organizations. And the authorial remuneration they received sometimes even amounted to more than their regular income from a day job, giving rise to occasional envy among their colleagues and friends.

Conclusion

The above examination of the production, publication, and consumption of Chinese SF reveals that thaw-era SF writers were generally more prolific than writers of mainstream literary fiction. Many emerged as "brand names" of PRC SF, including Tong Enzheng, Ye Yonglie, and Zheng Wenguang. They maintained close connections with other SF writers and had their own professional groupings and fan organizations. Thaw-era PRC SF entertained the reader while popularizing science and technology. It was more closely associated with exploring liberal strains of thought than merely profiting from commercial success. Though it could be considered popular fiction, its publication venues were not confined to genre fiction magazines. Some prominent thaw-era SF writers published extensively in mainstream literary magazines. Serialization of thaw-era SF in newspapers could be instrumental to an individual work's popularity "since it ensures longevity and, if successful, generates ongoing audience loyalty."[100] In brief, thaw-era

PRC SF appears to have been "open to a mass audience and remains conscious of its viewers/readers, and is determined to please them."[101] It engaged positively and enthusiastically with what Bourdieu describes as "worldly or commercial success."[102] Chinese SF "is not just a matter of texts in themselves, but of an entire apparatus of production, distribution (including promotion and advertising), and consumption."[103]

In short, during the post-Mao era the generic identity of SF truly coalesced and PRC SF "was restored to a highly defined categorical place and function."[104] My examination of SF in this chapter shows that thaw-era PRC SF expanded Bourdieu's framework of the field by tacitly challenging mainstream literary fiction's exclusive claim as high literature. Bourdieu argues that "in any given field, agents occupying the diverse available positions (or in some cases creating new positions) engage in competition for control of the interests or resources which are specific to the field in question."[105] According to Randal Johnson, "In the cultural (e.g., literary) field, competition often concerns the authority inherent in recognition, consecration and prestige. This is especially so in what Bourdieu calls the sub-field of restricted production."[106] Such authority stems from symbolic, cultural, and political capital. In post-Mao Chinese literature, restricted production amounts to mainstream literary fiction. Though SF was a non-mainstream popular genre located at the lower end of the literary hierarchy, it competed for cultural capital in the 1980s. Thaw-era SF practitioners were competing for such capital by engaging in cultural practices that had been the hallmark of literary fiction and high culture in general. These practices included winning national literary awards; canonizing the classics; helping to facilitate adaptations of this genre to other media such as radio and film; and founding new professional associations and journals with a focus on the genre.

In addition, post-Mao thaw SF competed with mainstream serious fiction for the attention of readers interested in political themes. SF increasingly broached socio-political themes that had been considered the special province of mainstream fiction and literary reportage. The transition of PRC SF from socialist realism to social realism – along with other contemporary literary and intellectual trends – echoed the changes in mainstream literature during the post-Mao cultural thaw. In this way, PRC SF gradually moved towards the nation's high-culture establishment. Jeffrey Kinkley has observed that "either sophistication of aesthetic conception (form) or seriousness of social-moral commentary (content) may elevate works from any of these basically popular genres onto the plateau of 'high literature.'"[107] As one of these long-time popular genres, thaw-era SF experienced elevation as its practitioners' accomplishments mainstreamed SF as an increasingly serious literary genre. SF's rising trajectory in the PRC became even more prominent with the advent of New Wave SF during the twenty-first century. SF has arguably become one of the PRC's top cultural exports to the West, as a number of foreign-language translations of PRC SF have won major international SF prizes. If we apply an international context to Bourdieu's framework of the cultural field, post-Mao Chinese SF's rising trajectory suggests a bourgeoning of cultural capital for this literary genre. The primary origins of this latter-day amassing of cultural capital for PRC SF date back to ground-breaking changes the genre underwent during the post-Mao thaw.

Having surveyed the major issues and developments in PRC SF during this dynamic era, I will turn to analysis and assessment of this period's most prominent PRC SF by Zheng Wenguang, Ye Yonglie, Tong Enzheng, and Xiao Jianheng in chapters 2–5, respectively. Chapter 6 focuses on the specific subgenre of tech-SF, which is unique to the thaw era. Chapter 7 examines Chinese SF's fledgling media convergence from print to electronic media. Chapter 8 is the book's conclusion, which ties together strands from the preceding chapters and provides overarching assessments of thaw-era PRC SF.

2 A Study of Zheng Wenguang's Mars Series

Though he studied astronomy for only one year at Sun Yat-Sen University in 1949, Zheng Wenguang's association with space was lifelong. Known as "the father of Chinese science fiction," Zheng was also an astronomer and a popular science writer by profession (see figure 2.1).[1] The first few images that readers associate with Zheng's narratives are rockets and journeys to outer space, whose unlimited expanse licenses an outward reach of Zheng's imagination. In Zheng's narratives, journeys to space go farther and farther, from landing on the moon, to flying to the vicinity of Mars, to landing on Mars, to flying to the vicinity of the sun, and eventually to flying out of the solar system. In space, Mars seems to be the planet that most fascinates Zheng. The trajectory of Zheng's writing starts with the short story "From Earth to Mars" ("Cong diqiu dao huoxing," 1954), to "The Mars Pioneers" ("Huoxing jianshe zhe," 1957), and ends with the novel *Descendant of Mars* (*Zhanshen de houyi*, 1983).[2] During intervals between completion of the three Mars narratives, Zheng also published works with such subject matter as exploring the moon, the sun, the Milky Way, and Earth's interior. Among these non-Mars narratives, *Flying toward Sagittarius* (*Fei xiang Renmazuo*, 1978) is the most famous and is often regarded as Zheng's representative work. In comparison, *Descendant of Mars* is less known, but it is probably Zheng's best work in terms of characterization, narrative techniques, technical trivia, and its critical concern about human interventions in nature.

This chapter focuses on Zheng's Mars series, which includes "From Earth to Mars," "The Mars Pioneers," and *Descendant of Mars*. My discussion also relates Zheng's Mars series to his non-Mars narratives and his theoretical writings about the genre. Through a close reading of these three interlinked narratives, I underscore three major changes that emerge in Zheng's works during nearly three decades of creative writing. First, the central protagonist undergoes a transformation from

Figure 2.1. Zheng Wenguang (1929–2003) (courtesy of Shen Zhonglan and Wu Yan).

a juvenile enthusiastic about space exploration to a passionate young scientist preoccupied with interstellar exploration, and finally to a middle-aged scientist who leaves Mars with misgivings about its human colonization. The thematic concerns shift from encouragement of juveniles to explore the universe after completing their schooling, to praise for human conquest of nature and colonization of other planets, and finally to scepticism about interference with an extraterrestrial planet's natural development. Zheng's Mars series also unfolds through steady improvement in literary quality: from a children's story with simple plotline interspersed with clusters of scientific explanation and technical descriptions, to a literary work of imagination, complicated plot structure, and vivid characterization. These changes correspond to the author's changing views about SF: instead of seeing it as a utilitarian genre with only a blurred boundary between the scientific essay and 1950s-era fiction, he came to view SF as an organic combination of artistic narrative and scientific imagination. These changes also bear witness to how Chinese SF has been influenced by translated Soviet SF of the 1950s and translated American SF of the 1980s. These transformations thus reveal how Chinese SF gradually moved from its 1950s belonging to the SF of the generalized "socialist bloc" and by the early 1980s had entered the ranks of worldwide SF with its particular socio-cultural and political characteristics.[3]

Among Zheng's three Mars narratives, my close reading focuses on *Descendant of Mars*, and includes two dimensions of reading this novel. The first is to situate the novel within the Chinese literary scene of the early 1980s. I argue that *Descendant of Mars* reveals the later Zheng's heartfelt scepticism about human interference with nature and climate, specifically Mao's radical wars against nature in the 1950s and 1960s. Zheng also extended his reflection of human violence towards nature to both Chinese history and world history. His changing views over the span of his writing career reveal how Chinese SF writers started to reject ideological control of the Communist Party under the influences of the liberal intellectual trend of "bidding adieu to the revolution" and "contemplative literature" during the post-Mao cultural thaw. SF provided Chinese writers with a space to respond to China's social, political, and literary changes by examining the impact of China's revolution and Mao's radical mass movements on the country's ecological system.

In the second dimension of reading, I situate *Descendant of Mars* within the topography of world SF. Zheng's presentation of earthlings' massive engineering project on Mars positions this novel as a terraforming text. It echoes the Western terraforming narratives written in the mid-twentieth century in motifs, technical trivia, and ideological implications. Furthermore, the characters' positions and debates on space colonization and terraforming resonate with dialogues about climate change and environmental ethics in today's world. Therefore, *Descendant* contributes to global terraforming texts and ongoing debates about the Anthropocene.

From the 1950s to the 1960s: Popular Science Writing and Early SF Stories

During the 1950s and prior to writing his first SF narrative about Mars, Zheng wrote more than a hundred science popularization essays about artificial satellites when he was working for the Chinese Science Popularization Association. His selection of the topic of satellites derived in part from the influence of Soviet popular science primers and SF works. Though the first satellite was not launched until the Sputnik mission of 1957, the idea of launching such a satellite into an orbit around Earth had long since appeared in works by the scientist Konstanty Ciołkowski (1857–1935) and the SF writer Alexander Belyaev (1884–1942).[4] Zheng taught himself Russian in the 1950s, so he could read Russian writings about satellites prior to their translation into Chinese. He admired Belyaev for writing about satellites in *The Star KETs* (1936), which was based on Konstanty Ciołkowski's theories about rocketry and astronautics:

"There is no doubt that man-made satellites will become a reality. Soviet Russia and many other countries have been working on the project. Though these satellites will initially be little more than a metal ball, eventually they will house large structures, scientific laboratories, and astronomical observatories."[5] These Russian-language writings formed a solid foundation for Zheng's imaginative writings on space exploration.

After having written so many essays on artificial satellites, Zheng wanted to explore new subjects. He was advised to write a Mars-themed story by an editor at *Chinese Teenagers News*.[6] By this time, Zheng had read Aleksey Tolstoy's (1882–1945) *Aelita* (1923), a novel about travelling to Mars by rocket ship, and another novel entitled *The Hyperboloid of Engineer Garin* (1927). Zheng faulted Tolstoy's two novels for their weak characterization. He argued that the two works aim merely to transmit scientific knowledge, and flat characterization results in their mediocrity as literary works.[7] Although Zheng was determined not to slip into Tolstoy's error of poor characterization, his first Mars story is no better than Tolstoy's novels in characterization and plot development.

Zheng's first SF story, "From Earth to Mars," was published in May 1954 in *Chinese Teenagers News*. As observed by Nicolai Volland, the work is "the interplay of science, science popularization, and science fiction, as well as the youth as pioneers."[8] In the story, after her father rejects her request to travel with him to Mars, a girl named Zhenzhen, her younger brother, and a friend steal a spaceship and set out on their own on a voyage to the red planet. Consequently, the father and his colleagues launch another spaceship to search for the youths and bring them back. The remainder of the narrative consists of the children's experiences in space travel, including the spaceship's encounter with a meteor shower and their observations of Mars from above its northern polar region.

This work of fiction is not a Mars narrative per se. None of its characters actually land on Mars. The use of a spaceship is self-evidently a pretext for rapidly covering the enormous distances of space. It seems no real concern of the author to explain the technology of the spaceship. Though Zheng had taught himself meteorology, geology, geography, and astronomy in the early 1950s, his knowledge of Mars was still very limited. He later admitted that he had no choice but to avoid direct depictions of the Martian environment in this narrative.[9] However, the story does popularize aspects of astronomy such as gravity, meteors, and composition of the Martian atmosphere. Some passages come "verbatim from Zheng's translations of Soviet literature."[10] At the end of the narrative, the narrator points out that he is just telling an imagined story about the future, and encourages young readers to explore Mars when they grow up. This somewhat unreliable narrator and meta-fictional ending might amount to stylistic experimentation on Zheng's part. It also serves as a bridge to connect reality with an imminent future, and safeguards the author from being accused of writing far-fetched fantasy. The story became an immediate hit with both juvenile and adult readers. The narrative's exposition on astronomy provoked a burgeoning interest in celestial observation among readers nationwide.[11]

Encouraged by the success of "From Earth to Mars," Zheng published the short story "The Second Moon" ("Di er ge yueliang") later the same year,[12] about a young protagonist named Xiaoping who takes a tour of an artificial moon. "The Second Moon" offers more expository material about gravity, centrifugal force, and technical facts than Zheng included in "From Earth to Mars." This scientific and technological material not only serves an educational function, but also enhances the credibility and authenticity of the narrative. Volland argues that Zheng's narrative strategy in this story was directly influenced by Soviet SF narratives such as Belyaev's *The Star KETs*.[13] In addition, the material about technology underlines the importance of modern science and technology, which is a message that Zheng believes SF should transmit.[14]

Zheng published two more short stories about space exploration: "The Conquerors of the Moon" ("Zhengfu yueliang de renmen," 1954) and "The Exploration of the Sun" ("Taiyang tanxian ji," 1955). Neither provides a breakthrough in plot development or characterization. The main technological icon is still a spaceship, which conveys scientists and younger protagonists to the moon or to the vicinity of the sun. Through dialogues between scientists and younger protagonists, these stories provide expositions of astronomical phenomena such as sunspots and technological advances such as heat shielding on rocket ships.

In 1957, Zheng wrote his second Mars story, "The Mars Pioneers," which won him a literary prize at the Moscow International Youth Festival. This story can be read as a continuation of "From Earth to Mars" and as an abbreviated version of *Descendant of Mars*. The narrative adopts the story-telling framework of "From Earth to Mars." But this time the story does not unfold from within the narrator's imagination, and is instead a public narrative recounted by the Mars pioneer Xue Yinqing at a traditional Chinese mid-autumn festival. At the beginning of the narrative, the narrator points out that Xue was a member of the youthful audience thirty years ago when the narrator gave a talk at the planetarium. This echoes the narrator's expectation at the end of "From the Earth to Mars" that some young readers will land on and explore Mars when they grow up. Therefore, the author's imaginary explorations in "From the Earth to Mars" bear fruit in "The Mars Pioneers." In the story, Xue, Yu Wen, and other scientists land on Mars in 1988 when Mars is at its closest proximity to Earth (during a period called the Mars opposition). In this trip, they conceive the "Yu Wen Plan" to transform Mars into humankind's second planetary home, and will build a Mars base as a jumping-off place for further exploration and colonization of others planets. Afterwards, over four thousand young people from fifty-one nations arrive at Mars to implement the plan. Though the team is ethnically diverse, the initial nationalist interest in terraforming represents the agenda of CCP-ruled China. However, this multinational team foresees political engagement with multinationals in post-1970s Mars narratives such as Kim Stanley Robison's *Mars* trilogy, along with many Chinese space exploration narratives such as Liu Cixin's *The Three-Body Problem* (*Santi*) trilogy. The author describes some technical trivia, such as generating power by using the temperature difference between day and night; synthesizing water from the oxygen and hydrogen in the Martian atmosphere; improving Martian soil in order to plant grains, trees, and vegetables; and setting up industrial and research facilities. These technical ideas and events are fully developed twenty-five years later in *Descendant of Mars*.

Similar to other stories that Zheng wrote at around this time, this narrative makes no mention of class struggle, and instead generates tension and dramatic interest through problems related to production and experimentation. Volland characterizes this narrative approach as "political-ideological minimalism" and traces its influence from translations of 1950s Soviet SF and scientific non-fiction.[15] He also argues that the "subdued nature of politics in translated [Soviet] science fiction ... shows the genre's lingering roots in the conventions of middlebrow literature."[16] Volland's observation is correct only on the narrative's plot structure, since political themes still figure significantly in these Chinese narratives. "The Mars Pioneers" deals with Chinese political themes, specifically Mao's political imperative that "humankind must conquer nature."[17] In "The Mars Pioneers," readers can find a rosy communist future where modern science and technology reign supreme, and particular praise for the young scientists who are conquering nature. While Xue recounts his experiences while exploring Mars, the narrator remarks, "In my mind, I envision a solemn scene in which humans are conquering nature."[18] At the end of the narrative, Xue proudly enumerates the pioneers' achievements on Mars, such as exploiting underground mineral deposits, accurately forecasting

Martian weather, and cleverly utilizing cosmic rays to help power the interstellar spaceship. Agricultural production on Mars also comes across as stunningly impressive: pioneers grow giant wheat from stalks that weigh five kilograms each, raise pigs that weigh thirty tons each, and raise doves that are the size of eagles. These hyperbolic portrayals echo Mao's attempts to forge "a self-reliant" new China "in the face of international isolation, and regain strength in the world."[19] They also reveal the author's uncritical adherence to the Maoist political dogma that "the earth could be miraculously transformed through ideologically motivated determination."[20]

Zheng's uncritical adherence to Party ideology is also reflected in his discussions about SF in general. His 1956 essay "On Science Fiction" is probably the first to discuss this genre in the PRC and includes his definition of SF: "Science fiction is a literary form depicting how human beings will fight against nature in future."[21] He points out that SF should "reveal the power of modern science and technology, depict the glorious future of humankind, showcase the conquerors of nature, and single out scientists for praise with respect to the war between humankind and nature."[22] These thematic concerns are all manifested in Zheng's 1950s narratives about Mars, the moon, and the sun.

In addition to Zheng's political concerns in SF, he also points out that SF follows many of the cultural traditions articulated in time-honoured Chinese myths and folklore, and embodies characteristics of romanticism.[23] He emphasizes two important elements of SF – imagination and "basic scientific laws (*kexue yiju*)" – that correspond to the sense of estrangement and emphasis on scientific cognition that Darko Suvin identifies as central to SF. Zheng argues that SF permits its writers to formulate bold speculations and sometimes even fictitious technological apparatuses – as long as these technological ideas are based on sound scientific principles. He draws upon three novels in particular to drive his point home: Grigory Adamov's *The Ousting of the Ruler* (1946), Alexander Belyaev's *The Star KETs* (1936), and Jules Verne's *From the Earth to the Moon* (1865). Zheng asserts that even though it sounds unfeasible in *The Ousting of the Ruler* to use underground heat to increase the temperature of Antarctica in order to exploit its water resources, Adamov's idea has a solid scientific basis.[24]

Zheng's essay also advises readers to read popular science primers and SF so that they can gain a firmer grasp of scientific knowledge.[25] This suggestion reveals his emphasis on the educational function of SF, along with his own practice of intertextual play in SF writing. Volland has noted that Zheng's ideas about science and technology move back and forth across the borderline between popular science essays and SF.

He argues that Zheng's 1950s publications show how "ideas were recycled and repackaged across different genres" along a spectrum between popular science at one end and SF on the other.[26] In fact, this practice of recycling and repackaging technological conceptions is also evident in some of Zheng's works written between 1978 and 1983. The practice of blurring borders bears the influences of Soviet SF.[27] It is also a legacy from early Chinese SF, especially the works of Gu Junzheng (1902–80) written in the 1930s and 1940s. Gu's SF narratives are full of essay-like paragraphs that explain aspects of science and technology in great detail. Rao Zhonghua dubbed these imbedded short essays "knowledge clusters" (*zhishi yingkuai*), praising them as a "courageous experiment."[28] Rao supported Gu's approach, saying that it is fine to intersperse such short scientific essays within fiction as long as the author does so in an artistic way. In contrast, SF writer and critic Xiao Jianheng looked askance at these "knowledge clusters" as a major flaw in Gu's stories. He argued that they compromise the aesthetic and artistic quality of Gu's stories.[29] In spite of the critics' contrasting views on "knowledge clusters," Zheng continued with this practice of inserting lengthy scientific explanations in his early SF narratives.

In March 1956, Zheng was invited to attend the National Young Writers Convention, the first time that he attended such a meeting as a literary writer instead of as a popular science writer. It was here that Zheng realized that the literary merits of his SF works were mediocre in comparison with those of most mainstream writers. He also discovered that mainstream literature has had much closer ties to the country's political agenda. SF critic Wu Yan has written a sensitive psychological analysis of Zheng's dissatisfaction with his own creative writing of the 1950s. He argues that one of Zheng's efforts to improve the literary quality of his works was to incorporate more political elements in his narrative.[30] This effort is reflected in an unfinished narrative called "The Communist Capriccio" ("Gongchan zhuyi changxiang qu"), whose setting was the Great Leap Forward (1959–62). It was serialized in the magazine *Chinese Youth* in 1958. More than three decades later, Zheng admitted that this piece was a failure for its lack of scientific imagination and its preoccupation with political matters, because it was too difficult for him to navigate through the tumultuous political situation at the time. For example, it was relatively easy for realist literature at that time to portray Mao as the party-state's paramount leader for the foreseeable future. However, in an SF work set in the year 2000, a novelist sacrificed credibility if portraying Mao as still the paramount leader at the age of 107.[31] In addition, a narrative about Chinese national politics entailed difficult predictions about the future direction of the international communist movement. These concerns led Zheng to temporarily abandon SF writing at the end of the 1950s. He remarked, "After the failure of 'The Communist Capriccio,' I found it is hard for me to anchor the direction of my creative writing in science fiction."[32]

This uncertainty about China's future political direction is also reflected in a story that he planned to write, but never completed. This abortive story features a man who discovers alarming physical changes in his body one evening. His hair turns red, his voice changes, and his arms grow longer and longer. Eventually, the protagonist flees the city to take refuge in the countryside, where his arms turn into wings. In retrospect, Zheng was not sure if his imaginative scenario of rapid physical changes resulted from his fear of the Great Leap Forward and previous CCP political movements or from his presentiments about the Cultural Revolution. Zheng never finished this story, much less sought a publishing outlet for it. Many years later, he said he still could not figure out how to further develop the plot. He said, "I am not sure if my new wings represented my freedom of heart and mind, or if it was just my individual fantasy of alienation from onerous social realities."[33] He thought about attributing the protagonist's transformation to aliens on account of the idea that alien technology could disguise the story's social and political dimensions. Later, he realized that this strategy would not succeed in Mao-era China because Marxist-Leninist doctrine made no provision for the possible existence of space aliens in the universe. Any narrative about space aliens was regarded as irredeemably tainted by corrupt bourgeois ideology. This also explains why there are no space aliens in any of Zheng's works written in the 1950s. Even though space aliens started to appear in Zheng's later narratives from the late 1970s and early 1980s, these aliens do not undertake direct communication with human beings. Normally, they are from a higher civilization that is friendly overall yet wary of earthlings. For example, in his short story "The Turquoise Butterfly" ("Kongque lanse de hudie," 1982), space aliens are presumably transformed into butterflies in order to observe human civilization first-hand. In *The Mirror Image of the Earth* (*Diqiu de jingxiang*, 1980), the aliens on the lemon-like planet avoid direct contact with people from Earth, and depart the planet before earthlings can land on it.

Zheng concluded that the period of the Great Leap Forward was not an appropriate time to write SF, and his career as a creative writer stagnated from 1958 to 1978. During those two decades, he published three semi-academic books: *The Philosophical Significance of the Kant-Laplace Nebular Hypothesis* (*Kangde xingyun shuo de zhexue yiyi*, 1974), *Ancient Chinese Theories about the Universe* (*Zhongguo lishi shang de yuzhou lilun*,

1975), and *The Origin and Development of Chinese Astronomy* (*Zhongguo tianwenxue yuanliu*, 1975). The publication of these academic works not only furthered his career as an astronomer, but also helped set the stage for his future writing of the novels *Flying toward Sagittarius* and *Descendant of Mars*.

From 1978 to the Early 1980s: Resuming Creative Writing and Theoretical Exploration of the Genre

Zheng resumed his career in creative writing in 1978 with the publication of his first full-length novel, *Flying toward Sagittarius*. The novel adopts a storyline similar to that of "From Earth to Mars": three young people take a journey into space and return to Earth with the help of a rescue spaceship nine years later. Among the three young people, two are brother and sister, as in "From Earth to Mars." The novel covers almost all of the topics found in Zheng's 1950s stories, such as landing on the moon, launching satellites into a near-Earth orbit, and building research stations on Mars. However, the novel goes beyond the author's earlier works by extending his imaginative reach out of the solar system. In addition, the young people's journey to space is involuntary, the result of a conspiracy hatched by an enemy country, which can be easily identified as the Soviet Union. This scenario reflects the serious deterioration of Sino-Soviet relations since the end of the 1950s. The enemy country dispatches four robots to a Chinese aerospace base to block the Chinese space mission. The robots initiate the launch when the spaceship "the Eastern" is still under inspection. Three high school students are visiting "the Eastern" when it takes off. The spaceship's original flight plan was to fly to Mars to transport supplies to the scientific laboratories there. However, it flies out of the solar system instead, and soars towards Sagittarius as the result of excessive acceleration. During this unexpected space travel, the young people teach themselves astronomy. Through their lengthy conversations, the author provides an updated exposition on the fundamentals of astronomy, much as he did in his writings of the 1950s. Zheng's protagonists travel through dark nebulae and galactic nuclei, pass by a supernova, escape the gravitational attraction of a black hole, and even approach the speed of light. Given the fact that China just experienced the Cultural Revolution, during which time most kinds of literature and art had been banned, it is not a surprise that the novel became a best seller immediately after its publication. It was especially popular with young and technologically minded readers because of its technological focus, unbridled imagination, spy-thriller elements, and war episodes.

Though the novel drew upon many of the motifs found in Zheng's earlier works, it also bore the imprint of the post-Mao cultural thaw. For example, the narrative showcases Chinese people's life in the near future equipped with modern technology such as self-driving cars, videophones, and automated kitchens. The depiction of modernized material life in the near future appears in many SF stories of Zheng's contemporaries. In addition, the author added two new narrative ingredients: an enemy country and a love interest. The Cold War framework became central to many Chinese SF works during this period, such as Tong Enzheng's "Death Ray on a Coral Island" and Ye Yonglie's detective thriller SF. Zheng's depiction of youthful love echoes a contemporary trend in mainstream literature: the call for humanism.

During this period, Zheng wrote several essays about SF, which reveal continuity and change in his views about the genre. Zheng was very consistent in emphasizing the romantic and scientific characteristics of SF, but the balance had tilted from an early-career focus on science popularization to a late-career artistic appreciation. His views on the thematic concerns of SF changed from praising the struggle of humankind to conquer nature, to depicting characters in a specific social environment, and finally to expounding a philosophy of life and humanism. Zheng's SF narratives written during different periods provide footnotes to his changing views about SF.

In his 1979 essay "A Miscellany on Literature and Art about Science" ("Kexue wenyi zatan"), Zheng reiterated his long-held view that SF originated in ancient fantastic narratives and developed into a new genre with the assistance of advances in modern science and technology.[34] He argued that the genre performs the social function of depicting people's lives in specific social environments, as well as the scientific function of disseminating scientific and technological knowledge. Science and technology should be an unobtrusive component of a narrative's plot structure instead of being shoe-horned into the narrative. This emphasis on the organic integration of science and literature shows that Zheng became more cognizant of the boundary between scientific non-fiction essays and SF than he had been during the 1950s.

In "Response to Lü Chen, the Hong Kong Journalist from *Open the Book Monthly*," Zheng admitted that his views about SF had evolved gradually. In the 1950s, his reading was limited to the works of Soviet writers, along with those of Jules Verne and H.G. Wells. It was only in the 1970s that he was able to come into contact with and read contemporary European and American SF. The latter course of reading has contributed greatly to his more well-rounded views about the genre.[35] He pointed out, "A good SF work expounds a philosophy of life and brings readers a sense of artistic appreciation."[36] In the "Postscript" to *In the Deep Ocean* (*Dayang shenchu*), he added, "Science fiction uses romantic narration and scientific fantasy as a reflector in order to portray human life."[37] Zheng criticized the way that some critics used the criteria of popular science writing in their evaluations of SF, and thus blamed some SF works for not having provided enough scientific knowledge to readers. While SF is neither futurology nor science popularization, people should not "underestimate its functions of scientific enlightenment, promoting scientific thinking, and spreading scientific views about the world and the universe."[38]

In his preface to the collection *The Shark Scouts* (*Shayu zhencha bing*), Zheng emphasized that he strove to depict flesh-and-blood characters. As he put it, they generally freed themselves from the spiritual shackles imposed on China by the "Gang of Four" and the authoritarian system of ultra-centralized rule over the past two thousand years. In sum, they were "modernized socialist new humans."[39] This collection includes three novellas: *The Shark Scouts* (*Shayu zhencha bing*, 1978), *The Crane and People* (*Xianhe yu ren*, 1979), and *The People from the Pacific* (*Taipingyang ren*, 1978). The last two novellas were Zheng's favourites.[40] The technical ideas in *The People from the Pacific* are recycled from his popular-science essay collection *Flying Away from the Earth* (*Feichu diqiu qu*, 1956). The novella is about how scientists conquer a small planet and help the apemen on that planet flourish. These ideas are based on Soviet scientist Konstanty Ciołkowski's assumption that human beings will be able to conquer small planets in the universe someday. The narrative also depicts a love triangle between two brothers, who are both scientists, and a female astronaut. Zheng was satisfied that he skillfully wove technical ideas into a narrative with a complicated love interest. For similar reasons, he liked *The Crane and People*, a story about how a neurosurgeon uses electronic pulses to stimulate human brains to restore the memories of amnesiacs. Zheng complained that this novella had been understudied by critics. He argued that even though this narrative does not embody unusual technological themes or an intricate plot structure, it is poetic with its nuanced and elegant diction, and its sensitive depiction of the characters' psychology.[41]

Zheng's views about the genre in these essays are best manifested in *Descendant of Mars*.

Descendant of Mars

Descendant, published in 1983, is framed within a story about the future history of Mars as recounted by Xue Yinqing, who time-travels back to the past. Unlike the two earlier Mars narratives, the novelist adopts a critical authorial tone about human interference in the Martian ecosystem. The story-telling framework had been evident in Zheng's early stories since the 1950s, but his framing of the future history of Mars within the narrative also bears a more recent influence from Ray Bradbury whose works were first translated into Chinese around 1980. Zheng claimed that he had been deeply touched by the poetics of Bradbury's *The Martian Chronicles*.[42] Throughout *Descendant*, we can see references to Bradbury's work.

Descendant involves two layers of first-person narrators. It begins with a prelude. A river in flood delays a group of strangers, who must spend one night together in a farmer's house. The first-layer narrator, Yuan Fang, a hydraulic technician, describes his encounter with these strangers: a middle-aged geologist named Xue Yinqing, a young truck driver named Xiaoshun, and the host couple Old Cao and his wife. At night, Xue tells Yuan about his experiences on Mars. From here, the narrative is taken over from Yuan by the second-layer narrator Xue, who provides a first-person narration of his own five-year sojourn on Mars from 2078 to 2083. However, from the very beginning, Xue is unreliable. In the prelude, he mentions that he is looking for Dragon Head Gold Mine, but no one has ever heard of it. Neither has anyone heard of the newspaper *Mars Times* or the exploration of Mars that he repeatedly mentions. The mystery is solved only at the end of novel when Xue asks Yuan what year it is now. It turns out that Xue has travelled back to 1983, a century prior to the end of his Mars trip. So Xue suspects that all of his experiences on Mars have been nothing more than a dream. This unreliable second-layer narrator destabilizes the authenticity of Xue's story.

Xue gives a detailed account of how the "Yu Wen plan" is carried out on Mars. In the preliminary phase, the exploration team settles in Sun Valley as their base, erecting large glass domes. These domes simulate the air composition, temperature, and pressure on Earth so that people can live and work inside without wearing spacesuits. Meanwhile, the team dispatches three groups to carry out geological and atmospheric surveys of Mars. The second phase transforms the Martian atmosphere to make it suitable for humans to breath and create a self-sustaining ecosystem that can fully support human habitation. Settlers expand their territories from Sun Valley to Hellas Basin and five other regions. They build underground cities that radiate outwards from the central region of Sun Valley. In the cities, they create a complete societal infrastructure by constructing hospitals, schools, research institutes, and theatres, creating a Martian calendar, and founding the planet's first newspaper, the *Mars Times*.

Hellas Basin, a huge impact crater, is chosen to implement the team's bold atmospheric transformation. Taking advantage of steam and lava from a volcanic eruption, the team creates artificial precipitation to form a lake, which will not only store water, but also create a local climate and increase the oxygen content and temperature of the atmosphere. They also hope the local climate will cause atmospheric circulation, which will melt the ice caps at the North and South Poles and bring water to Hellas. In this way, the Hellas Basin will become the cradle of Martian civilization, much as Earth's earliest major civilizations emerged within fertile valleys of the Tigris and Euphrates, the Nile, the Indus, and the Yellow Rivers. In addition, the team grows grains and vegetables, and plants trees not only to supply the colonists with food, but also in hope of creating a vibrant ecosystem. However, the forced-air blockade artificially created by the team to sustain the local climate in Hellas Basin changes the natural atmospheric circulation on Mars. When air turbulence from the South Pole confronts the forced-air blockade in Hellas Basin, it creates a global climate anomaly. Frigid cold fronts and violent windstorms sweep across Mars, destroying all the facilities on the planet's surface, and finally even set off a nuclear explosion. The team leader Yu Wen dies in the explosion, and the human colonists are forced to retreat underground. Yu's body is blasted out of the planet's atmosphere together with the explosion debris, and ends up in orbit around Mars. Xue glorifies Yu's death by saying that Yu has metamorphosed into a moon orbiting Mars, and dubs Yu "the descendant of Mars."[43] The author uses the term "Mars" as a pun: it is the name of both the red planet and the Roman god of war. Yu becomes a symbol of a descendant of both the planet Mars and of the god of war.

Terraforming is a plot motif, which "involves processes aimed at adapting the environmental parameters of alien planets for habitation by Earthbound life, and it includes methods for modifying a planet's climate, atmosphere, topology, and ecology."[44] The technical ideas of terraforming in *Descendant* remind readers of Grigory Adamov's 1946 novel *The Ousting of the Ruler*, which recounts a water diversion project, and short stories dealing with solar energy, large-scale generation of electricity, and artificial climate change published by *Znanie-Sila* (Knowledge is power) magazine in the early 1930s. In his study of terraforming texts, Martyn Fogg indicates that it contains two subsets of planetary engineering: terraforming alien planets and terraforming Earth.[45] *Descendant* involves both sets, represented by the "Yu Wen Plan" on Mars and Mao's war against nature on Earth. However, Mao's geoengineering projects on Earth are not depicted directly; instead, they are sporadically recalled and mentioned by characters throughout the narrative. Hence, the author creates an analogy between these mammoth engineering projects on Mars and Mao's mass mobilization campaigns on Earth. The novel locates terraforming in the near future, in the politico-economic context of an Earth that closely resembles contemporary social relations. Through this analogy, the terraforming motif functions as commentary on Chinese society. There is a lengthy conversation between the protagonist Xue and the team leader Yu Wen, who compares the terraforming projects on Mars to those on Earth: "If we can develop Antarctica and transform the Sahara and Taklimakan deserts, I do not see why we cannot transform Mars into a habitable place for human beings. I do not mean to simply build small-scale labs and work stations that undertake scientific research. I have a plan to exploit Mars. We will construct both villages and cities on Mars. We will farm, mine, develop industry, engage in scientific research, and build entertainment facilities. Mars should have its own opera theatres and gymnasiums, just as we have on Earth."[46]

In the early 1950s, the traditional Chinese ideal of "harmony between heaven and humankind" was abrogated in favour of Mao's insistence that humanity must conquer nature. Mao's triumphalist rhetoric unfolded during mass campaigns to resettle Han Chinese migrants in remote borderland regions in an attempt to open up wastelands and secure frontier areas during the 1950s and 1960s. These mass-mobilized migrations severely affected the mountainous regions of southwest China, the deserts of Xinjiang in the far west, the grasslands of Inner Mongolia in the northwest, and the "Great Northern Wilderness" in the northeast's Heilongjiang province.[47] The negative results of these campaigns are mentioned in the prelude of the novel. Old Cao in the host family complains to Xue that the natural environment in the area has changed dramatically during the last thirty years. "This area suffers floods every year, and the flooding has grown more severe each year. The groves of ancient old-growth pine trees around the upper reaches of the river valley were all clear-cut during the campaign of *pishan zaotian* (transform the hilly wilderness into farmland)."[48] However, the farmland has registered very poor crop yields because its soil is unsuitable for cultivating row crops. Old Cao recalls the good old days when those hills were covered with pine trees and orchards. Now the hills are a barren expanse of sand and rocks, and the river is muddy and turbid. Old Cao sighs, "Everything that farmers treasure has been washed away."[49] Through Old Cao, the author reveals that the Maoist warlike mobilizations to bend the physical world to human exploitation had disastrous consequences both for human beings and the natural environment.

Yu Wen and many of his team members, as Xue observes, "were involved in either the project to transform the Tibetan plateau, the initiative to exploit Antarctica, the project to re-engineer the sea bed of the Southern Pacific, or the campaign to transform the Taklimakan Desert" before they came to Mars.[50] The pioneering spirit of these team members has thus merely shifted from the frontiers of Earth to the frontiers of Mars. This pioneering spirit resembles and differs from the pioneering spirit in the twentieth century terraforming texts of America. Pak indicates that early 1950s American terraforming stories were informed by pastoral themes and the pioneering spirit of America's colonization; terraforming narratives also provide a space to explore issues such as interplanetary isolationism, political and economic oppression, and environmental ethics.[51] Similar to colonial settlers on the American continent, the Mars settlers in American terraforming texts see Mars as a new space where they can escape from the old system on Earth and create new socio-political foundations.

For example, in Bradbury's "The Taxpayer" (1958) originally published in *The Martian Chronicles,* the eponymous taxpayer is eager to "get away from wars and censorship and statism and conscription and government control of this and that, of art and science" on Earth.[52] Similarly, in "The Million Year Picnic" (1946), after the family of five lands on Mars, the father burns all the important documents they have brought from Earth, saying, "I'm burning a way of life."[53] Burning all of their files is a sign that they have cut themselves off from "civilization's legal, economic, and political structures, but above all its technocracy."[54] Pak argues that Bradbury "restructured the pastoral opposition between the country and the city" in traditional American pastoral texts "as an opposition between Earth and Mars" in his Martian narratives.[55] Many characters in *The Martian Chronicles* see Mars as a pastoral utopia where they can start a new life that contrasts markedly with what they experienced on Earth. In *Descendant,* though Yu's ambitions of making Mars a second Earth and of pressing earthlings to become settlers on Mars remind readers of *The Martian Chronicles,* Yu and his team members do not see Mars as a potential for pastoral retreat, nor do they wish to sever ties with Earth's civilization in the way that some of Bradbury's characters do. Instead, they view the potential Martian civilization as an extension of Earth's civilization, and see technocracy as an effective tool for achieving this goal. Though Xue in *Descendant* sporadically mentions that the community on Mars is very democratic (in contrast with authoritarian rule in China), and reveals his critical views about terraforming Mars and Earth, these discussions are not a rejection of the contemporary socio-political system in China or a desire to cut themselves off from Earth's civilization.

Yu and his team want to create a civilization similar to that on Earth. He emphasizes the rationality of human beings, and believes that people can develop a Martian civilization as rational as that on Earth. He envisions that human posterity will evolve physical features more suitable for the natural environment on Mars. He refers to Konstanty Ciołkowski's idea that human civilization cannot thrive indefinitely if confined solely on Earth, and should spread its reach to other parts of the universe.[56] Both Yu and his colleague Liu Yunyun refer to Arthur C. Clarke's work *2001: A Space Odyssey* in which human civilization has been generated in part by an alien civilization, and that some humans will eventually be transformed into a form of energy in the universe.

If terraforming is an overt motif in the novel, then the Mars syndrome is an underlying motif. In the narrative, natural conditions on Mars begin to warp human psychology. The earthlings have developed psychological problems related to the limited progress of terraforming projects on Mars. Xue refers to the abnormal behaviour and verbal communication as the Mars syndrome, which can be seen as a counterforce of terraforming, representing the resistance of the natural environment of Mars to the earthlings' ambition to adapt to this alien environment. It underscores the difficulty of adapting any organism to an unfamiliar environment. Everyone on Mars is changing "from polite to rude, from warm-hearted to cold-hearted, from calm to irritable, from lively to dull.... It is very likely that I am not transforming Mars, but being transformed by Mars, and being transformed into a Martian whom I cannot recognize myself."[57] Such psychological change also reminds readers of many Chinese people's psychological condition during Mao's Cultural Revolution.

The Mars syndrome not only warps human psychology, but also harms family life. For example, Yu and his wife have been deeply in love since they were newlyweds. However, their marital relations gradually deteriorate after their arrival on Mars. The extreme natural environment and arduous working conditions contribute to an escalation of small conflicts between the couple. The situation gets worse after Yu insists on bringing their son to Mars to become part of his social experiment there. The son becomes contaminated by water in Hellas Basin's artificial lake and develops an incurable cancer. Yu's wife eventually decides to make a total break with her husband. With the help of her friends, she absconds from Mars with their son. Yu's failed marriage symbolizes the acute risks involved in trying to preserve normal family life on Mars.

In addition, what happens to Xue's unborn child also reveals the author's pessimism about the future for humans on Mars. Xue and his wife Ruhong are expecting their baby – "the first citizen of the universe."[58] Xue even compares the birth of their first baby with the moment when the first ape walked upright on Earth. Unfortunately, both the expectant mother and her deformed baby die in the delivery room. The death of Xue's unborn baby and the mysterious disease that Yu's young son contracts remind readers of the death of Peggy on Ganymede in Robert Heinlein's *Farmer in the Sky* (1950). Such sickness and death among these extraterrestrial pioneers "underscore notions of fitness to habitation involved in terraforming."[59] After the death of his wife and the baby, Xue repeatedly asks himself, "Why did Ruhong's pregnancy end up in such a deadly way? Is it because she had been exposed to too much radiation? Or do the natural conditions of Mars prohibit earthlings from reproducing themselves?"[60] Xue's reflections suggest that earthlings must struggle with and transcend the limits of their humanity in order to successfully make a home on Mars. The death of the first Martian baby also has dark implications for the sustainability of the Martian colonial project: all human offspring conceived on Mars might well be doomed to being stillborn. The Mars syndrome reveals how the use of technology within a community can affect individuals. The psychological changes and physical problems can readily escalate to a crisis that is beyond the ability of Yu Wen to control. Such crises are compounded by dust storms, magnetic storms, and seismic quakes, and eventually thwart the "Yu Wen Plan" with grim deaths and accidents.

In addition to leading to psychological problems and wrecking family life, the biggest impact of the Mars syndrome is that many people's views about the wisdom of colonizing Mars gradually grow darker: initially supportive, people increasingly grow suspicious and even go so far as to disapprove of the Mars colonization. The author stages the perspectives on Mars exploitation within a variety of narrative voices, which result in reflection on relations between humankind and nature.

As an omniscient first-person narrator, Xue maintains a certain distance from his group of "new socialist men" of strong will, passion, and professionalism – led by Yu Wen and Liu Yunyun. They continue to manifest the pioneering spirit of the socialist builders on Earth whom I discussed earlier in this chapter. Yu and Liu also embody the ideological position of the time – Deng Xiaoping's emphasis that science and technology are advanced productive forces. When Xue eulogizes the pioneers' achievements, he also expresses his own critical and sceptical view about the purported great feats of humankind on Mars. From the very beginning, Xue questioned whether it is necessary to travel a vast distance to exploit Mars when so many problems remain unresolved on Earth? Xue's scepticism about the "Yu Wen Plan" intensifies as the projects on Mars go awry. In Zheng's early narrative "The Mars Pioneers," he describes these accidents and unexpected difficulties in order to reveal the strong will and optimism of new socialist man about changing the world for the better. In contrast, the accidents and deaths in *Descendant* motivate Xue to reflect on humans' radical transformation of nature. The entire narrative is interspersed with Xue's thoughts on the Mars exploitation.

Descendant includes an episode about the discovery of alien life on Mars. In contrast with the assumption of the exploration team that there was no Martian civilization in the past, Xue infers that there should have been – on the basis of Darwinian evolution and Herbert Spencer's popular geopolitical notion of "survival of the fittest." Xue's inference proves correct. The exploration team locates metal fragments and the remains of organisms within the geological strata that indicate there was intelligent life and an advanced civilization on Mars in the past.

When discussing the discovery of alien life in Heinlein's *Farmer in the Sky* and Clarke's *The Sands of Mars*, Pak indicates that terraforming narratives in the 1950s "show a distinct engagement with the politics of imperialism, nationalism, and utopia."[61] "When these themes interact with the trope of alien life, terraforming is used to explore the extension of human moral environments towards others."[62] Zheng's novel resonates with Heinlein's and Clarke's works in this way – specifically, by using the tropes of terraforming and alien life to "open up ethical debate on issues of responsibility and respect for nature's otherness" and the politics of imperialism in interplanetary colonization.[63]

Xue's reflections on alien life forms and the difficulty of human adaptation to living on Mars explore the ethics of planetary colonization and environmental ethics on Earth. When a windstorm destroys domes and forces people to withdraw underground, Xue feels that "nature on Mars is like an intelligent and powerful life force that vigorously makes humans retreat to an underground cage."[64] Xue quotes Friedrich Engels's caution against the conceptualization of nature as standing in opposition to humanity: "Let us not flatter ourselves overmuch on account of our human victories over nature. For each such victory nature takes its revenge on us."[65] He comments directly on the team's Mars project: "Mars did not have its own ecological system prior to our arrival there. Yet if we want to introduce life to Mars, we must consider how to establish a balanced ecosystem. We need to make careful calculations about water sources, oxygen content, energy, and climatic cycles."[66] Xue further relates these problems to humankind and ecosystems on Earth: humans have already had too many bad experiences of throwing the ecosystem out of balance on Earth. Whenever people start to develop a region's economy, the first thing they destroy is its ecological balance. He concludes, "When we transform nature, nature will take its revenge on us."[67] Here again, Xue refers to Mao's geoengineering projects on Earth.

Furthermore, Xue speculates that the extinct Martian civilization may have developed to the stage of generating electricity through nuclear fusion. Abnormally high levels of radiation in Devil Valley seem to provide evidence of nuclear power stations. Xue speculates that this civilization might have died out as the result of natural environmental changes, nuclear explosions, wars, or plagues. We can see that whatever caused the extinction of Martian civilization may be highly relevant to risks now faced by human civilization on Earth – climate change, pollution, thermonuclear wars, pandemics, and mass extinctions of species. These problems have resulted at least in part from human activities, especially since the Industrial Revolution. Scholars such as Ian Baucom,[68] Dipesh Chakrabarty,[69] and Pieter Vermeulen have theorized about the contradictory nature of human life: it is not only "a biological, psychological, and linguistic phenomenon," but also "plays in the same league as, say, heat waves, volcanoes, and Antarctic ice."[70] We can read Zheng's speculation on the extinction of life on Mars as an analogy of the future of human life on Earth. The analogy shows that the possibility of our extinction is not merely a projection into the distant future, but emphatically also a likely reality within a shorter time frame.

The author further examines human history on Earth. Xue once has a dream after a windstorm. In the dream, a giant armour-clad Martian with an axe in hand, who resembles the Roman god of war, asks Xue, "Why have you invaded our territory?"[71] Xue replies, "This war between nature on Mars and human earthlings will last for many generations."[72] When later pondering this scene, he compares human endeavours on Mars to empire-building on Earth. He refers to Isaac Asimov's Galactic Empire series, and questions why the term "empire" is used in space exploration. "The galaxy is so vast that there must be some intelligent and rational beings on some planets other than Earth. Why do we call such a place an 'empire'? Can we not build a rational interstellar community with advanced technology and civilization, a democratic, equal, and peaceful society? Must we suffer under yet another first emperor of the Qin dynasty whose hands are stained by Chinese intellectuals' blood – or yet another Hitler who would lord over a brutal empire within the vast territory of the galaxy?"[73] Xue's comment on the first emperor of Qin and Hitler enhances the novel's piquant social commentary on imperialism and nationalism. At the end of the narrative following Xue's return to Earth, he asks, "When will this Sodom get its retribution?"[74] This is the author's implied rebuke to human violence against nature and people's inhumanity to each other.

Xue's reflections and the tension between his critical view of the Mars colonial project and the Party's rhetoric that glorifies conquering nature are diffracted in the author's treatment of Xue's time travel back to the past, the time when Zheng wrote this narrative. After Yu dies, several voices on the Mars project speak: some people want to withdraw from Mars and return to Earth because science and technology are not sufficiently advanced to colonize Mars sustainably. Others insist upon continuing with the colonial project under Liu Yunyun's leadership. In spite of the controversy, a third group of two thousand volunteers arrives during another period of Mars opposition. Just as Robinson fails to bring matters to resolution in his *Mars* trilogy, Zheng does not settle the debates about terraforming. In this way, the work's "multiple perspectives encourage readers to continually synthesize a complex array of political positions."[75] Xue subsequently returns to Earth to receive medical treatment. However, his spaceship encounters a black hole on its way back. When Xue accelerates to escape the black hole, his spaceship accelerates to ultra-light speed and takes him back to Earth of one century earlier, in 1983. This time travel to the past has two areas of significance. First, it reveals the author's opposition to human colonization of Mars. Time travel gives the author a convenient excuse to terminate Xue's career on Mars. Second, it gives people hope that by getting a second chance, Xue might be able to influence Yu Wen and change the flawed plan for transforming and colonizing Mars.

This analysis of the novel reveals the author's scepticism about Mao's past wars against nature and future colonization of other planets. We also can now better understand the author's reflections on human history and his concerns about human life as a geological force in the Anthropocene. The thematic concerns of *Descendant* situate the novel within the mainstream early reform-era PRC literary trend of "contemplative literature" and the broad intellectual movement to "bid … adieu to the revolution" around 1980.

During the period from 1978 to 1983, many of Zheng's narratives have thematic concerns in common with those of "scar literature" and "contemplative literature," which expose the dark side of Mao's Cultural Revolution, seek deeper explanations of recent calamities, and call for a contrasting humanistic spirit or ethos. Echoing the literary trends in mainstream Chinese literature, Zheng wrote a series of SF short stories and novellas with the Cultural Revolution as the social background, such as the novellas *Star Labour Camp* (*Xingxing ying*, 1980), *Philosopher* (*Zhexuejia*, 1982), and "Destiny Nightclub" ("Mingyun yezonghui," 1982). These stories all depict the use of modern technology to persecute Chinese intellectuals during the Cultural Revolution. In *Star Labour Camp*, the "revolutionary" leftists use anti-hormone therapy to transform intellectual inmates into ape-men. The third person omniscient narrator cries, "This is an abominable crime, not only committed against all of humankind, but also against Mother Nature herself!"[76] In *Philosopher*, a special kind of mineral emits bio-electricity to stimulate human brains. Under its effects, both the first-person narrator and the philosopher recall their physical and spiritual suffering in labour camps or "cowsheds" (*niupeng*) during the decade-long catastrophe of the Cultural Revolution. In "Destiny Nightclub," ultrasonic equipment is used to force intellectuals in a great northern wilderness labour camp to make bogus confessions of imaginary crimes. In these stories, Zheng incorporates his personal experiences and feelings during the Cultural Revolution when he was forced to "remould" himself through manual labour in the countryside around Panjin and Anshan in the far northeast (Manchuria) from the mid-1960s to the early 1970s.[77]

In addition to those stories about the Cultural Revolution, Zheng also extended his reflection on the dark realities to human history, and to human endeavours to explore the universe. In the preface to his short story collection *A New Anthology of Zheng Wenguang*, Zheng writes, "As a historian of science, I have paid great attention to the development of human civilization, and have pondered various contemporary issues we face by viewing them in the context of our long history."[78] For example, his novella *The Mirror Image of the Earth* does not overtly explore the Cultural Revolution, but reflects broadly on the violent history of human civilization. In the narrative, a spaceship lands on an alien planet with an atmosphere similar to that of the Earth. In a cave the astronauts discover holographic films left behind by intelligent aliens. The film contains scenes of first Emperor Qin burning books and burying the literati, Xiang Yu torching the Epang palace, Zheng He's voyage to the Western Ocean, and even the Maoist Red Guards' conflicts during the Cultural Revolution. The astronauts find that the aliens do not trust them and are afraid that human beings "might attack them any moment with machine guns and tanks, or with old weapons like booby traps, spears, swords, and bricks."[79] At the end of the narrative, one astronaut asks, "Are we, people from the Earth, so terrible?" Another answers, "Some of us indeed resemble a fierce flood or a savage beast."[80] This short conversation is Zheng's lament for not only what happened during the Cultural Revolution, but also for widespread violence throughout the history of human civilization.

This reflective tone in *The Mirror Image of the Earth* continues in *Descendant,* in which Zheng extends his concerns about violence on Earth to human activities elsewhere in the universe. In *Descendant,* he uses Mars exploration as a device to estrange the reader from the familiar world in order to examine the violence that has accompanied human history and has similarly damaged nature. Through the failure of the atmospheric transformation project on Mars, Zheng questions the radical campaigns to transform nature during the Mao era. He cautions the reader that scientific research and technological development without consideration for their social repercussions will likely precipitate political and ecological catastrophes on both Earth and Mars.

Zheng's novel echoes Western terraforming narratives of the mid-1950s by using the terraforming motif to engage in socio-political and environmental ethics discourse. When we read this novel more than thirty years after it was first published, we can see that the variety of narratives on terraforming in the novel sounds similar to discussions about terraforming in Robinson's *Mars* trilogy and current debates on climate change. Though the term "Anthropocene" had not yet been coined when Zheng wrote *Descendant,* the idea of human existence as a geological force is evident in his narrative. The novel features geoengineering as a form of climate change mitigation. The failed atmospheric engineering project in Hellas Basin on Mars and Mao's war against nature on Earth demonstrate that terraforming is an extension of anthropogenic climate change, and powerfully illustrate a connection between climate change and geoengineering.

3 A Scientific Holmes in Post-Mao China: Ye Yonglie and His SF Thrillers

Ye Yonglie has been a prolific writer of SF, science popularization narratives, playscripts, and reportage literature (see figure 3.1). The publication of *Xiao Lingtong Travels to the Future* in 1978 brought him national fame in the PRC among juvenile readers. Beginning in the late 1970s, Ye shifted his focus to a mature readership through a series of stories featuring a tech-savvy detective named Jin Ming as the protagonist. From 1979 to 1983, Ye published such SF thriller novellas as *Disguised* (*Qiaozhuang daban*, 1980), *A Strange Case of Pandas* (*Guobao qi'an*, 1980), *Black Shadow* (*Heiying*, 1980), *Secret Column* (*Mimi zongdui*, 1981), *Veiled Strife* (*An dou*, 1981), *Disappearing without a Trace* (*Bu yi er fei*, 1982), and *As If Awakening from a Dream* (*Ru meng chu xing*, 1983). This SF thriller series won Ye great popularity among mature PRC readers, including fans from the burgeoning scientific intelligentsia as well as general readers of detective thrillers.

This chapter focuses on Ye's SF thriller, a subgenre that Ye almost single-handedly originated and promoted in the PRC. Ye's creative incorporation of the detective thriller within a standard variety of Chinese SF narrative was a major contribution to the revival of entertainment fiction and SF during the post-Mao thaw.[1] When reading for pleasure started to re-enter the daily routine of Chinese people after the end of the Cultural Revolution, demand surged for popular fiction. SF thrillers played a significant role in meeting this pent-up demand. Much like the popular genre of sentimental romances (often dubbed "mandarin-duck-and-butterfly fiction") in the early twentieth century, post-Mao SF thrillers were often initially serialized in newspapers or magazines and utilized a formulaic plot. In addition, post-Mao SF thrillers typically borrow narrative techniques from such genres of Western popular fiction as thrillers, spy novels, and detective fiction. The enthusiastic popular reception of Ye's SF thrillers demonstrates his

Figure 3.1. Ye Yonglie (1940–2020) and the author at Ye's Shanghai residence in July 2019 (courtesy of the author).

successful integration of popular literary features from the Chinese and Western traditions of entertainment fiction. Moreover, Ye's ubiquitous protagonist Jin Ming presents a new image of a highly educated Chinese professional who exhibits martial arts savvy and high-tech expertise. This new type of PRC protagonist provides a curious twist on the post-Mao party-state's elevation of the intelligentsia's role in striving to achieve the Four Modernizations.

Bridging the Dichotomy between SF and Thrillers

Ye first utilized the Chinese term *jingxianshi kexue huanxiang xiaoshuo* (literally, "thriller-style science fiction") to refer to SF thrillers in an article published in the *Guangming Daily* on 28 February 1980.[2] He wrote, "This year, my focus will be on writing science fiction. I'm very fond of thrillers and will try to combine the features of both science fiction and thrillers. I will write *jingxian shi kexue huanxiang xiaoshuo*."[3] Half a year later in July 1980, Ye dropped the suffix "-style" (*shi*), switching to the term *jingxian kexue huanxiang xiaoshuo* (SF thriller) in the preface to *The Mysterious Suit* (*Shenmi yi*, 1980).[4] In October 1980, Rao Zhonghua and Lin Yaochen utilized Ye's updated term "SF thriller" in the preface to an edited volume entitled *Science Fantasy* (*Kexue shenhua*), praising Ye's *The X-3 Case* (*X-3 an jian*, 1980) as an example of a successful SF thriller.[5]

In the preface to *An Anthology of Chinese SF Thrillers*, Ye claimed that the Chinese category of the "thriller novel" (*jingxian xiaoshuo*) encompasses features of detective fiction (*zhentan xiaoshuo*), the mystery novel (*tuili xiaoshuo*), the spy novel (*jiandie xiaoshuo*), and other types of fiction that feature shocking crimes and political conspiracies.[6] He included Western classic detective fiction, Soviet spy novels, and Japanese *suiri shōsetsu* (mystery fiction) under the category of the thriller.

Ye's creative blend of SF and thriller stems from his personal fondness for thrillers and his aspiration to increase the popularity of SF in China. Ye has long been aware of the popularity of thriller fiction in Japan and the West. He also noticed that thrillers attracted Chinese readers as well. In 1979, the magazine *Juvenile Literature and Arts* published a special issue on the thriller, and the first print run sold out within three days.[7] What first piqued his interest in SF were two Soviet SF thriller narratives he read during his student days at Beijing University in the 1950s. One was an illustrated book entitled *Secrets at a Shooting Range* (*Shejichang de mimi*, 1955), a counterintelligence novel featuring the implanting of a miniature camera in a dog's eye in order to spy on an enemy military base. Another was a collection of five thrillers entitled *The Bizarre Glue* (*Qiyi de touming jiao*, 1956). The eponymous story is about injecting a kind of transparent glue into a large hydrogen balloon that can carry passengers into the sky. These two narratives impressed him so much that he wanted to blend SF and the thriller when eventually writing his own SF thrillers.[8]

Ye's early fascination with Chinese translations of the Soviet SF thrillers is paralleled by his fondness for Chinese translations of British mystery novels by Arthur Conan Doyle and Agatha Christie. Sherlock Holmes narratives have been familiar to Chinese readers since the first decades of the twentieth century. For example, Conan Doyle's *A Study in Scarlet* (1887) was translated into Chinese by Lin Shu (1852–1924) and first serialized in newspapers in 1907. The novel first came out in book form in 1914 under the Chinese title *Xialuoke qi'an kaichang* (Sherlock's first bizarre case). Strong sales of this popular novel led to numerous other Chinese translations of the Holmes series. Many PRC publishers reprinted old Holmes translations during the post-Mao cultural thaw, often in illustrated editions. For example, the Lingnan Fine Arts

Publishing House published an illustrated fifty-seven-volume Holmes series during the early 1980s.

In the early months of 1979, Agatha Christie achieved celebrity among PRC readers when cinematic versions of her novels *Death on the Nile* and *Murder on the Orient Express* were first screened in China. The prominent magazine *Yi Lin* and the Chinese Film Publishing House subsequently published Chinese translations of those two Christie novels in the latter half of that year. Soon afterwards, Christie's series of Poirot detective novels also came out in Chinese translation. The PRC's enthusiastic reception of detective and mystery fiction by Doyle and Christie spurred Ye to write his own flavour of detective fiction. Ye commented, "I was inspired by Conan Doyle's Holmes series.... I feel that I should concentrate on conjuring a lone protagonist to form the basis for an entire series of SF thrillers."[9] Ye points out that the influence of Conan Doyle comes across clearly in the first eight narratives of his Jin Ming series, such as "The Case of a Killing Umbrella" ("Sha ren san an jian," 1980), *The X-3 Case*, and *Veiled Strife*.[10]

In his letter to the Japanese literary critic Noguchi Masami, Ye argued that his Jin Ming series should not be classified as detective SF, but instead as mystery (*suiri*) SF because of the similarity of these narratives to Japanese *suiri shōsetsu*. His Jin Ming series bears an especially close affinity to the Japanese subgenre of socially engaged mystery fiction (*shakai suiri shōsetsu*). Ye added that the relative lack of social engagement in Conan Doyle's novels is a shortcoming that he avoids in his Jin Ming series.[11]

In his essay "Responses to Questions about SF Thrillers" (1983), Ye pointed out that he may not have been the first novelist to have written a SF thriller, for many foreign writers preceded him in developing this blended genre. They include Isaac Asimov in *The Caves of Steel* (1954) and *The Naked Sun* (1957), Shizuko Natsuki (1938–2016) in *Portal of the Wind* (1981), and Hiroshi Sano (1928–2013) in his short stories "Transparent Assassination" (1960), "Metallic Sound Syndrome" (1961), and "A Prostitute Soaring in the Sky" (1968).[12] Ye added that a novelist's scientific and technological know-how contribute to success in the two key features of the thriller: "pungent sensationalism" and "the power of logical analysis and subtle and acute reasoning."[13] He recommended that Chinese SF writers take the advantage of the "protean nature of the thriller, which has always been capacious enough to incorporate devices from the detective story tradition."[14] Ye encouraged his peers on the SF literary scene to make their own SF more readable by reading Conan Doyle and Agatha Christie with an eye to learning from two British novelists' mastery of suspense, plot twists, and compact structure.[15] Much like Sherlock Holmes, the detective protagonists in PRC SF thrillers should crack crime cases and solve mysteries with the aid of expertise in modern science and technology. At the same time that they enjoy entertaining tales, Chinese readers of SF thrillers should feel inspired to extend their knowledge of science and technology even further.[16]

The post-Mao SF thriller made its debut in 1979 with the newspaper serializations of Wu Boze's (1933–2005) novella *Invisible Man* (*Yin xing ren*) and Ye's short story "Hovering between Life and Death" ("Shengsi weibu").[17] In the same year, Ye also published his novellas *Cat and Mouse Game* (*Yuqin guzong*), *The Mysterious Suit (Shenmi yi)*, and *The Violinist* (*Xian wai zhi yin*), along with two film scripts. Near the end of 1980, Ye started to publish the Jin Ming series, which includes such renowned narratives as *Disguised*, *Veiled Strife*, *The X-3 Case* (later reprinted under the new title *Guobao qi'an*, 1980), *Secret Column*, *Black Shadow*, *Disappearing without a Trace*, and *As If Awakening from a Dream*.

Ye encapsulated his formula for the SF thriller in three phrases consisting of twelve Chinese characters: *tichu xuannian*, *cengceng bosun*, and *pianmo jiemi*. This means to "create suspense" in the beginning of the narrative, "peel away layer after layer of uncertainty" in the middle, and "solve the mystery" at the end.[18] He assured writers that if they apply this formula to a SF thriller, they will succeed in conjuring an intricate and fascinating plot.[19]

In 1981, Ye compiled and published *An Anthology of Chinese SF Thrillers*, which contains twenty Chinese stories and novellas published between 1939 and 1980. In his preface, Ye identifies Gu Junzheng's novella *The Dream of Peace* (*Heping de meng*, 1939) as the first Chinese SF thriller, which recounts intrigues of Japanese and American spies during the Second World War. Science enters the picture prominently when the Japanese espionage authority attempts to manipulate the American populace into a spirit of defeatism through the use of hypnosis. Ye claims that *The Dream of Peace* contains such features of the SF thriller as plot twists, scientific motifs, and leaps of imagination. Ye also cites Yu Zhi's "The Missing Brother" ("Shizong de gege," 1955) as another early Chinese SF thriller. In this narrative, a teenage boy becomes locked in a factory freezer and hibernates in a cryonic state for fifteen years. Local scientists eventually retrieve the boy's body from the freezer and use advanced technology to revive him. When compared with *The Dream of Peace*, Ye believes that this story has a stronger Chinese flavour for its setting in Mao-era China.[20]

In this anthology, Ye categorizes the fictional works according to subgenre. For example, Ye groups three stories within the subgenre of the "international conspiracy SF thriller": Tong Enzheng's "Death Ray on a Coral Island," Wang Xiaoda's "The Mysterious Waves" ("Shenmi de bo," 1980), and Wei Yahua's "The Incident of a Flying Blanket" ("Feitan de fengbo," 1979). Similarly, Ye applies the subgenre label of "espionage SF thriller" to three other stories: Liu Husheng's "The Mystery in Deep Ocean" ("Shenhai yi an," 1980), Liu Zhaogui's "The Mystery of β" ("β zhege mi," 1979), and Wang Bao'an's "The Case of Theft at the International Exposition" ("Wanguo bolanhui shang de qie an," 1980).[21]

The Jin Ming Series

Ye's most popular SF thrillers belong to his Jin Ming series. Throughout, Jin Ming often insists that he depends upon both heaven above and Earth below. Ye explains that "heaven" refers here to the Communist Party's leadership, while "Earth" refers to the populace in the PRC. Jin Ming utilizes three main tools that help him solve various cases he is investigating: the Party's leadership, support from the PRC populace, and scientific methodology.[22]

Every narrative's plot within the Jin Ming series is highly formulaic. Many episodes reflect a Cold War mindset in their utilization of a common framework found in much international espionage fiction. There is an "underlying feeling of national insecurity in the face of international relations" that the critics David Stafford and David Seed attribute to the rise of British spy fiction at the turn of the nineteenth century.[23] The world of the Jin Ming series is dangerous and treacherous in which China is the target of envy and hostility from the Soviet Union, the United States, or both. The villainous spy organizations in this series typically encroach upon China under the sponsorship of an adversarial foreign government or an insidious international consortium. At the same time, this series abounds with paranoia about domestic enemies, a theme repeated endlessly in Mao Zedong's ideological preoccupation with class struggle. In many of Ye's narratives, the villainous spies are usually either overseas Chinese or unscrupulous PRC citizens who have been bought off by foreign spy organizations. These villains typically worm their way into a Chinese research institute or military base in order to pilfer a technological invention that has military or commercial value. Sometimes the villain even murders a prominent scientist or sabotages research facilities. (However, Ye presents a more positive image of overseas Chinese in his later SF thrillers after the Chinese government adopted a more welcoming and less suspicious policy towards them.) At that point, the detective Jin Ming and his assistants march in to investigate the case and inevitably uncover and then destroy the enemy's scheme so as to safeguard the party-state from insidious subversion from abroad.

In his research on British spy fiction, David Seed claims that early Western spy fiction appealed to readers by promising them special access to what took place in the shadows behind official history.[24] In the Jin Ming series, the appeal for readers is in the way the omniscient narrator grants readers special access to the secret procedures used to crack cases by the PRC's national police, the Public Security Bureau (PSB). Another area of appeal to readers stems from fancy gadgetry and other high-tech devices used in counter-espionage missions. For example, *A Scientific Holmes* starts with a short prologue: "Nowadays, all over the world spies are equipped with modern technology to tap into the intelligence gathered by other countries."[25] At the end of the narrative, the narrator repeats a point made in the prologue: "Nowadays, enemy countries use modern espionage technology to collect intelligence, so we must use modern technology to combat this spying. This is how counter-intelligence now functions in the new international order."[26] In the Jin Ming series, enemy agents usually target such fields as the life sciences, artificial intelligence, or electronics. For example, "The Case of a Killing Umbrella" recounts the extraction of snake venom in order to manufacture a poison and its antidote. *The X-3 Case* features a cloned animal and a memory-recovery machine. *Veiled Strife* explores the technology behind identifying suspects by their fingerprints. *A Case of Counterfeit Currency* (*Zhizui jinmi*) portrays the enemy's use of printing technology to manufacture counterfeit currency and presumably even destabilize the target country's economy. *Secret Column* explores how to control human brain functioning through electronic devices, along with extending the human lifespan through rejuvenating hormones. Many high-tech motifs that Ye utilizes also appeared in SF writings by his peers in the PRC.

Jin Ming holds the rank of chief detective in PRC's Public Security Bureau. The pronunciation of his name is almost identical to that of the Chinese word *jingming*, meaning "highly astute." In addition, his given name Ming is exactly the same Chinese character found in the brilliant military strategist Zhuge Liang's (181–234) courtesy name of Kong Ming. In fact, one of Jin Ming's nicknames is "Detective Zhuge." Jin Ming's top sidekick is named Ge Liang, which is the same as the final two characters of the name Zhuge Liang.[27] From the way Ye coins names for some of his main characters, we can see that he generates resonances between these contemporary protagonists and the most astute famous personage of ancient imperial China.

When Jin Ming first appears in "The Case of a Killing Umbrella," Ye introduces him at some length: "Jin Ming is not Holmes, as depicted by British author Arthur Conan Doyle; nor is he the short Belgian detective Hercule Poirot, as depicted by Agatha Christie. Nor is he Chief Inspector Morse, as depicted by British author Colin Dexter. Jin Ming is a Public Security Bureau investigator who lives in socialist China. He cracks mysterious cases with modern equipment and his breadth of scientific knowledge."[28]

Though Ye tries to differentiate Jin Ming from the images of famous Western literary detectives, his publishers still used Holmes to promote the Jin Ming series by heralding Jin Ming as "a scientific Holmes." For example, when Ye's novella *Veiled Strife* was serialized in the *Wenhui Daily* (*Wenhui bao*), the editors altered the title to *A Scientific Holmes*, and the revised title continued to be used when the novella was reprinted in *An Anthology of Chinese SF Thrillers*.

In each narrative within the Jin Ming series, Ye begins with two or three paragraphs that introduce Jin Ming in a somewhat different way in order to emphasize whatever personality traits rise to prominence in a given narrative. For example, Ye notes at the outset of *A Scientific Holmes* that aside from "scientific Holmes," Jin Ming has another nickname: "Dr. Police Officer."[29] Ye also offers a physical description of Jin Ming as a lean, muscular, and dexterous man of medium height in his forties. Jin Ming is swarthy because he works outdoors most of the time. His eyes are bloodshot from habitually staying up late, yet they gleam and sparkle. In *Black Shadow*, Jin Ming is presented as a renaissance man with extensive learning and a broad range of skills. Jin Ming can speak numerous Chinese dialects as well as several foreign languages. He is also good at music and photography, and talented in soccer, archery, and martial arts. He can ride motorcycles, steer motorboats, and pilot airplanes. He also has a solid grounding in literature, fine arts, and history.[30]

In 1981, Ye responded to a question from a British journalist about the difference between Jin Ming and Sherlock Holmes. Ye noted that the identity and self-image of the two protagonists differ fundamentally. Jin is a late twentieth-century Chinese government PSB officer with a PhD in law enforcement, while Holmes is a late nineteenth-century British private detective with high-level but mostly informal education in investigatory practices. Moreover, Jin cracks cases in order to make his homeland more secure from largely foreign enemies, while Holmes takes on cases largely for the personal pleasure of matching wits with clever criminals. Ye also claimed that commentators should not try to draw too many parallels between the Jin Ming series and detective thriller series written in "capitalist" countries.[31]

Chinese intellectual protagonists in "scar literature" and "contemplative literature" are often portrayed as weak or even frail, and thus susceptible to bullying by villains often associated with the Party's repressive policies, such as during the Anti-Rightist Campaign or the Cultural Revolution. However, Jin Ming complements his lofty educational background and case-cracking savvy with rugged physical skills such as martial arts and archery. Unlike many of the lightweight bookworm protagonists in thaw-era fiction, Jin Ming fearlessly confronts villains, daringly rescues victims, and dutifully protects the homeland from mostly foreign threats.

Readers' Reception, Critics' Commentary, and Ye's Response

Most of Ye's SF thrillers were initially serialized in newspapers or magazines. For example, "A Killing Umbrella" was serialized in the first two issues of the magazine *Science and People* (*Kexue yu ren*) in 1980; *The X-3 Case* was serialized in *Yangcheng Evening News* (*Yangcheng wanbao*) from 19 February to 14 March 1980. In January 1981, the novellas *Veiled Strife, Black Shadow, Disguised, A Case of Counterfeit Currency,* and *Secret Column* were simultaneously serialized in such magazines and newspapers as *Wenhui Daily, Yangcheng Evening News, Xi'an Evening News* (*Xi'an wanbao*), *Science and Life* (*Kexue shenghuo*), and *Changjiang Daily* (*Changjiang ribao*). Among these newspapers and magazines, *Wenhui Daily* and *Yangcheng Evening News* had the largest circulation, each exceeding one million. Ye points out that serialization was instrumental to the rise in popularity of Jin Ming among readers of that period.[32]

Once Ye's SF thrillers flooded the market, serious critical attention began to be paid to the genre as a whole and specific works within it. The positive reviews normally came from other SF writers as well as the newspapers and magazines that serialized Ye's works. For example, *Yangcheng Evening News* published an article by Zhou Haiming on 14 February 1982 entitled "Jin Ming Was Praised as a Superhero in Japan." In the article, Zhou introduces the Jin Ming series, quoting a Japanese commentator in the Japanese magazine *SF Houseki* (issue 6, supplement, 1981): "The hero Jin Ming was created by a Chinese author, and works for and belongs to the Chinese people. He presents a glorious image in Chinese SF history."[33]

The relatively critical reviews were from literary critics and popular science writers. The Shanghai newspaper *Literary News* (*Wenxue bao*) and the journal *Reading* (*Du shu*) were two major venues for articles on the SF thriller subgenre and criticisms of Ye's works from April 1981 to early 1983. They focused on the formulaic approach in Ye's writing and the lack of scientific content in SF thrillers. *Literary News* published Xiao Lei's article, in which Xiao did not directly attack the

SF thriller genre, but instead criticized the formulaic approach to the writing of PRC SF in general. He complained that these SF writers had been taking shortcuts in their narratives by leaning heavily upon formulas such as "fantasy plus love interest," or "fantasy plus thriller." He argued that they had not dared to face social realities, nor could they effectively reflect them. The literary value of their narratives was thus even less than that of sentimental romances such as mandarin-duck-and-butterfly fiction and talent-meets-beauty fiction. Xiao concluded that over-reliance on formulaic writing had caused a crisis in PRC SF.[34]

Ye responded to this sweeping rebuke. He took issue with Xiao by arguing that such formulas have appeared in other genres, too – not just in SF. In Ye's view, there was nothing wrong with formulaic writing. He further argued that most SF writers have both literary cultivation and broad scientific knowledge. They have been cross-fertilizing literature and science. Unfortunately, they have often been excluded or even criticized by both sides. The real crisis confronting PRC SF was that "these seedlings of SF will not be able to survive if the realms of both literature and science attack them."[35]

Reading published another critical article entitled "Some Questions about the SF Thriller." The author Zhao Shizhou faulted the SF thriller for what he saw as its lack of science content. Though many SF thrillers contained a lot of scientific terms, they did not offer substantial scientific content. Many SF thrillers were merely ordinary thrillers. In addition, Zhao noted that many narratives duplicated one another with the same sort of science-based themes, such as brain science.[36]

Three months later, *Reading* published Ye's response. Ye argued that as long as the science fantasy in a SF thriller is based on scientific principles, it does not matter how much scientific content the narrative as a whole contains. SF writers had been keeping up with advances in science, Ye maintained, and often incorporated some of the latest research findings in their narratives. For example, the 1980s witnessed great advances in brain science, so it was not surprising to see many SF writers incorporating this theme in their narratives. Even though they were dealing with the same theme, they used a variety of narrative techniques and plot construction to articulate a given scientific concept.[37] Ye pointed out that as a new subgenre, the SF thriller had developed very quickly in the PRC. Many SF thriller writers were relative novices, and it was inevitable that their writings would be flawed. However, this should not be justification for dismissing the SF thriller subgenre. Instead, we should encourage writers to improve the quality of their narratives.[38]

Ye went on to point out major problems he had observed in PRC SF thrillers, including characterization, literary quality, scientific content, and theoretical exploration of the genre.[39] Using his own work as an example, Ye advised writers how to write about enemy countries. Some years earlier, he had used "S Country" and "M Country" to refer to enemy countries, which were easily identified as Soviet Russia and the United States. After some critics pointed out that this practice was not appropriate, he avoided references to specific enemy nations in his subsequent writings. In addition, some writers often depicted overseas Chinese as spies or secret agents in the employ of enemy countries. Ye called for writers to study the PRC government's recent and more sympathetic policies on overseas Chinese, in order to avoid such stereotypes. They should present a more positive image of overseas Chinese in order to bring them into the fold through SF works. Some narratives set the narrative entirely in a foreign country, and the detective and other characters were all foreigners. PRC writers should avoid writing such narratives, Ye asserted. Instead, they should write SF thrillers in a distinctive national style, and portray the astuteness of their own Chinese detective.[40]

Ye also tried to clarify some misunderstandings about the genre. For example, there were accusations that SF thrillers advocated murder, merely because there were detailed depictions of murder. Ye argued that the Chinese classic novel *Romance of the Three Kingdoms* contains a great deal of fighting and killing; Lu Xun's short story "Medicine" also depicts the consumption of a steamed bun soaked in the blood of an executed convict. However, we cannot accuse such narratives of having advocated murder. Another misconception was that writers of SF thrillers were interested in nothing other than the popularity of their narratives and achieving large print runs. Ye argued that there was nothing wrong with writers of popular fiction having such intentions. Even Zhao Shuli's (1906–70) classic revolutionary narratives amounted to popular fiction and enjoyed a large readership.[41] In addition, the popularity of a work was not necessarily associated with low literary quality or thematic shallowness.[42]

While defending the SF thriller, Ye also admitted that the literary quality of some SF thrillers was mediocre. For example, some writers aimed solely at constructing a thrillingly twisting plot and paid no attention to characterization. Some thrillers lacked any sort of engaging societal themes and merely provided superficial rhetoric about defending the nation's sovereign territory. Other works occasionally showed poor taste by depicting vulgar or erotic incidents. Occasionally an SF thriller writer was unfamiliar with the detective's milieu and spun a farfetched plot or created wooden characters. Ye also criticized the way some writers used technology merely as a prop or peddled misconceptions about science, knowingly or not.

Ye pointed out that neither critics nor writers had adequately explored the theory and practice of this new subgenre. In these discussions, Ye almost single-handedly defended the SF thriller from critics who had dismissed or misconstrued the subgenre, while providing guidance to his peers in the literary scene on how to write an effective SF thriller.

Black Shadow

Black Shadow is unique in the Jin Ming series, because it does not portray espionage or international conspiracies and focuses instead on a mystery about China's political movements. Jin Ming's efficient and dedicated police work contrasts with the protagonist Lou Shan's bizarre and dramatic experiences during the Cultural Revolution. This novella reveals Ye's effort to incorporate themes relating to society and history within the SF thriller. Ye claims that the significance of this novel within the realm of Chinese SF is equivalent to the importance of Bai Hua's film script *Bitter Love* (*Ku lian*, 1979) within the canon of mainstream PRC literature.[43] After achieving fame as landmark narratives, both *Bitter Love* and *Black Shadow* were subsequently castigated by party officials and other regime propagandists for having supposedly promulgated "spiritual pollution" and "bourgeois liberalism."[44] *Black Shadow* shares features of both "scar literature" and "contemplative literature," while echoing Deng's affirmation that "Science and technology are productive forces"; the novel also appears to have been a response to the central government's call for "looking ahead to the future."[45]

Black Shadow was written in the autumn of 1980. As soon as it was finished, it was serialized in *Yangcheng Evening News* between January and March 1981 under the original title *Black Shadow in Ghost Mountain* (*Guishan heiying*). In April 1981, Beijing's Geology Press published the novella in book form with a print run of 118,200 copies. During the following year, the narrative was published again by two different publishers in Beijing and Guangzhou as an illustrated book.[46] In the postscript, Ye notes that he was able to complete the entire narrative within just two months because the fate of his protagonist Lou Shan during the Cultural Revolution greatly resembles Ye's personal experience of that era. "The decade-long catastrophe left scars" on both Lou Shan and the novelist himself. Therefore, he "made great effort to render the protagonist's fate and emotional life."[47] Ye concludes, "The dark era finally ended, but its profound historical lessons are worth remembering forever."[48]

The novella creates suspense like a detective thriller. The author utilizes enigmatic chapter titles, such as "The Strange Cave in Ghost Mountain," "The Strange Cases," "The Mystery of the Codes," and "A Victorious Return." They reveal the author's creation of suspense at the beginning, peeling away layer after layer of mystery in the middle, and solving the mystery at the end. The plot also fits the popular formula of "fantasy plus love interest." The narrative recounts how a group of scientists find traces of a wild man in an uninhabited area of Ghost Mountain and call him Black Shadow. They suspect that Black Shadow is a spy. As detective Jin Ming and his colleagues investigate the case, it turns out that Black Shadow is an entomologist named Lou Shan who has gone into hiding at Ghost Mountain during the country's "Iron Broom" movement in order to protect his late father's scientific invention: an invisibility suit. Lou Shan's father, Lou Jinyu, has invented an invisibility suit. Though living overseas, Lou Jinyu has always wanted to share his invention with his homeland of China. However, he is unsure about the wisdom of doing so, given the instability of the political situation. Therefore, he first sends his son to China to attend university. During his studies there, Lou Shan falls in love with a classmate, Wei Ying, and the two become engaged. Lou Jinyu returns to China in hopes of attending Lou Shan and Wei Ying's wedding. But soon after he arrives, a political storm called the "Iron Broom" sweeps the country. Lou Jinyu and Lou Shan are arrested as spies in the service of foreign enemies, and are locked up. The general director of the people's militia, Dai Chuan, knows about Lou Jinyu's invention and has tried to obtain it. However, Lou Jinyu is afraid Dai would use the invisibility suit to intercept, monitor, or even assassinate more innocent people. Therefore, he refuses to give the invention to Dai, who poisons the old man out of vindictiveness. Before Old Lou dies, he tells his son about the invention. Lou Shan absconds with the invisibility suit and flees to Ghost Mountain to live in hiding. After several decades, Jin Ming and several scientists finally find Lou Shan. By this time, the "Iron Broom" movement has long passed, and Lou Shan can finally present the invisibility suit as a gift to the Party and reunite with his fiancée, the entomologist Wei Ying.

As a work of SF that PRC readers might expect to teach them about science and technology, the narrative contains many explanations about scientific concepts such as blood types, aliens, electronic waves, and light waves. The novella also links *Black Shadow* and the invisibility suit to similar motifs in "The Daoist Adept of Lao Mountain" ("Laoshan daoshi") in Pu Songling's (1640–1715) *Strange Stories from a Chinese Studio* (*Liaozhai zhiyi*), the story of "Ali Baba and Forty Thieves" in *One Thousand and One Nights*, and *Robinson Crusoe*. The novella also refers to inventions in other contemporary SF works. For example, the narrative's description of a "chameleon suit" was borrowed from Ye's earlier story "The Mysterious Suit" ("Shenmi yi," 1979). In addition, the scene in which Lou Shan wears the invisibility suit to escape police searches is similar to the scene in Wu Boze's *Invisible Man*.

The images of Lou Shan and his father represent the scientists who never lost their faith in the Party's absolute rule in spite of mistreatment at the hands of the party-state. Scientists, teachers, and professors had nearly always been the main characters in PRC SF since the 1950s. However, they were frequently sketched out as two-dimensional figures rather than as truly rounded-out characters. They were often only vehicles to transmit scientific and technological knowledge to juvenile readers. Authors seldom paid attention to the characterization of these scientists and professors. However, in this novella Ye explained that he could relate Lou Shan's fate and experience to his own during the Cultural Revolution, so he had worked hard to sketch the emotional life and character of the protagonist. Similar to the main character in Bai Hua's *Bitter Love*, Lou Shan and his father are patriotic intellectuals who have returned to their homeland from abroad. They have always been loyal to the country and the Party, in spite of the suffering and persecution they experienced during the Cultural Revolution. This is a typical portrayal of Chinese intellectuals in the early Deng era. In Deng Xiaoping's speech at the 1978 National Science Conference, he criticized the frequent political persecution of educated professionals during the Cultural Revolution: many distinguished scientists, professors, and engineers were labelled "bourgeois academic authorities," and many young scientists and technicians whom the Party had trained were reviled as "revisionist seedlings." Deng blamed the "Gang of Four" for degrading educated professionals, conveniently obscuring Mao Zedong's leading role in this state of affairs. Deng recommended that the PRC government break away from outmoded rules and conventions to nurture and promote talented professionals in science and technology.[49] What Deng described during the Cultural Revolution is exactly what happened to Lou Shan and his father. Though the novella has a bright ending, Lou Shan regrets that he is too old to continue in his father's footsteps, so he urges young scientists and technicians to continue scientific research and contribute to socialist construction. Lou Shan's return to the society from which he had been estranged symbolizes the return of science and technology to China after the end of the Mao era.

In the narrative, Lou Shan expresses his bitterness by using his family's secret code to write letters to his fiancée Wei Ying. In these letters, he recalls how he and his father were persecuted in the "Iron Broom" movement, which is literary shorthand for the Cultural Revolution. The sufferings of Lou Shan and his father and the armed political struggles between rival civilian cliques remind the reader of the violent chaos of the Cultural Revolution. At one juncture in the narrative, Lou Shan compares his own society with the dark social reality of early twentieth-century Chinese society that Lu Xun describes in "Diary of a Madman": "Pitch-dark. I don't know whether it is day or night. The Zhaos' dog has started barking again. The fierceness of a lion, the timidity of a rabbit, the craftiness of a fox."[50]

Besides exposing dark realities of the Cultural Revolution, the novel also touches upon the theme of humanism. In mainstream literature, Dai Houying's novel *Ah! Humanity* was often "read as a plea to revive humanism, thus implicitly rejecting Mao's theory that there is no human nature, only class nature."[51] *Black Shadow* also praises the spirit of humanism that survives in ordinary people's lives, even in the darkest times. In the novella, Yu Shi'an, a senior police officer and a Communist Party member, realizes that Lou Shan and his father are innocent of the trumped-up charges against them, and have been wrongly persecuted. So he turns away from his Communist comrades on the Municipal Party Committee and saves Lou Shan's life. But a ruthless high-ranking cadre from the Municipal Party Committee discovers what Yu has been doing and assassinates him. Here human nature prevails over class nature. The spirit of humanism also pervades the relationship between Lou Shan and Wei Ying. Their love breaks the taboo against intimacy and marriage with someone from a very different social class. Wei Ying is a Communist Party member. She does not reject Lou Shan, even though the Party would have prevented her from marrying him because of Lou Shan's questionable overseas family background and lack of Party membership. The unfailing love between them helps sustain Lou Shan through the decades of living in isolation on Ghost Mountain. Lou Shan quotes Li Bo's (701–62) poem "Infinite Longing for You" ("Chang xiang si") and Wen Yiduo's (1899–1946) "Colour" ("Secai") to express his love and longing for Wei Ying. Their relationship is finally fulfiled with their reunion at the the novella's conclusion.

Though Jin Ming is not the protagonist in the narrative, he plays a vital role in solving a mystery and reintegrating Lou Shan into his society. Through Jin Ming's focalization, the reader not only learns about basic aspects of police procedure and forensics, but also about the dark side of the PRC's political movements. The reader also becomes acquainted with Jin Ming's personality, work ethic, and breadth of scientific knowledge. While Lou Shan and his father represent well-educated Chinese adults who fall victim to totalitarian political movements, Jin Ming stands for a new generation of Chinese professionals who have eluded victimization and protect the Chinese populace. Lou Shan and Jin Ming in *Black Shadow* become a synthesis of personal and social heroism. Their achievements and cheerful voices humanize a society that had been traumatized by violence and chaos during much of the twentieth century. The bright ending of the narrative implies that the pain of the past will be relieved by the protagonist's hopeful future prospects.

Black Shadow was a major success. Ye Yonglie and *Yangcheng Evening News* received numerous readers' letters about the novella after it was serialized in the newspaper in 1981. One reader even insisted that he must have been the model for Ye when he created his protagonist Lou Shan.[52] In spite of the popularity and the upbeat spirit of *Black Shadow*, it was severely criticized by influential state-run newspapers in 1982 and 1983. On 3 November 1983, the front page of *China Youth Daily* published an article entitled "A Black Shadow of Thought: On the Detective Science Fiction *Black Shadow*."[53] It was not the first time that Ye's works had been harshly criticized. For example, in previous years, Ye's short story "The Miracle on the World's Highest Mountain" was accused of having promulgated "fake science"; his novella *The X-3 Case* was rebuked for supposedly having advocated commercialization; and his novella *Reap As You Have Sown (Zi shi qi guo*, 1981) was castigated for its supposed "tendency of bourgeois liberalism."[54] In contrast with those denunciations, Ye received strong support from his fellow writers and editors. Before publication of critical article in *China Youth Daily*, the fourth issue of *Literary Scene* (*Wentan*) published an open letter in August 1982 entitled "On the Criticism of Science Fiction" co-signed by twelve SF writers and editors such as Tong Enzheng, Liu Xingshi, and Wang Xiaoda. However, this public request that state media adopt a less strident tone in critiquing Ye's fiction was not persuasive. The subsequent article on *China Youth Daily* escalated the criticism of Ye's works, alleging political wrongdoing. Though *Black Shadow* is about the persecution and suffering of intellectuals during the Cultural Revolution, the article in *China Youth Daily* accused the novella of having disobeyed the Four Basic Principles of Deng Xiaoping. And it went further: "The protagonist Lou Shan has very negative and dark thoughts. He cold-shoulders the Party, and he does not trust the Party; he has no confidence in our Socialist homeland. He is merely concerned about his own future and wants to be a free individual."[55] The article then pressed on with a point-by-point denunciation of the novella. For example, the angry reader accused Ye's work of having advocated "feudal" thinking on account of Lou Shan's quotation from Lu Xun's "Diary of a Madman," which supposedly compared socialist China to the "feudal" Zhao family in Lu Xun's story. Furthermore, Lou Shan, it was alleged, does not really love his homeland of China and its people because he has hidden himself away on a mountain. The article also accused Ye of having prevented his protagonist Lou Shan from perceiving the bright side of life in present-day China; for example, Ye did not allow Lou Shan to learn about the toppling of the "Gang of Four" until many years later. The most problematic issue for the critic was that Lou Shan is supposedly pursuing nothing other than personal freedom. Therefore, the narrative was actually spreading doubt and distrust, and the real theme of the novella was to advocate individual freedom. At the end, this article warned readers of the spiritual pollution pouring into China from SF.[56] In another Shanghai daily newspaper, one commentary denounced Ye's novella as a literary work that describes how "a man turns into a ghost" in socialist China. Therefore, "it sketches the Chinese nation in completely negative terms and exposes the horrors of the Cultural Revolution to the point of distortion; and in so doing, it smears China's socialist society, thereby negating the values of socialism."[57]

The harsh criticism of *Black Shadow* for spreading spiritual pollution and bourgeois liberalism echoed the political climate at the time. On the one hand, Deng Xiaoping had repeatedly confirmed the importance of science and technology, and the role of the intelligentsia in advancing the Four Modernizations. On the other hand, Deng warned the PRC populace against adopting bourgeois liberalism. On 16 January 1980, Deng Xiaoping drew the new line clearly in a speech that was later circulated to Party branches throughout China. He pointed out that many youth had become infatuated with "bourgeois liberalism" and did not appreciate the distinction between "socialist" democracy and "bourgeois" democracy. Deng made it clear that literature and art in "socialist democracy" must observe his Four Basic Principles: the socialist road, the people's democratic dictatorship, the leadership of the Communist Party, and Marxism-Leninism-Mao Zedong Thought.[58]

Along with Ye's *Black Shadow*, other works of SF were also denounced by state-run media as unhealthy and vulgar. Criticisms of *Black Shadow* played a role in Ye Yonglie's decision in 1983 to abandon SF and launch his career as a writer of reportage literature. Ye described his departure as "a victorious escape."[59] He said, "In my conversion from a science fiction writer to a reportage literature writer, my interviewees are not scientists anymore. My official job affiliation was also transferred from the Standing Committee of Shanghai Science and Technology

Association to the Chinese Writers' Association. From that point on, I have firmly anchored myself in the field of Chinese mainstream literature. As a good horse, I would never turn back to munch the grass of yesteryear."[60] This statement, especially his sardonic use of the term "victorious escape," not only reflects how Ye felt deeply offended by these political attacks, but also reveals that he may have seen the writing on the wall about the party-state's imminent crackdown on science fiction during the "Campaign to Eliminate Spiritual Pollution" from late 1983 to early 1984.

4 Tong Enzheng and the Motif of Alien Invasions

"As an archaeologist by profession, I am drinking today's wine, and writing stories about the future."[1] This is how Tong Enzheng described his dual identity as archaeologist and SF writer while having dinner with an old friend in 1979. Tong is an archaeologist known for his research and scholarly articles on the history of early southwest China (see figure 4.1). His academic training in history and archaeology provided him with a unique perspective to explore history – the historical past and the imagined future – in his creative writing.

Tong's creative writings are mainly short stories and novellas, and include one full-length novel. Tong's literary works fall into three groups. The first contains narratives directly inspired by his archaeological works. Tong uses deductive logic, historical knowledge, and scientific imagination to conjure fascinating narratives connected with archaeological discoveries. This category includes such narratives as *Dense Fog over the Old Gorge* (*Guxia miwu*, 1960), "A Guest from Fifty Thousand Years Ago" ("Wuwannian yiqian de keren," 1962), "Magic Flute in the Snowy Mountains" ("Xueshan modi," 1978), "The Mysterious Stone Tomb" ("Shenmi de da shimu,"1980), "The Man Who Followed Dinosaur Tracks" ("Zhuizong konglong de ren," 1980), and "Song of the Stalagmites" ("Shisun xing," 1982). The second group deals with international political or commercial conspiracies, such as "Death Ray on a Coral Island" and "Behind the Leaden Curtain of Time" ("Zai shijian de qian mu houmian," 1989).

Tong's third and final type of literary works portrays breakthroughs in electronics, space exploration, and contacts with highly intelligent extraterrestrial organisms. This category includes such works as "The Miracle of an Electronic Brain" ("Dianzi danao de qiji," 1962), "Lost Memory" ("Shiqu de jiyi," 1963), "The Robot Who Disappeared" ("Shizong de jiqiren," 1962), "The Return of an Astronaut" ("Yuhangyuan de guilai," 1979), "The Death of the World's First Robot"

Figure 4.1. Tong Enzheng (1935–97) (courtesy of Liu Xingshi).

("Shijie shang diyige jiqiren zhi si," 1982), *Faraway Love* (*Yaoyuan de ai*, 1982), "The First Defeat" ("Diyici shibai," 1984), and *New Journey to the West* (*Xin xiyouji*, 1984).[2]

Among Tong's SF works, four narratives are about alien invasions and human-alien encounters: "A Guest from Fifty Thousand Years Ago," *Faraway Love*, "Song of the Stalagmites," and "The First Defeat." Tong was the first PRC SF author to write about alien invasions of Earth.

In addition to creative writing, Tong also published non-fiction essays on SF around 1980. These essays had two major concerns – to separate SF from popular science writing, and to emphasize the literary nature of SF. His well-argued expository essays and high-quality creative writings combine to make him a leading representative of PRC SF writers from the late 1970s to the mid-1980s.

This chapter focuses on Tong's expository essays on SF, as well as his SF narratives about extraterrestrial invasions of Earth and other contacts between humans and extraterrestrial beings. Among other things, these expository essays reveal how Tong and some of his contemporary PRC SF writers attempted to cross the boundaries between *kexue wenyi* and mainstream literature, combining features of popular literature with those of mainstream literature. I mentioned in chapter 1 that Tong won a prestigious mainstream literary prize with his short SF story "Death Ray on a Coral Island" in 1978. This award for a SF story challenged the domination of the Chinese literary scene by realist or "serious" literature. Tong's alien narratives demonstrate similar features of crossing boundaries, articulating differences, and destabilizing hierarchies by situating human beings within a space-time window, and exploring the possibility of there being multiple civilizations in the universe.

Essays on Science Fiction

During the early post-Mao reform and opening era, Tong Enzheng and many of his contemporaries took issue with the received wisdom about SF since the 1950s and 1960s. Tong's short essay entitled "My Understanding of Literature and Art about Science" ("Tantan wo dui kexue wenyi de renshi," 1979) was one of the earliest essays to distinguish SF from popular science writing.[3] It immediately became a target of criticism by some in the old guard who defended the scientific significance of SF. These exchanges of views developed into a heated debate about the nature of SF: is it literature or science? If we situate this debate within the history of Chinese SF, these discussions can be seen as a writerly movement devoted to the development of the literary potential of SF.

In this essay, Tong distinguished between literature about science (here referring mainly to SF) and general popular science writing (*kepu zuopin*), and summarized three of his main ideas. First, the major goals of these two genres differ. The main goal of popular science writing is to transmit scientific knowledge; whatever literary qualities it may exhibit are merely to make the writing more interesting and attractive. In contrast, literature about science promotes a scientific world view and a scientific mode of thinking; and science is more of a tool to facilitate plot development than a body of knowledge to transmit. Second, the writing methods are different. Popular science writing is based on evidence-based science and technology, and holds fast to scientific principles. Literature about science is based on imagination, and the scientific content in these works can often be obsolete or even preposterous. Third, the structure of the two types of writing differs significantly.

Popular science writing aims to introduce scientific knowledge, so its structure tightly adheres to a scientific theme while hardly ever indulging in irrelevant elaborations or witty asides. In contrast, literature about science follows the rules of imaginative writing, characterized by a freewheeling artistic imagination, vivid characterization, the creation of suspense, and twists in the plot.[4]

This short essay soon became a target of Lu Bing's critical essay, "Literature without a Soul." Lu took a contrary stance on literature about science. He argued that literature about science is merely part of the larger category of popular science writing. Launching an outspoken criticism of Tong's views on this topic, Lu argued that if a work of literature about science forfeits its scientific content, it sinks to the level of soulless literature.[5] Lu's and Tong's divergent conceptions of literature about science escalated to even more heated discussions during the following years. In essence, these discussions reflect contrasting ways of conceptualizing SF among SF writers, literary critics, popular science writers, and scientists. What is the primary concern of SF: its literary merit or its scientific content? Tong firmly supported the view that SF is a genre of imaginative literature, and thus called for an unabashedly literary type of SF.

When Joan Gordon discusses American SF, she lists the positive qualities of SF, including "scientific verisimilitude and plausibility, stimulating and innovative ideas, and that nebulous attribute, a sense of wonder."[6] Meanwhile, several negative elements have also been associated with SF, such as "a lack of psychological depth or convincing characterization, clumsy or merely serviceable prose, wooden dialogue, awkward intrusions of information sometimes referred to as expository lumps or info-dumps, and unlikely or wildly extravagant plots."[7] These negative tendencies are often trotted out as "proof of SF's non-literary status" in dismissals of SF by its detractors from outside the field.[8] Similarly, the shortcomings of some SF works were also used to attack Chinese SF works by various critics, writers from China's literary mainstream, the field of popular science literature, and the party-state's Bureau of Propaganda. While Chinese SF writers valued the positive features of SF, they also engaged in discussions of how to improve its literary quality.

In another essay, entitled "My Experiences of Writing Science Fiction" ("Chuangzuo kehuan xiaoshuo de tihui," 1979), Tong addressed five key issues of SF writing: the purpose of writing SF, the tension between artistic hyperbole and scientific truth, verisimilitude, characterization, and plot. When discussing the purpose of writing SF, he again distinguished popular science writing from SF, focusing upon its two key functions. The first is to promote a scientific world view. That involves problems of scientific methodology to approaching new phenomena with sensitivity, and cultivating a courageous spirit of seeking and upholding a vision of truth. The other key function is to popularize scientific knowledge in such a way as to give readers the tools they need to transform the objective world. Tong affirmed that SF, as a subgenre of literature and art about science, has been more focused upon promoting a scientific world view than on popularizing scientific knowledge.[9] The tension between artistic hyperbole and scientific truth was crucial for SF writers, Tong suggested. Since literary principles guide the approach of most SF writers to writing, scientific themes should accord with plot development and characterization. In addition, scientific themes within a SF work should not be evaluated for scientific accuracy. Instead, SF writers should be allowed to make innovative, bold, and extrapolative leaps of imagination in their works as long as their conceptual frameworks do not violate basic scientific principles. Tong approvingly cited an analogy that another Chinese SF writer, Ye Yonglie, had made: the relationship between SF and science resembles the relationship between historical fiction and history. Writers of historical fiction should enjoy the liberty to inject the element of imagination into a historical novel's characterization and plot development. Ye had cited the example of the contrasting characterization of the historical figure Cao Cao in the classic historical novel *Romance of the Three Kingdoms* (*Sanguo yanyi*) versus the ancient historical text *Records of the Three Kingdoms* (*San guo zhi*). Both depict the history of the late Eastern Han dynasty (ca. 184–220). Cao Cao is presented as a founding emperor of brilliant talent and bold vision in *Records of the Three Kingdoms*, but is portrayed as a villainous careerist who achieves high position through unscrupulous scheming in *Romance of the Three Kingdoms*. However, the villainous and fanciful characterization of Cao Cao in the novel does not dampen readers' enjoyment when they read *Romance of the Three Kingdoms*.[10]

Tong Enzheng argued that since SF is a literary subgenre, characterization should be an SF writer's primary concern. Engrossing themes and curious scientific principles are all enhanced by the creation of well-rounded characters. He criticized the stereotyped characterization found in most contemporary Chinese SF, especially the one-dimensional intellectuals such as professors, researchers, engineers, and technicians, who play no function other than merely to transmit scientific knowledge or further the development of the plot. SF writers should emphasize the individuality of intellectuals in their narratives. Furthermore, SF narratives should also include other types of characters such as factory workers, farmers, and cadres. In this way, SF can reflect the diversity of society and reveal that scientific development receives popular support from the masses. In addition, Tong recommended that writers should speculate about future developments in science on the basis of actual laws of nature; they should also conjure new varieties of societal organization on the basis of existing ideas about the evolution of society, and explore people's psychological and emotional responses to these changes within the society of the future.[11] Tong himself performed such thought experiments in his alien narratives *Faraway Love* and "The First Defeat," as discussed later in this chapter.

Tong insisted that SF writers must improve the readability of their works through heightened attention to plot, deductive logic, and suspense. He pointed out that traditional Chinese fiction since the advent of *chuánqí* narratives of the Tang and Song dynasties drew much of its vitality from the influence of traditional performing arts, which often feature intricate plotting with many twists and turns in order to hold an audience's attention. Contemporary SF writers should thereby learn techniques of effective plot development from wide reading in traditional Chinese fiction. By doing so, SF writers could avoid slipping into the mediocre and formulaic narrative that was widespread at that time. Tong claimed that formulaic SF was so predictable that readers quickly lost their appetite for it; the conflicts and ironies in everyday life were much more interesting and complicated than the stilted moments of suspense and inevitable resolutions of three-part formulaic narratives.[12]

Tong's insistence on the separation of SF from popular science narratives and his advocacy for a more literary type of SF marked a major shift in Chinese SF from the nakedly utilitarian popularization of knowledge about science and technology to an artistic and literary form comparable with mainstream Chinese literature. Chinese writers who followed Tong's call for a more literary approach to Chinese SF were not only defying the old paradigm of an overwhelmingly didactic Chinese SF, but also questioning the diminished role that had been assigned to Chinese SF vis-à-vis mainstream Chinese literature.

Tong's First Alien Narrative and Other SF Works Prior to 1979

The images in Western SF of intelligent extraterrestrials have gone through three major phases, according to Gwyneth Jones: first as invaders, "competitors, and deadly enemies" at the turn of the twentieth century, such as in H.G. Wells's *The War of the Worlds* (1897); second, as "aliens that could be pitied, admired or defended" during the period from the end of the Second War to the 1960s; and third, as relatively colourful aliens who play useful roles as "immigrants, ethnic minorities, underprivileged guest-workers, and wily diplomatic opponents" from the 1970s to the present day.[13] Similarly, M. Keith Booker and Anne-Marie Thomas trace the genealogy of alien invasions in Western SF and analyse how these narratives serve as commentaries on real-world socio-political phenomena at the time of writing. For example, the alien invasion in Wells's *The War of the Worlds* serves as a commentary on British colonial expansion during the late nineteenth century. The American narratives of alien invasions in the 1950s responded to a "paranoid sense of threat that was central to American culture in the peak Cold War years."[14] As Cold War tensions eased in the 1960s, the alien invasion subgenre receded into the background of contemporary SF, and portrayals of alien invasions in such works as Thomas Disch's *The Genocides* (1965) and Michael Crichton's *The Andromeda Strain* (1969) are less threatening than those portrayed in narratives from the 1950s.

The motif of alien invasions grew prominent in cinema with the uptick in Western SF films during the 1970s and 1980s. Cinematic space aliens sometimes come across as benevolent, as in Steven Spielberg's *Close Encounters of the Third Kind* (1977). In the 1980s, alien invasions often functioned as satire or criticism of American politics and government, or U.S. religious rhetoric, as in Greg Bear's *The Forge of God* (1987) and Octavia Butler's "Xenogenesis" trilogy (1987–9).

Narratives involving space aliens or alien invasions of the Earth appeared in Chinese SF much later than in Western SF. Lao She's *Cat Country* (*Mao cheng ji*, 1932) is one of the earliest Chinese SF narratives portraying extraterritorial beings, who are cat-like Martians, presented as the Martian equivalents of humans on Earth for the purpose of social satire and allegory. By the middle of the twentieth century, the use of space aliens in SF had become taboo, and stayed that way in the PRC throughout the entire Mao era (1949–76). Any PRC narrative that featured space aliens would have been considered guilty of harbouring an evil and corrupt bourgeois ideology. Therefore, there were practically no Chinese alien narratives in the 1950s except for Tong Enzheng's "A Guest from Fifty Thousand Years Ago."

"A Guest from Fifty Thousand Years Ago" was Tong Enzheng's first short story, written in 1959 and published in the third issue of *Juvenile Literature and Art* (*Shaonian wenyi*) in 1960.[15] The narrative begins with a boy's discovery of meteorite fragments. The meteorite is a piece of metal from a wrecked rocket launched by Martians. In the story, Mars gave rise to an advanced civilization, which launched an Earth-bound rocket fifty thousand years ago. However, after the rocket had settled into an orbit around Earth, a mechanical breakdown prevented the rocket from leaving its orbit to land. In the narrative, the astronomy professor Li Mingzhe relates this satellite-like Martian rocket to the star Tianyi (in the constellation of Draco), which was described in the "Treatise on Celestial Offices" ("Tianguan shu") by Sima Qian (145–86 BCE) in *Records of the Grand Historian* (*Shiji*). "Treatise on Celestial offices" is the earliest Chinese text on astronomy and astrology. The treatise records that the ancient Chinese astronomers divided the sky into five celestial palaces: east, west, south, north, and middle palaces, which host thirty-one constellations. The opening section of this treatise describes the star Tianyi as a "partly hidden and partly visible" star in the "middle palace."[16] Professor Li also solves the mystery of why Tianyi suddenly disappeared in 1645. He explains that the Martian rocket was shattered by a meteor in 1645 and to the Earth in pieces. This collision was recorded by a Chinese historian from the early Qing dynasty: "During the fifth month in the second year of the Shunzhi reign, a heavenly body from the east crashed to Earth in the vicinity of Guangzhou. Red flames erupted from the ground amidst a thunderous roar."[17]

This is one of the few Chinese SF narratives about a Martian civilization since Lao She's *Cat Country* was published in the 1930s. How could this story have been accepted for publication in Mao-era China, when Mao had categorically insisted that there was no such thing as an extraterrestrial intelligent being? It is important to note that this story enjoys some poetic licence because it is categorized as children's literature; it was published in a juvenile literary magazine, after all. One protagonist is a "young pioneer" (similar to a Boy Scout in the West) who thirsts after knowledge and embodies an admirable spirit of adventure. Astronomy Professor Li and his colleagues are portrayed as patient educators who foster young people's curiosity and enthusiasm for modern science and technology. The interaction between this young pioneer and the astronomer corresponds to the Party's educational agenda of transforming young people into "workers with both knowledge and a socialist way of thinking."[18] Furthermore, the notion of an advanced Martian civilization is downplayed and overshadowed by the potential benefits earthlings might gain from their discovery of the type of metal alloy used in the Martian rocket. The author does not directly depict any Martians, merely mentioning their civilization in passing in order to explain the origins of the rocket. The narrative emphasizes that human beings will benefit from this small chunk of metal alloy. When Chinese scientists determine the exact composition of the metal alloy, they will be able to manufacture it so as to "further master rocket technology for interstellar navigation … and accelerate our plan to conquer the universe."[19] Such "correct" political messages have safeguarded the story from accusations of advocating "bourgeois ideology" about alien civilizations.

The story's references to Chinese history and archaeology resonate with the author's academic training in history and archaeology. Tong's childhood overlapped with the Sino-Japanese War (1937–45), during which time his family frequently moved from one region to another to avoid the perils of warfare and shifting battle fronts. After the war, Tong's family settled in the Hunanese provincial capital of Changsha, where Tong completed his primary and secondary schooling. After Tong's father moved the family to Sichuan after a job transfer in 1956, Tong entered Sichuan University as a history major.[20] During the summer of 1959, Tong joined his university's archaeological dig at a nearby Neolithic burial site, and soon decided to focus more on archaeology than history. Upon Tong's return from this awe-inspiring archaeological dig, he wrote his first novella, *Dense Fog over the Old Gorge*.[21] The narrative was soon included in a collection of juvenile fiction and published by the Shanghai Juvenile Press in 1960. The novella depicts two archaeological excavations at a cave site in Sichuan that were undertaken by an American team in 1932 and a Chinese team in 1959. A key incident is the dramatic unearthing of a precious ancient bronze sword and its possible connections with the mysterious disappearance of the ancient state of Ba around 316 BCE. In contrast with "A Guest from Fifty Thousand Years Ago," this novella has strong political overtones in its portrayal of the American archaeological team's theft of Chinese cultural relics and their participation in espionage. In spite of these political overtones, the narrative stands as a relatively polished literary work. The Chinese SF historian Dong Renwei praises *Dense Fog over the Old Gorge* for having overcome the early-to-mid-Mao-era pigeonholing of Chinese SF as a subgenre of mere juvenile literature or science popularization literature. This novella stirred the reader's imagination at both the literary and scientific registers through its intricate plot, vivid characterization, and descriptive prose.[22] The unmistakably literary quality of this Mao-era novella foreshadows Tong's thaw era polemical writings that assert the literary nature of SF.

Tong's literary talent led to his first full-time job as a screenwriter at Sichuan Emei Film Studio directly following his graduation from Sichuan University in 1961. However, he was soon transferred back to Sichuan University to work as a research assistant to Professor of Archaeology Feng Hanji, and eventually rose to become a full-fledged archaeologist. Ever since his time as a research assistant, Tong's career followed along the two tracks of archaeology and fiction writing.

After publishing "A Guest from Fifty Thousand Years Ago" and *Dense Fog over the Old Gorge*, Tong wrote SF narratives about electronic technology and robots, such as "The Miracle of an Electric Brain," "Lost Memory," and "The Robot Who Disappeared." Like almost all other PRC novelists, Tong suspended all his efforts at creative writing during the decade of the Cultural Revolution. In 1977, publishers such as Shanghai Juvenile Press, China Juvenile Press, and People's Literature Press had begun to ask for permission to reprint his old works. In May 1978, he attended the National Popular Science Writing Forum in Shanghai, where he enjoyed a reunion with veteran SF and popular science writers such as Gao Shiqi, Zheng Wenguang, Ye Yonglie, and Xiao Jianheng. After the forum, Tong published newly revised editions of *Dense Fog over the Old Gorge* and the short story "Death Ray on a Coral Island."

Like most other PRC novelists, Tong was sensitive to the fluctuations in the PRC political climate. The late 1970s were a watershed in Tong's SF writing career. Most of his narratives prior to 1979 smacked of Cold War thinking. Western powers appeared repeatedly as arch-villains in Tong's pre-1979 fiction, such as in "Death Ray on a Coral Island" and his revised edition of *Dense Fog over the Old Gorge*. In 1978, Tong made substantial revisions to *Dense Fog over the Old Gorge* by strengthening his condemnation of "imperialist cultural pillage" and accentuating the Maoist themes of ideological conflict and class struggle. His 1978 edition of this novella also inserted a new fictional character in the form of a communist cadre to lead the archaeological team and guide its research agenda. The overtly political tone substantially lowered the literary quality of this novella.

"Death Ray on a Coral Island" was completed in 1964, but was not published until August 1978 in *People's Literature*. Tong explained that this story was not published in the 1960s because "the content of the story was not compatible with the political atmosphere at that time."[23] This incompatibility with the political situation could refer to the patriotic spirit of the overseas Chinese scientists whom Tong portrays in the narrative. The main themes of the story are the patriotism of overseas Chinese scientists, "opposition to global hegemony," and "support for world peace."[24] This story gives voice to a Cold War mentality, with Superpower A (America) functioning as a villainous realm. The narrator, Chen Tianhong, recounts how he returned to China from a Southeast Asian country in order to help China secure his mentor's invention of a high-efficiency atomic battery with important military and aerospace applications. His mentor had been killed by spies from Superpower A after they failed to obtain the blueprints for the battery.

Chen thereupon snatched a sample atomic battery and its blueprints before boarding a China-bound private jet. Although Chen's jet was shot down by enemy forces, he was rescued by a fellow overseas Chinese scientist named Hu Mingli, who had been conducting research while living on a coral island. Hu Mingli invented a laser rangefinder while living in the United States, but was so outraged about how the U.S. government commandeered his invention for military use that he left the United States for good. His classmate Blain, who worked for a European corporation, helped Hu set up a research lab on the coral island. Hu subsequently discovered that Blain's European corporation had collaborated with the U.S. government. Near the story's finale, Blain fatally wounds Hu while attempting to seize Hu's latest invention, a laser gadget, and pass it on to the U.S. government. Before dying from his wounds, Hu destroys the warship on which Blain is a passenger, thereby preventing Blain from handing over Hu's laser gadget to the U.S. government.

A major irony of the story is that Hu uses his laser gadget to destroy a U.S. warship, even though he has adamantly opposed military applications of the devices he has invented. After Hu dies from his wounds but before the coral island is destroyed, Chen flees the island and returns to China with the high-efficiency atomic battery in hand. Because the story's plot includes incidents of espionage, international conspiracies, and murder, Ye Yonglie anthologized this story in *An Anthology of Chinese SF Thrillers*. After winning the PRC's Best Short Story Award in 1978, "Death Ray on a Coral Island" was soon adapted as a radio drama, feature film, and illustrated book. In spite of the story's popularity, Tong did not consider it his finest SF work; instead, he attributed its sensational success to the void of high-quality literature during the immediate aftermath of the Cultural Revolution. Tong suggested that "Death Ray on a Coral Island" appealed to readers who had thirsted for imaginative literature at a time when it was still rare in the PRC. He modestly likened the typical reader of that time to a famished person who views even a plain dish of everyday fare as a rare delicacy.[25]

After the success of "Death Ray on the Coral Island," Tong published other SF narratives during the following twelve years prior to his relocation to the United States in 1991.[26] Among these narratives, *Faraway Love*, "Song of the Stalagmites," and "The First Defeat" all feature space aliens. Starting in 1978, the PRC's diplomatic relations with the United States and other Western countries underwent a dramatic change as Deng Xiaoping emerged as paramount leader of a major economic reform program that opened up the PRC to foreign capital investment. This rapid shift in the PRC's economic policies and diplomatic posture was reflected in Tong's space alien narratives after 1978, and the paranoid atmosphere of threat from imperialist Western powers receded from his works. In *Faraway Love*, the Cold War mentality was replaced by a spirit of cooperation amongst international scientific teams.

Faraway Love

Faraway Love was completed in 1979 and first published in two instalments of the literary magazine *Sichuan Literature* in 1980 (issues 5 and 6). This novella unfolds through the recollections of the participant narrator, UFO researcher Qi Mo, about his encounter with a UFO and his romance with a cloned alien woman named Joan 101 in a secret undersea observatory built on Earth by space aliens. Qi has been dispatched to investigate a UFO that has landed in a deep trench on the floor of the Pacific Ocean. Though Qi's nuclear-powered submarine crashes into a reef, an intelligent robot named Hali rescues Qi and escorts him to a nearby underwater research station. There Hali introduces Qi to the beautiful Joan 101, who was cloned in the form of an adult human female. Both Joan 101 and Hali were created by aliens of the Jima civilization on Planet TX-II, which revolves around a star in the Lyra constellation, roughly one million light years away from Earth. Twelve thousand years ago, the Jima civilization had dispatched nine spaceships to explore part of the universe. After this expedition landed on Earth, they discovered its tribes of humans were living in primitive conditions. Before the Jima aliens departed from Earth, they built a science observatory on the ocean floor and left their clone Joan 101 and robot Hali to stay in the observatory, gathering information. This undersea observatory regularly dispatched UFOs to track the development of human tribes and societies. Joan 101 then collected the information into reports that she sent back to TX-II. Hence, Qi praises Joan 101 as "the messenger from Planet TX-II."[27]

Qi gradually develops an emotional attachment to Joan 101 during his ten-day stay in the underwater observatory. Yet now that a human being has finally learned of the underwater observatory, the alien supervisors of Joan 101 and Hali decide to order both to leave, because the Jima civilization does not want to interfere in the development of human civilization. Joan 101 and Hali arrange for Qi to be transported safely to a beach before they board a UFO in preparation for their return to their mother planet. The underwater observatory remains intact for eventual use by human beings. As the UFO starts to rise into the sky, its metallic exterior flashes the phrase, "Let us never forget one another."[28]

The influence of Steven Spielberg's *Close Encounters of the Third Kind* comes across vividly in *Faraway Love*. At the beginning of the narrative, the participant narrator Qi characterizes his investigation of the UFO as a "close encounter of the third kind." Qi explains there are three types of encounters between human beings and UFOs: a UFO sighting, the discovery of alien objects or other evidence left behind by a UFO, and direct contact between human beings and a UFO. Like most other foreign movies, *Close Encounters of the Third Kind* was not allowed to be publicly screened in the PRC, but it premiered in Hong Kong in March 1978. As early as 1979, Tong served as executive director of the government-run Sichuan Film Association, and thus enjoyed high-level access to foreign movies that had not been officially approved or released for public screening in the PRC. Unlike the American feature film in which aliens emerge from the UFO and and travel with protagonist Roy Neary, the aliens in Tong's novella never appear in the flesh. Instead, they have dispatched the robot and clone to observe humans and other life forms on Earth. The human protagonist Qi never leaves Earth with Joan 101, nor do any other humans board the aliens' UFO as they do in Spielberg's film.

With a Cold War mentality receding from Western SF in the 1970s and 1980s, the visits of space aliens to Earth were less and less analogous to invasion or other threats from the Communist Bloc. Similarly, their visits to Earth were less and less symbolic of invasion or other threats from capitalist countries in a PRC novella such as *Faraway Love*. Qi's own scientific occupation requires him to collaborate with Western scientists at the International UFO Research Institute, whose very existence has helped to reduce historical tensions between the Communist Bloc and capitalist countries. This collaboration between Chinese and Western scientists differs strikingly from Tong's pre-1979 SF narratives, in which any association with "enemy" representatives from the West inspired fear and even paranoia in Tong's PRC protagonists.

In this novella, space aliens from Planet TX-II are benevolent and likable, particularly their cloned representative Joan 101. When Qi first meets Joan 101, he is struck by her stunning beauty. He recalls, "She looks like a fairy.... Her gaze is so mild, and her face is radiant with wisdom and equanimity."[29] When Qi asks Joan 101 if the Jima civilization plans to conquer Earth, Joan 101 replies that the Jima civilization has no such designs on Earth, whose inhabitants it looks upon with kindness and patience. Since human societies on Earth are still at only modestly developed, the Jima civilization wishes only to observe unobtrusively and avoid any interference. Once human societies on Earth develop to a relatively advanced level, the Jima civilization will help humankind develop even more advanced science and technology. This caring and benevolent image of aliens, the optimistic view of humankind benefiting from science, and the evolution of an alien species of far more intelligence than *Homo sapiens* remind readers of similar images and views in Arthur Clarke's novels, such as *Childhood's End* (1953), *2001: A Space Odyssey* (1968), and *Rendezvous with Rama* (1973), which were first translated into Chinese in the 1980s.

In *Faraway Love*, Tong writes of archaeological discoveries that point to the possibility that aliens visited Earth long ago. After Joan 101 leaves Earth, Qi discovers that the Nazca Lines in South America were actually runways constructed by aliens from the Jima civilization. Many years ago, when the aliens from Jima reached Earth's orbit in their spaceships, they landed on the surface with smaller airplane-like shuttle vehicles. To make their landings safer, they built runways on South American plateaus: the Nazca Lines that archaeologists continue to research. In addition, Jima aliens also established a "science city" as a base of operation on the island of Atlantis in the Atlantic. During the Paleolithic age, humans visited Atlantis and were amazed by what they saw. References to Atlantis then made their way into ancient Greek myths and even writings by Plato such as *Timaeus* and *Critias*. However, before their departure from Earth the aliens from the Jima civilization obliterated their science city so thoroughly that the entire island upon which it sat sank below the waves of the Atlantic Ocean.[30]

Tong drew upon ideas from Charles Darwin, Herbert Spencer, and Karl Marx to flesh out his own ideas about the universe and space-age morality. Through the conversation between Qi and Joan 101, readers learn that intelligent life in the universe develops in accordance with evolutionary shifts from low to high, from simple to complex, and from disorder to order. When there is enough scientific knowledge, economic productivity achieves a qualitative change for the better, and a revolutionary society that is free from oppression and tyranny is established. The intelligent denizens of this new society uphold the principles of a sublime and altruistic morality. Even human beings on Earth are likely to aim for similar goals. This depiction of an advanced alien civilization closely resembles Clarke's view of a civilization so advanced as to seem almost god-like, as it has in Tong's narrative, on Planet TX-II. Joan 101 presents herself as a bridge between humankind and the Jima civilization on Planet TX-II, much like Overlord Karellen in *Childhood's End*. Tong's optimistic views of space-age morality contrast strikingly with those in twenty-first-century SF, such as notions about a "dark forest" in Liu Cixin's *The Three-Body Problem*.

Tong's depiction of the romance between Qi and Joan 101 echoes the humanistic trend in the "contemplative literature" of that period, when many of Tong's SF-writing contemporaries such as Zheng Wenguang and Ye Yonglie included a love interest in their narratives. These romantic elements not only increased the readability of their stories, but also responded to the return of humanism in mainstream PRC literature during the thaw era. In *Faraway Love*, Qi is portrayed as both a devoted scientist and an affectionate man. Though it has been forty years since Joan 101 left, Qi continues to dispatch the message "Never forget" every year on the anniversary of her leaving. The amatory connection between Qi and Joan 101 also highlights the empathy of her alien species for human earthlings. When Qi first realizes that he harbours feelings of love for Joan 101, he hides his emotional attachment to her. He simply assumes that an alien of superior intelligence would be too coldly rational to fall in love or even understand the relatively primitive amatory feelings of human earthlings. Shortly before Joan 101 leaves, Qi overcomes his inhibitions and expresses his love for her. To his surprise, she replies, "I understand. I love you, too."[31] Symbolically, this interplanetary love interest between two different species reveals Tong's optimism about possible future interactions between earthlings and intelligent life from different planets.

Alien Archaeology

"Song of the Stalagmites" deals not directly with an invasion from space aliens, but with the artefacts left behind by the visit of an alien civilization to Earth. It can be read as an archaeological story in which Tong skilfully combines historical records, accounts of archaeological excavations, and scientific hypotheses. Though "Song of the Stalagmites" was first published in 1982 in *Juvenile Science*, a popular science magazine with a juvenile readership, the story does not cater solely to juvenile readers. The story is of an archaeological team that excavates a stalagmite in the city of Chengdu. The narrator is an archaeologist who uses a conceptual framework from his profession to present his scientific hypothesis that the stalagmite is an artefact from a space alien civilization. His hypothesis is based on historical records, and his deductive reasoning is painstakingly logical. By the end of the narrative, when he concludes that the unearthed stalagmite is actually a monitoring device left behind from a space-alien civilization, the reader likely finds his hypothesis plausible and even convincing.

The story starts with a short prelude quoting the Tang poet Du Fu's (712–70) eponymous poem "Song of the Stalagmites" ("Shisun xing"), in which Du Fu criticizes the superstitious explanation that the two stalagmites were the "eyes of the sea." He points out that they are actually tombstones of ancient officials. Then Du Fu relates the stalagmites to the political conflict of his time. He argues that many treacherous court officials confused the emperor with their talk. They were just like those who groundlessly explain the origin of the stalagmites and prevent the populace from seeing the truth. Following this prelude, the narrator observes that the two stalagmites are relics of Chengdu and thus symbols of the past. If we offer a scientific hypothesis that the stalagmites are actually relics of an advanced interstellar civilization, the stalagmites will become symbols of the future. He further points out that the excavation project in which he has recently participated has linked these two symbols.

The first half of the story reviews Chinese historical records of the stalagmites in Chengdu. Their earliest mention is in "Divination and Validation of Meteors in Han Dynasty" ("Han liuxing xingshi zhanyan"), which is included in "A Treatise on Literature" ("Yi wen zhi") within *The History of the Han Dynasty* (*Han shu*):[32] "There are ten stalagmites in Chengdu. They are the remains of meteorites that landed during the reign of King Yi of Zhou [Zhou yi wang, 899–72 BCE]. One of these stalagmites has disappeared every two hundred years. One must not touch these stalagmites, as that would be highly inauspicious. Some elders have said, 'Since they arrived from the Milky Way, they should be left alone for the Milky Way.'"[33] The stalagmites are mentioned again in the gazetteer *Chronicles of Huayang* (*Huayang guo zhi*) compiled by Chang Qu (291–361) during the Jin dynasty (265–420).[34] Chang's account claims there were three stalagmites in Chengdu. By the time Du Fu wrote his poem, there were only two left. During the late Tang, the stalagmites were mentioned again in Du Guangting's (850–933) *Evidential Miracles in Support of Daoism* (*Daojiao lingyan ji*).[35] Du's account claims that a grand commandant surnamed Liu asked his subordinates to chisel out a small piece from a stalagmite and make Liu an ink stone from it. However, when the subordinate tried to chisel, a bolt of lightning knocked him to the ground. Two subsequent attempts failed in the same way. Grand Commandant Liu realized that the stalagmites seemed protected by an unknown force, and had an attendant tie the stalagmites together with an iron chain.

The second half of the narrative interprets these historical accounts with the aid of scientific hypotheses. The excavation team unearths a stalagmite that had been buried underground horizontally. Before leaving the worksite at the end of the day, the team places the stalagmite upright. However, when returning next morning, the team discovers that the stalagmite has disappeared. Inspired by historical accounts, the narrator hypothesizes a connection between the stalagmite and visiting aliens. He suspects that the stalagmite is a monitoring device that an advanced alien civilization sent to monitor the development of human civilization. According to this hypothesis, the space aliens launched ten rockets that carried these monitoring devices. This echoes the account in "Divination and Validation of Meteors in Han Dynasty" that the stalagmites were originally from meteors. Since the casings of the monitors were made of a special metal alloy, they felt as heavy as stones. Because they were arranged vertically, humans described them as stalagmites. The space aliens had programmed one monitor to return to the home planet of alien civilization every two centuries, to deliver the data collected on Earth. This could explain why there were only two stalagmites remaining by the time Du Fu mentioned them. One of the last stalagmites rocketed back to the aliens' home during the eleventh century. However, since Grand Commandant Liu had tied the two stalagmites together with an iron chain, when one of the stalagmites rocketed into the sky, it pulled the other one along for a short distance before the second stalagmite fell back to the ground, where it rested horizontally. Because of its horizontal alignment, the rocket apparatus within the monitor was unable to lift the last stalagmite off the ground. Therefore, the last stalagmite had remained on Earth until its discovery by the excavation team. Since the excavation team left the stalagmite standing in its proper vertical position, its long-dormant rocket had fired up and launched it into space. The last stalagmite-like monitor thus was finally able to return to the space aliens' home planet.

Later the narrator and his colleagues come across more evidence to support this hypothesis. During the evening when the last stalagmite rocketed into space, radar systems all over the world detected a rocket launch in the vicinity of Chengdu. The rocket's exhaust caused the soil in the launch area to appear scorched and left small green beads, which matched Du Fu's account of jade beads left behind by the vanished stalagmite. In addition, the scorched earth tested positive for radioactive elements, which must have been present in the rocket exhaust.

Tong's view on alien civilization in this story is consistent with that revealed in "A Guest from Fifty Thousand Years Ago" and *The Faraway Love*: a highly advanced civilization of space aliens has been monitoring Earth's human civilization but has refrained from interfering in the development of human civilization. As in his two earlier space alien narratives, Tong again used the term *gaoji zhihui shengwu* (beings of advanced intelligence) to characterize the space aliens. However, Tong did not specify the location of the space aliens' home planet in "Song of the Stalagmites," but instead simply used the generic term "cosmic space" (*yuzhou kongjian*).

Tong's narrative is interspersed with the narrator's reflections on the mysteries of the universe. He comments on limitations of Einstein's theory of general relativity about space-time. He argues that the theory cannot necessarily be applied to the entirety of the universe. There might well be alternate versions of space-time elsewhere. The narrative ends with a series of questions from the narrator: "Among these numerous stars in the sky, from which planetary system might intelligent beings be observing and monitoring us at this moment? What do they look like? What are their thoughts? Two millennia might well be a relatively short cycle of observation for them – what is their standard unit of duration? How many unsolved mysteries are there in the vast reaches of space?"[36] He conveys a sense of frustration about how limited human understanding of the universe remains, even in an age of rapid scientific progress.

"Song of the Stalagmites" is apolitical. It contains few political or ideological features in characterization or plot development. In "The Icons of Science Fiction," Gwyneth Jones argues that SF understandably often has little to say about politics or economics: "The sense of wonder invoked, at coming face-to-face with the workings of the cosmos, should be freed as far as possible from the economic and political constraints of 'real' science, and it is no accident that some of the most beloved images of SF are enshrined in narratives of pure encounter."[37] Her comments reference canonical SF novels such as Arthur C. Clarke's *Rendezvous with Rama* (1973), Frederik Pohl's *Gateway* (1979), and Jack McDevitt's *The Engines of God* (1994), in which encounters with space aliens or their artefacts take place in the midst of humankind's space exploration. The relative absence of economic and political constraints "allows us to discuss social, political, and psychological permutations of human otherness."[38] However, Jones also points to a negative side of such encounters with space aliens, involving a frequent "descent into the banal: the center of these stories is a vastness, an inhuman majesty that cannot be reduced to human terms."[39] Tong overcame this common defect of "inhuman majesty" by placing his encounter between humans and space alien artefacts in the recognizable setting of Chengdu, and by relating these encounters to Chinese historical accounts. In doing so, Tong familiarized his strange artefacts so that readers could speculate about advanced civilizations in a more concrete way, imagining how space aliens' curiosity about earthlings might be tempered with a commitment to avoid interfering in the development of Earth's primitive civilization. The story's matter-of-fact narrative tone, non-theatrical plot, lack of ideological conflict, and minimalist characterization enhance the credibility of the story's scientific hypotheses.

The First Defeat

"The First Defeat" was written for a collection of space alien invasion stories called *Tales from the Planet Earth*, edited by Frederik Pohl and Elizabeth Anne Hull and published in 1986. The collection contains nineteen short stories that revolve around the theme of a human and a space alien co-existing within one physical body. The Chinese version of "The First Defeat" was published in the tenth issue of the literary magazine *Young Writers* in 1984. The story was translated into English by Dingbo Wu, and adapted by Hull with the English title "The Middle Kingdom."[40]

The story is told from the first-person perspective of a space alien invader. He begins his narrative with a prologue that provides background information about his life and his civilization. An Inter-Stellar Alliance of Civilizations (ISAC) is composed of highly intelligent beings from different planets. After ISAC learns of the existence of Earth and its human civilization, it sends a delegation to study its civilization and exploit its natural resources. Because of the vast distance between the interstellar federation and Earth, the aliens are dispatched by mental projection technology at a speed faster than light. After they arrive, the aliens take up residence in human bodies. Each alien's mind occupies an individual human's brain. Even after an alien's mind occupies a human host and manipulates that human's behaviour, that host still retains his or her memories, intelligence, and skills. The aliens set up a base of operations on the Hawaiian island of Maui. The narrator is one of five aliens who have been dispatched to China to search for their host humans and convey them to Maui. Unfortunately, the narrator cannot force his will upon Wu Li, a Chinese engineer working on the production of radionuclides, because of the strength of Wu's patriotism and indomitable willpower. After the narrator returns crestfallen from China, he reports what happened to a delegation of space aliens.

This short story makes for a strong contrast with Tong's three earlier space-alien narratives. Most notably, "The First Defeat" depicts a direct encounter between humans and space aliens, not merely alien artefacts, robots, or clones. As for the story's backdrop, the setting of "The First Defeat" encompasses both China and America, while the earlier narratives are all set in China. The space aliens' invasion of Earth is not peaceful, nor are the invaders empathetic and patient observers. In this narrative, they are ruthless invaders who are in collaboration with the

U.S. government. In the prologue, the alien narrator spells out the invaders' purpose for visiting Earth: they will not only study Earth's civilization, but also exploit its radioactive resources. They then establish a station in Borneo for shipping the radioactive materials by rocket to a larger spaceship orbiting Earth – and finally send the materials to their home planets by photon rocket.

This story resembles Western space-alien invasion narratives from the end of the nineteenth and early twentieth centuries that serve as critiques of European colonial expansionism during the heyday of imperialism. However, Tong's story offers an ideological twist. In the original Chinese version, these exploitations on Earth by the space aliens receive support from the U.S. government, which helps them build their base in Maui.[41] The story's change of stance on an invasion from space aliens, especially the aliens' friendly association with the U.S. government, derives from a change of political climate in China during 1983 and 1984 – the "Campaign to Eliminate Spiritual Pollution," which aimed to root out Western-inspired liberalization of thought from the Chinese populace. This political circumstance not only affected Tong's change in approach to the motif of a space-alien invasion, but also shaped the didactic tone of the story. The alien narrator's attempt to abduct the Chinese engineer and force him to relocate to the United States is a parable for Western governments' luring of Chinese scientists to work for them in the prosperous and technologically advanced West.

The story's narrator chooses Engineer Wu in Beijing as his human host. Wu shares a cramped apartment with his wife and two children, working hard day and night on technological innovations for processing radioactive material. However, when he presents his production plan to Party cadres in his factory, they reject it. This episode reveals some of the problems that Deng Xiaoping's reform initiatives encountered during the thaw era when his new leadership team attempted to shift the PRC economy from a Maoist centrally planned model to a more modern mixed economy subject to market forces. Taking advantage of this situation, the alien narrator merges with Wu's body and tries to lure Wu into abandoning the PRC in favour of the United States. He tells Wu if Wu and his family emigrate to the United States, the Americans will not only build a factory for him to utilize his technological innovations, but also guarantee that he will enjoy an affluent life there. In this conversation, the narrator's identity becomes virtually identical with that of an American. However, Wu responds, "I'll contribute my knowledge solely to my motherland [the PRC]. No riches of any kind in the world could tempt me to betray her."[42] Wu thus refuses to go along with the alien's scheme, adding, "My country is moving ahead with construction and is revitalizing herself. Duty bound to my motherland, I won't leave her."[43] When the alien mocks Wu that what he has been saying amounts to mere empty dogma, Wu refuses to concede: "No, it's not empty dogma. It is the faith mixed in my flesh and blood. It is the principle of my life. It is my sublime spirit."[44] When the the alien considers using force to take Wu to Maui, Wu replies that he would rather die than betray his own country. At this moment, the factory director drops by with the good news that the Municipal Party Committee and the Chemical Industry Bureau have just decided to approve Wu's plan and implement his project without delay. Wu is also appointed deputy director of the factory. This Disney-like finale echoes Deng Xiaoping's instructions to Party committees in research institutes and science and technology units about supporting innovation and cherishing scientific talent.[45] Realizing that he could not persuade Wu to go to the United States with him, the alien narrator decides to leave Wu to his destiny, but he "could not help feeling affection as well as admiration" for him.[46] He concludes, "Our control over Earthmen can only reach the limit of their physical lives. If someone adheres to a certain principle above his own life, our control will come to an end. The Chinese are unusual."[47]

This story touches upon an interesting question about communication between humans and space aliens. When a human body is taken over by a space alien, what is the connection between a human's free will and an alien's imposed will? In the narrative, "possessed" humans commit suicide or suffer from schizophrenia because of the conflict. Tong did not offer a creative resolution of this issue, but merely answered the question simplistically: a human being's core faith cannot be manipulated by an alien force, no matter how advanced that alien civilization might be. Through the alien's failure to abduct the Chinese engineer, the author asserts Chinese intellectuals' presumed loyalty to their native country and their assumed resistance to the lure of prosperity and technological advancement in the West.

This thematic concern was echoed in mainstream PRC literature and cinema at the time, such as in Bai Hua's film script *Bitter Love* and in the film *The Herdsman* (*Mumaren*, 1982) directed by Xie Jin (1923–2008). Wu's declaration of loyalty to his motherland also serves as Tong's response to many in the PRC who suspected him of trying to emigrate to the United States. Tong's family had close ties with the United States even prior to Tong's birth. His father graduated with a degree in mechanical engineering at Harvard University in the 1920s. While a teenager, Tong was enrolled in a school run by American missionaries, Changsha's Yali Middle School, from 1947 to 1950.[48] In addition, Tong was one of the first PRC writers to visit the United States after the end of the Cultural Revolution. He was a visiting scholar at UCLA in 1980 and at Harvard University in 1981, and visited other American universities over the next few years. Because of his frequent visits to the United States during the thaw era, some of Tong's colleagues publicly accused him of wanting to betray his homeland and emigrate. It is not surprising that Tong would use the protagonist of Engineer Wu as a mouthpiece for declaring how loyal he remained to his native country, even in the face of the lure of the West. However, the publication of this story is a bit self-contradictory. The English version of the story is included in a collection of SF stories written by an international team and edited by two Americans, but the ideological message of the story is to resist the lure of the prosperous West and its "bourgeois spiritual pollution." The omission and revision of political messages in the English-language adaptation of this story betray this dilemma.

Conclusion

Tong did not achieve aesthetic breakthroughs in his space-alien narratives about invasion, but his works are high in the literary quality of his limpid prose style, plausible plotting based on the logic of cause and effect, and relatively true-to-life characterization. These narratives valorize human intellect and rationality, and embody an optimistic faith in the rising trajectory of human civilization, including its eventual expansion beyond the confines of Earth. Tong celebrates the seemingly unstoppable co-evolution of human beings and their advancing technology. His narratives are also aligned with the values of "classical" SF: "scientific accuracy, intellectual rationality, and the self-evident materiality of the physical world."[49]

At the same time, Tong's space-alien narratives also reveal characteristics that were rare or non-existent in PRC SF from the 1950s and 1960s. Unlike his forebears, Tong was willing to blur or break boundaries, parody early texts and generic conventions, and adopt a self-conscious narrative persona with multiple allegiances. Specifically, these narratives often break the Mao-era PRC taboo of writing about space aliens. He did not just expand the SF subject matter by examining the human condition through its interaction with space aliens; more importantly, he moved beyond the idea of a unity coalescing around a single central authority by writing about multinational research collaboration as well as multiple worlds in the universe "without a totalizing or structuring center, and in a constant state of flux."[50] Furthermore, Tong's space alien narratives connect China's historical past with both present-day Chinese society and alien civilizations.

Tong bridged a historically oriented imagination with contemplation of the unknowns of the universe. He treated historical curiosities such as the Chengdu stalagmites, the Nazca Lines, and mythical accounts of the lost island of Atlantis as forensic evidence of encounters between space aliens and human beings. His extensive appropriation and reinterpretation of historical texts in "A Guest from Fifty Thousand Years Ago" and "Song of the Stalagmites" not only blur the boundaries between reality and imagination, history and fiction, past and future, but also destabilize history.

Moreover, Tong's renderings of alien invasions, from monitoring and protecting Earth's civilization to controlling earthlings and exploiting Earth's resources resonated with the PRC's ambivalent relations with the West during this period. His depictions of space aliens and their invasions serve as a mode of social and political critique, and reflect the author's own political sensibility within a highly politicized society.

5 Posthuman Conditions in Xiao Jianheng's SF Narratives

In his discussion of posthumanism in SF, Colin Milburn identifies three main varieties of posthuman narrative: biological, technological, and cultural.[1] Biological posthuman narrative deals mostly with qualities of mind and body, with a focus on the evolutionary future of human beings and the psychological changes they are likely to undergo. Technological posthuman narrative focuses "on the synthetic, engineered successors of humanity or the idea of humans and machines linked ever more closely in the circuits of technoculture."[2] Cultural posthuman narrative explores the "epistemic sense," or how we know that someone lives within the posthuman condition, and discovers that "human nature is a tenuous construct open to modification and revision."[3] Though Milburn's discussion is based on Western SF texts, many Chinese SF narratives also venture into one or more of these three realms. This chapter probes the posthuman contours of Xiao Jianheng's narratives about organ transplantation and robotics. Xiao's SF narratives showcase a diversity of posthuman qualities in his scenarios of Earth's future.

Xiao engaged in SF writing during two separate stages of his career. The first began in 1956 when he published his first popular science script, "The Story of Bubbles" ("Qipao de gushi"), and lasted through 1965, the year prior to the eruption of the Cultural Revolution. The second began with Xiao's resumption of SF writing in 1977 and lasted until the mid-1980s. Xiao graduated from the Nanjing Engineering Institute in 1953 with a bachelor's degree in electronic engineering. He launched his career in creative writing in 1956 right after taking sick leave from a vacuum tube factory in Beijing and returning to his hometown of Suzhou. When the Shanghai Science Education Film Studio solicited draft film scripts, Xiao responded by writing his first science-popularization work, "The Story of Bubbles," which won an award. The success of this debut greatly encouraged Xiao, motivating him to devote his energy to science popularizing

Figure 5.1. Xiao Jianheng (b. 1930) (*left*) and Wu Yan (SF writer and scholar, *right*) in Harbin in 1980 (courtesy of Wu Yan).

and SF writing.[4] Xiao published his first robot story, "A Strange Passenger" ("Qiyi de lüke"), in 1960. In the following five years, he published seven SF stories, among which "Buke's Adventure" ("Buke de qiyu," 1962) and "An Amazing Machine Dog" ("Qiyi de jiqi gou," 1965) are the most renowned.[5] These stories focus on two major scientific themes: biomedical experiments on extending life and artificial intelligence.

Unlike most of his peers on the literary scene who held day jobs as professionals in government, industry, or academia, Xiao had earned a living by doing casual or transient labour in Suzhou after his employers in Beijing fired him for taking a long sick leave in 1956. This situation lasted till May 1978 when he was invited to attend the National Popular Science Writing Forum in Shanghai. Soon after he returned from the forum, he was appointed to a job on the Suzhou Municipal Science Committee. In the following year, he was transferred to the Suzhou Municipal Cultural Bureau, where he focused on creative writing (see figure 5.1).[6]

Xiao was a prolific fiction writer from 1977 to 1982, when he published such short stories as "Tracking Tigers in the Dense Forest" ("Milin huzong," 1977), "A Dream" ("Meng," 1979), "The Optimized Solution of the All-Purpose Service Company" ("Wanneng fuwu gongsi de zuijia fang an," 1979), "The Mystery of the Venusians" ("Jinxing ren zhi mi," 1979), "Professor Shalom's Confusion" ("Shaluomu jiaoshou de miwu," 1980), and "Qiao the Younger Fell Ill" ("Qiao er huan bing ji," 1982). Among these stories, "The Mystery of the Venusians" is the only one about an extraterrestrial alien encounter in space; all of Xiao's other stories deal with more down-to-earth scientific themes such as biomedical experiments about lifespan extension and raising productivity through robotics and artificial intelligence.

Xiao's SF narratives showcase a diversity of posthuman scenarios and reveal the author's speculations about a future posthuman era. His biologically oriented accounts of the posthuman appear in such stories as "Buke's Adventure" and "A Dream." His technologically focused accounts of the posthuman appear in stories such as "Qiao the Younger Fell Ill." The posthuman condition as an epistemological alternative to the cultural and linguistic traditions of humanism features prominently in "Professor Shalom's Confusion." These narratives explore scientific ideas in interesting ways while having affinities with traditional Chinese literary texts.

The Biologically Oriented Account of the Posthuman: "Buke's Adventure"

In Western SF, motifs of organ transplantation and bringing the dead back to life go back to the early nineteenth century, having first appeared in novels such as Mary Shelley's *Frankenstein* (1818) and H.G. Wells's *The Island of Dr. Moreau* (1896). In the early twentieth century, both the German SF writer Carl Grunert (1865–1918) and the Soviet Russian writer Alexander Belyaev (1884–1942) wrote about laboratories that keep severed heads on life support in "Mr. Vivacious Style" (1908) and *Professor Dowell's Head* (1925), respectively.[7] Chinese SF narratives that contend with these motifs did not appear until the 1950s. However, in traditional Chinese literature we can find at least two texts about organ transplantation and bringing the dead back to life. In his collection of essays and tales entitled *Brush Talks from Dream Brook* (*Mengxi bitan*, ca. 1083–93), Shen Kuo (1031–95) wrote about medicine for rejuvenation. In this account, a seventy-year-old Chen Yun with grey hair is given ointment by a younger man named Sun Xiling. Sun assures Chen that anyone who applies the ointment to his teeth will see his hair turn black. After some hesitation, Chen follows Sun's strange instructions. To Chen's surprise, his beard and his hair soon turn black again, and new teeth grow to replace old teeth that had fallen out. The collection of Hong Mai (1123–1202) entitled *Records of Yi Jian* (*Yi jian zhi*, 1162), includes an account of a Chinese surgeon who performs a jaw transplant on a patient suffering from osteonecrosis.[8] Both narratives are proto-science-fiction accounts, for the rejuvenating ointment and surgical transplantation of a jaw are merely more advanced versions of traditional Chinese methods of healing and might be plausible in the foreseeable future. Chinese SF writers revived this theme again in the 1950s. For example, Xiao Jianheng's "Buke's Adventure" portrays organ transplantation in animals and human beings.

Xiao wrote "Buke's Adventure" in 1961, saw it published the following year in a popular science magazine for juvenile readers, *We Love Science* (*Women ai kexue*), and later included in his collected SF stories that he published through Juvenile Publishing. The story brought Xiao nationwide fame as a writer of SF for juveniles, and it was the most popular one of the collection. "Buke's Adventure" was adapted as both a radio drama and an illustrated book, and was eventually translated into Korean. A post-Mao reprint of the book came out in 1979 and the print run was approximately one million copies.[9]

The story unfolds at a residential compound in a Chinese city, begining with the return of a missing dog named Buke, who belongs to Old Li, a neighbour of the narrator. Playing the part of a clown, Old Li works as a performer in a local circus troupe. Buke is a fellow circus performer but has become too old to keep up the pace, so Old Li adopts it as a pet and takes care of it. Reports surface one day that a truck accidentally ran over Buke on a local street, but the dog's body is nowhere to be found. Three months later, Buke returns to Old Li's house. Old Li soon discovers that Buke is not the same dog he owned before, because the colour of its fur has changed. The reader does not solve the mystery until after Buke goes missing again. It turns out that scientists at a medical research institute saved Buke's life on the day of the accident. Buke's heart and lungs were seriously injured, but the head remained intact. The scientists put Buke on life support, with a pump to circulate the blood and an iron lung to handle respiration. Then the scientists transplanted Buke's head onto the body of a different dog, enabling Buke to make a full recovery. Old Li and the narrator are invitated to visit the research institute, where they tour animal labs and inspect equipment used in experiments. The lab may remind readers of Ivan Pavlov's laboratory, for it has a large-scale kennel to house the experimental animals. Following the success of Buke's operation, the narrator beseeches the doctor to perform a similar transplant on his daughter, Young Hui, who lost her leg in an accident some years before. The doctors perform a leg transplant for Young Hui, and six months later, she is able to walk just like a normal person. Soon afterward, the doctors perform a hand transplant for a model worker, as well as transplants of the heart, lungs, and kidneys for other patients. The methodology of organ transplantations soon spreads to other regions within China and even overseas. At the end of the narrative, Buke and Young Hui perform together onstage with the rest of the circus troupe.

The story's editor, Yan Hui, praised Xiao for having made a breakthrough in skilfully marrying science and technology with storytelling. Though organ transplantation was not a new topic in either bioscience or popular science writings at that time, Xiao made his ideas about organ and body-part transplants more informative and entertaining through an imaginative futuristic story.[10] More importantly, the story conveys the strong potential of future bio-scientific advances to vastly improve the quality of life for humans and other animals with severely damaged organs or body parts. This theme not only reveals the story's influence from Soviet SF, but also resonates with the sociopolitical discourse of the revitalization of a new China in the Mao era.

Konstantin E. Tsiolkovsky (1857–1935) and Alexander Belyaev were the most influential Soviet writers on scientific themes in Mao-era China. Tsiolkovsky's writing about space travel and rocketry inspired many PRC writers to explore these topics in their own writings. Belyaev's SF narratives about organ and body part transplants in *Professor Dowell's Head* and *The Amphibian Man* (1928) likewise encouraged some PRC writers to take up this topic. *The Amphibian Man* came out in Chinese translation in 1958, while *Professor Dowell's Head* came out in translation in 1959. Soviet scientist Margarita Alekseevna Vorontsov's (1923–2015) monograph on organ reconstruction was also translated into Chinese in 1957 as *Reconstruction of Animal and Human Organs* (*Dongwu he renti qiguan de zaisheng*).

In addition, Ivan Pavlov's research on conditioned reflexes such as a dog salivating after hearing a bell ring also contributed to the emergence of Chinese SF narratives about biomedical experiments. Pavlov's writings arrived in China during the late 1920s in the form of English translations, as well as through Chinese-language writings by psychologists such as Pan Shu (1897–1988), Gao Juefu (1896–1993), Guo Yicen (1894–1977), and Chen Hanbiao (1906–82). Pavlov's theories became especially influential in the PRC during the 1950s after the CCP's repeated exhortations to "learn from the Soviet Union on all fronts."[11] For example, the PRC Ministry of Education invited four

Soviet psychologists to China to deliver lectures on Pavlov in 1952. At around the same time, the Translation Bureau of the PRC General Administration of Press and Publication appointed the psychologist Zhou Xiangeng (1903–96) to lead a team of fellow specialists to translate Pavlov's two-volume study, *Conditioned Reflexes* (1927). Furthermore, in 1953 the PRC Ministry of Health organized seminars on the theories of Pavlov.[12] These activities not only promoted Pavlov's theories among academicians and other professionals, but also influenced lay readers by popularizing Pavlov's findings about conditioned reflexes. The PRC historian of science and technology Cao Yu even called attention to the ringing political endorsement of Pavlovian theory through such Marxist-Leninist labels as "dialectical materialism" in the Mao era.[13]

Xiao Jianheng read widely on such matters through Chinese translations of Belyaev's fiction, Pavlovian treatises, and Soviet popular science writings. The severed head of a dog in "Buke's Adventure" reminds the reader of Professor Dowell's head in Belyaev's story, as well as the head of a dog that Russian doctor Sergei Briukhonenko (1890–1960) described in his account of a medical experiment he performed in 1926. However, the difference between Buke's head, Professor Dowell's head, and Briukhonenko's dog head is that the latter two heads are on life support through mechanical medical devices, while Buke's head has been transplanted onto another dog's actual body. Xiao's portrayal of the viability of Buke's severed head resonates significantly with the latest medical advances in organ transplantation during the early 1960s. In the mid-1920s, when Belyaev wrote *Professor Dowell's Head*, and Briukhonenko experimented on the severed head of a dog, they were largely unaware of tissue rejection and transplantation immunology, and they assumed that life support for a severed head merely required anonymous blood transfusions and medical gadgetry that facilitated circulation of the dog's blood. Yet by the time Xiao wrote the story about Buke in the early 1960s, medical science had already made advances in transplantation immunology. For example, in the early 1950s Dr. Joseph Murray led a team of physicians in Boston who performed a successful and long-lasting kidney transplant on a dog, having taken measures to reduce the likelihood of the recipient's rejection of the donor kidney. In 1954, Murray and his team went on successfully to perform a kidney transplant between genetically identical twins.[14] During the 1950s and 1960s, worldwide biomedical discoveries in immunological rejection "established the paradigm of transplantation immunology and provided the basis for immunological dogma that remains relevant today in the context of both tissue and stem cell transplantation."[15] Xiao obviously kept up with the latest advances and incorporated them in his fiction. The only difference is that Xiao's fiction nationalistically attributes all of these medical advances to PRC scientists. In "Buke's Adventure," the narrator summarizes news reports about doctors in Suzhou (the author's hometown) who successfully performed organ and body part transplants, and claims that these Suzhou doctors successfully dealt with the dangerous problem of heterogenic protein in organ transplants by drawing upon Pavlov's theory of trans-marginal inhibition – an organism's response to overwhelming stimuli.

The success of the PRC scientists' biomedical endeavours in Xiao's story about Buke echoes Mao Zedong's political rhetoric about how scientific experimentation is a necessary component in the PRC's march to become a major world power.[16] It is noteworthy that the author repeatedly underscores his notion of "believing in science," displaying an uncritical attitude known as scientism. During one scene in the story, Dr. Yao tells Old Li and the narrator, "Believe in science! We will definitely keep Buke alive."[17] The narrator also emphasizes that advances in science and medicine require sacrifice by both doctors and patients who are involved with experimental procedures. Before Young Hui undergoes a risky operation, the narrator comments, "Science sometimes requires sacrifice. Any new endeavor needs someone to give it a try for the first time. If science needs me for this, I won't hesitate at all; if this operation succeeds, it may help thousands of at-risk patients live and thrive."[18]

When explaining the Soviet readership's enthusiastic reception of Belyaev's *Professor's Dowell's Head* and Briukhonenko's accounts of his experiments with the severed head of a dog, Krementsov relates "both literary and physiological experimentation with severed heads" to "a particular cultural milieu of mid-1920s Russia, which was at one and the same time permeated by omnipresent death and by high hopes for the future, instigated by the decade of death and the subsequent 'resurrection' of the country."[19] Krementsov's comment also sheds light on the emergence of Chinese narratives of organ transplantation during the 1950s and 1960s. During the first half of the twentieth century, China also experienced more than its share of death and destruction, such as the overthrow of the Qing dynasty in 1911, over a decade of internecine conflict between regional warlords (1916–27), the invasion from Japan and the Second World War (1937–45), the civil war between the armies of the Nationalist party-state and the Communist party-state (1946–9), and the Korean War (1950–3). Mao's newly founded regime had just emerged from these disasters by the mid-1950s and seemed to have entered a revival. Therefore, literary experimentation with a sort of emergence from life support and revitalization resonated with the party-state's socio-political discourse of reconstructing and revitalizing China. In "Buke's Adventure," the narrator elaborates on the significance of the doctors' work: "If [doctors] could replace a failing organ with a healthy one, then the patient would recover and go on living. He would be able to continue to contribute to the building of our socialist country. If these experiments succeeded, we would not only be able to save thousands of people from an untimely death, but also significantly extend their lifespan."[20]

In the Maoist party-state's socio-political discourse of scientism during the 1950s and 1960s, there was no room for the PRC populace to question or doubt anything done in the name of science. "Buke's Adventure" does not reveal the ethical implications of organ transplants such as how or whether the authorities receive an organ donor's consent. To some extent, Mao Zedong's insistence that "humanity must conquer nature" desensitized the PRC public to ethical issues in biomedical experimentation.[21] Opposing biomedical experimentation on ethical grounds would be almost unthinkable for the PRC populace. At the end of *Professor Dowell's Head*, Dowell's head dies and the authorities arrest his disciple as a criminal suspect. In this way, Belyaev questions the ethics of keeping a severed head on life support with scientific gadgetry and medical know-how.[22] In contrast, Xiao's narrative delivers a much more optimistic ending, totally ignoring the ethical dimensions of human organ transplantation. Young Hui receives a new leg through her body part transplant, but the narrative provides no information whatever about the donor of the transplanted leg, merely commenting, "[Young Hui's] transplanted leg functions as well as her real leg, except that the color of its skin is slightly different from that of her other leg."[23] Xiao and his peers on the Mao-era PRC literary scene could not provide answers to the ethical issues that accompanied rapid advances in experimental biology and medicine during the 1950s and 1960s.

Mao Zedong's death in 1976 marked the formal cessation of the Cultural Revolution. The ensuing socio-political discourse of the PRC's recovery from a decade of nationwide catastrophe helped legitimize the re-emergence of SF narratives about revitalization and organ transplantation. "Buke's Adventure" was reprinted in 1979 and once again won popularity among PRC readers. The theme of organ and body-part transplants proved a stimulant to the imagination of PRC SF writers. In 1979, Ye Yonglie wrote the short story "After Losing His Nose" ("Shiqu bizi yihou") on the theme of a medical operation to reconstruct a mangled human nose.[24] Similar stories include Wang Yafa's "Qiangba's Eyes" ("Qiangba de yanjing," 1977) about a cornea transplant;

Zhang Yiwu and Wei Liao's "Water for Growing" ("Sheng zhang shui," 1978) and Fang Weigong's "Returning to the Athletic Field" ("Chongfan saichang," 1979) are both about reconstructive surgery on a leg. Gao Weibin's "After the Heart Stops Beating" ("Xinzang tingzhi tiaodong yihou," 1978) and Ying Wenhui and Chen Jiejun's "A Man without a Heart" ("Meiyou xinzang de ren," 1979) are both about heart transplants. Xiao Jianheng wrote two stories on the theme of cryogenics entitled "A Dream" and "Combat" ("Bodou," 1980). In these two narratives, scientists induce a state of hibernation in astronauts or patients using cryogenic deep freeze. Scientists intend to revive the hibernating astronauts when their training can be fully utilized, while doctors plan to revive the hibernating patients when effective new treatments for their illnesses are ready to be implemented.

High-Tech Visions and the Posthuman: Xiao's Two Robot Stories

In addition to narratives about cryogenics, Xiao wrote more stories about robots during the late 1970s and early 1980s. The Czech writer Karel Capek first coined the term "robot" in his 1920 play entitled *R.U.R.: Rossum's Universal Robots*; Capek's neologism "carried suggestions of heavy labor, even of slavery."[25] Since then, the definition of robot gradually narrowed and came to mean a "self-contained, maybe remote-controlled artificial device that mimics the actions, and possibly the appearance of a human being."[26] The term "cyborg" was coined in 1960 "in relation to survival in outer space," and means "a cybernetic organism, crudely a combination of human and machine."[27]

In traditional Chinese literature, the earliest robot was Yanshi's in "Questions of Tang" ("Tang wen") in *The Book of Lieizi* (*Lie zi*, ca. 307–13) compiled by Zhang Zhan (ca. 370). In this story, the craftsman Yanshi creates a sing-song robot that can pass as a genuine human performer. Yanshi presents his robot as a gift to the reigning Zhou dynasty king. The king finds the robot's musical performance amazing but flies into a murderous rage after noticing that the robot keeps staring at one of the king's royal concubines. The king even decides to kill the robotic performer. Yanshi intercedes to explain that his performer is not a genuine man, but instead a contraption built out of leather, wood, and glue. After carefully examining the robot, the king praises Yanshi's excellent craftsmanship.[28] In 1982, Tong Enzheng wrote a parody of this story entitled "The Death of the World's First Robot" ("Shijie shang diyige jiqiren zhi si"). In Tong's story, the robot dies of a heart attack stemming from its jealousy upon seeing the royal concubine flirt with young male courtiers.[29]

The SF critic Dingbo Wu identifies three more Chinese robot stories from pre-modern times. Zhang Zhuo's (ca. 660–740) *The Complete Records of the Court and the Commoners* (*Chaoye qianzai*) includes one tale about a robot monk who begs for alms, and another story about a robot dancing girl. Shen Kuo's (1031–95) *Brush Talks from Dream Brook* showcases a tale about a robot rat-killer.[30] In addition, Xie Zhaozhe's (1567–1624) *Five Miscellaneous Morsels* (*Wu zazu*) features a story about how the wife of the famous Three Kingdoms strategist Zhuge Liang builds wooden robots to help her handle household chores and harvest the wheat crop.[31]

Robotics became a central theme in Chinese SF shortly after the middle of the twentieth century. In 1960, Xiao Jianheng published "A Strange Passenger." In this piece of juvenilia, a group of Suzhou middle school students who specialize in science and technology send their robot off on a train trip all alone, managing the robot's actions by remote control. In 1962, Tong Enzheng published a similar piece entitled "A Missing Robot," which depicts a group of secondary school students who build a working robot. However, after a malfunction in the robot's transmitter, the robot goes haywire and winds up roaming the city streets aimlessly at night.

Since the late 1970s, robots, cyborgs, automated machines, and artificial intelligence have figured even more frequently in PRC SF. PRC SF writers have increasingly pitched their fiction to a broad adult readership, unlike the 1960s SF stories that appealed mostly to juveniles. Increasing emphasis upon robot stories in post-Mao PRC SF stemmed in large part from changes in policies of the PRC government on science and technology. Mao-era science policy channelled the lion's share of the country's resources into military applications at the expense of civilian uses. For instance, in Mao-era nuclear science, emphasis was placed on manufacturing nuclear bombs and nuclear-powered submarines, while the PRC failed to build or even design a single nuclear power plant, in comparison with Taiwan and South Korea. In contrast, the post-Mao leadership under Deng Xiaoping implemented a much more balanced science policy, which saw the PRC design and start building its first two nuclear power plants at Dayawan and Qinshan in the 1980s while also maintaining its nuclear weapons program. In other words, civilian applications of science and technology received far more resources and prioritization under Deng and his successors than they had under Mao, preoccupied as he was with military applications.

Post-Mao science policy placed special emphasis on high-tech research and development, which tended to produce strong economic returns through value-added products and other stimulants to societal advances. Naturally, high-tech applications such as robotics and automation resonated with the post-Mao turn in PRC policies on science and technology.[32] Many post-Mao SF narratives thereupon featured the use of robots and artificial intelligence in industrial and agricultural production in order to relieve human workers of the need to perform especially dangerous or repetitious tasks at work. Robots become firefighters, vehicle operators, pearl divers, and aquaculture farmers in SF stories such as Wang Qinlan and Wang Yi's "The Alarm at the Outside of Wusongkou" ("Wusongkou wai de jingbao," 1978), Deng Yanlu's "The Twenty-First Century Railway Trip" ("Ershiyi shiji tielu manyou," 1979), Li Shaoming's "Bright Pearls on the Ocean Floor" ("Haidi mingzhu," 1979), and Wang Jinhai and Dai Shan's "The Strange Encounters in the Ocean" ("Dahai qiyu," 1979). Military applications of robotics also appeared occasionally, such as the employment of robots as border guards in Yang Xunan and Tao Jinsheng's "Sentries in the Thick Forest" ("Milin shaobing," 1979). In the realm of spycraft, cyborgs play an important role as counterintelligence operatives in Liu Zhaogui's "The Mystery of ß" ("ß zhe ge mi," 1979). In the world of sports and entertainment, robots and cyborgs function as soccer players and opera singers in Wang Wen and Chi Fang's "A Novel Ball Game" ("Xinqi de qiu sai," 1978) and Wang Yafa's "A Strange Performance" ("Yichang qiguai de yanchu," 1979).

Xiao's peers on the post-Mao literary scene thus overwhelmingly celebrated the advent of robots and cyborgs as a sign of technological and societal progress. More sophisticated than the works of his peers, Xiao's post-Mao SF narratives sometimes questioned the wisdom of delegating so many tasks at home and workplace to robots and artificial intelligence, which might at some point supersede or even replace humans at the centre of society. In his work, Isaac Asimov formulated his Three Laws of Robotics to ensure that humans will always remain in control of robots, and promoted a consistently positive vision of robots. In contrast with Asimov, other Western SF writers have depicted a "grim future when [robots] have superseded humans in a 'triumph' of evolution," as presented in Sidney Fowler Wright's 1929 story "Automama."[33] Asimov has dismissed such fears as a "Frankenstein complex."[34] The SF critic David Seed argues that although *Frankenstein* does not portray robots or cyborgs, it invents a new narrative paradigm: scientists in a laboratory construct a living human body out of miscellaneous organs and body parts.

SF novels often portray scientists who construct robots or cyborgs in human form; the scientists' purpose is to "dissect or disassemble the body" in order to achieve their goal of reconstructing or modifying robots or cyborgs.[35] This common SF motif ratchets up readers' fears of finding themselves superseded or even replaced by robots, androids, cyborgs, or artificial intelligence. Xiao was aware of these fears and sometimes articulated them, but he tended to come down on the same side of this issue as Asimov, and felt mostly optimistic about advances in robotics and artificial intelligence. More often than not, he promoted positive images of robotics and artificial intelligence, and assured his readers that robots would not be able to supersede humans. The following paragraphs will focus on Xiao's two robot stories, "Professor Shalom's Confusion" and "Qiao the Younger Fell Ill." The two not only present the techno-centric vision of robots participating fully in our future lives, but also explore psychological and epistemological factors that robotics entails.

Xiao's literary experiment in "Professor Shalom's Confusion" assumes that robots are already indistinguishable from the human beings in their midst. Xiao sets out to investigate what effects this feat might have on human relationships and society at large. "Professor Shalom's Confusion" came out in 1980 in the mainstream PRC literary magazine *People's Literature*. In the narrative, Professor Shalom specializes in artificial intelligence and is called "the father of the modern robot."[36] Based on Shalom's theory of "human body simulation," Cola International Corporation has manufactured Cola III as its latest model of humanoid robots. The story humanizes robots by making them identical to humans in appearance and prioritizing their names over their identification numbers. In order to promote the sale of Cola III robots and out-compete their business competitors, the corporation convinces Professor Shalom to participate in its "waif transformation project." Professor Shalom agrees, not for the lucrative awards, but because he wants to see if robots could really pass themselves off as ordinary human beings in psychological and emotional complexity. The experiment will utilize intelligent robots to play the role of foster parents who will transform waifs and vagabonds into well-educated and genteel persons. If this experiment in social engineering succeeds, it will garner government financial support, which would make bulk purchases of the robots and use them as social workers to alleviate the social problems that thousands of vagabonds and waifs have caused. More specifically, each of these intelligent robots will become a new member of a human family, and function in it as a family member's partner, private tutor, nurse, butler, or secretary.

The experiment takes place within a typical middle-class family. The robotic parents, known as Mr. and Mrs. Brown, are well versed in psychology, philosophy, literature, and the arts. They brim with parental patience and affection for their children. The Browns soon adopt a homeless child named Andy, who has a bent for sketching. Andy's mother, Jane, had given birth to him out of wedlock, and later abandoned him at the age of five to fend for himself on the street. Yet Andy still cherishes memories of his mother. Mr. and Mrs. Brown take very good care of Andy and have made progress in transforming Andy into a well-educated and genteel young man with a talent for drawing and painting. The corporation decides to organize a painting exhibition for Andy in order to showcase the success of the project. However, the day before the beginning of the exhibition, Andy goes missing and fails to return to the comforts of his middle-class family. Professor Shalom finds Andy's disappearance most puzzling. Why did Andy fail to develop an attachment to the comforts of home, not to mention the parental love the Browns gave him? Why did he abandon a bright future as a budding painter? Through the assistance of a housemaid in a local hostel, Professor Shalom discovers why Andy abandoned his family. Though Mr. and Mrs. Brown parented Andy with patience and love, Andy could not stand the way that Mrs. Brown caressed him because she did so in a manner identical to the caresses that Jane had previously given him. This reminded Andy of how much he still missed his original mother. Andy left home to search for Jane, since his robotic stepmother turned out to be a poor substitute.

Xiao sets his story in an unnamed Western country. According to widespread suspicions of the West among the PRC populace at the juncture, this foreign country "represented the pinnacle of an 'immoral' capitalist system, where scientific and technological advances served to benefit not 'the people,' but a few capitalists in their pursuit of ever-larger profits."[37] In the narrative, Mr. Hobert, the owner of Cola International Corporation, is a representative of the capitalist system. In contrast to the lofty scientific motivation of Professor Shalom, Hobert's motivation for launching this experiment in social engineering derives solely from his pursuit of ever-larger profits. Hobert's exploitative personal relationship with Jane symbolizes the immorality of the type of capitalist boss who cares more about profits than anything else. It turns out that Jane is Hobert's former mistress, and Hobert is Andy's biological father. According to Marxian views of class-based social relations, Jane is an exploited proletarian. Hobert's rejection of Jane reveals the cold-blooded brutality of many bourgeois bosses. Ironically, when Hobert belatedly discovers that Andy is his son, Andy has already disappeared, and Hobert will probably never meet Andy again. The failure of Hobert's experiment in social engineering turns out to be a logical conclusion for a story about science in a society rife with class-based exploitation.

Aside from criticizing the capitalist system, Xiao provides a scenario for the consoling suggestion that robots will never be able to supersede humans within the core societal unit of the family, no matter how advanced technology becomes. David Seeds has observed that robot narratives often involve the "duality between creator and created," or "experimenter and subject," similar to the main scenarios in *Frankenstein* and Michael Crichton's *The Terminal Man* (1972).[38] In "Professor Shalom's Confusion," there is a similar duality between Professor Shalom and the robots. Both the creator and the created are lacking in empathy, and are initially clueless about why Andy has abandoned the comforts of home and family. Professor Shalom comes across as a kind-hearted and honest scientist, but as an ageing bachelor he lives alone and is uninterested in raising a family. Shalom's lack of a human touch resonates with the mechanical parenting of the robots he has designed such as the Browns; none of them can understand Andy's deep emotional attachment to his biological mother. The failure of this experiment forces Shalom to acknowledge that all human beings have uniquely cherished memories and a complex psychology. Through artificial intelligence, robots can learn and think; they have an extraordinary memory, use rigorous logic, and make accurate judgments. However, robots cannot adequately understand humanistic values or emotional complexities. Scientists like Shalom design robots to select the optimal course of action in a given situation. In contrast, when human beings weigh their options in the face of a dilemma, they do not necessarily select the optimal course of action. Instead, they often make decisions on the basis of emotional attachments. These emotional attachments often lead to a course of action that diverges sharply from what an outside observer would consider the optimal choice. Even though Jane did not fulfil her parental responsibility to look after Andy properly and provide for him, Andy still chooses to search for this flawed human while abandoning his seemingly flawless robotic step-parents.

In 1982, Xiao's second major robot story, "Qiao the Younger Fell Ill," also came out in *People's Literature*. The setting is wholly contemporary: the post-Mao PRC, with its focus on social and economic reforms. The narrative unfolds at a conference on economic reform convened by a provincial bureau of consumer goods manufacturing. The Accurate Watch Factory has dispatched its general engineer and vice director Qiao Ming to attend the conference. Yet the conference-goers soon discover that a robot named Qiao the Younger has been impersonating Qiao Ming at the conference. Much like the experiment in social engineering in "Professor Shalom's Confusion," the robot Qiao the Younger is also part of an experiment. Qiao Ming has become increasingly fed up with attending endless meetings in the wake of his promotion to vice director of his factory. In his opinion, these meetings last far too long, occur too frequently, and achieve little or nothing substantial. Instead of solving the key problem of incompetent management of the factory, these endless meetings merely waste time.

Fortunately for Qiao Ming, his wife is an AI engineer who has helped manufacture an advanced robot that is virtually indistinguishable from a human adult. This robot belongs to the same Cola III prototype featured in "Professor Shalom's Confusion." It resembles Qiao Ming so closely that it looks like a twin brother, and is named Qiao the Younger. The purpose of creating this lookalike robot is to discover if it could relieve engineers and research technicians from their unproductive administrative and clerical tasks.

From that point forward, Qiao the Younger serves as a stand-in for Qiao Ming at routine meetings. However, this conference is important. Managers at Qiao Ming's factory become worried after they learn that he has sent his lookalike robot to attend the conference in his stead. They are afraid that higher-level officials will feel angry and insulted if they notice a robot at the conference. They initially order Qiao the Younger to go back to the factory. However, the head of the consumer goods manufacturing bureau, Director Li, insists that Qiao the Younger remain at the conference after he discovers that he is a robot. Li wants to conduct an informal experiment to see how much useful information the robot can actually collect at the conference. Director Li comes across as an open-minded reformist leader who has a clear understanding of the factory's main problems. The factory has enough manpower, capital, and equipment to be much more productive than it is. However, bureaucratic red tape, incompetent management, and endless meetings have blocked the factory from lowering production costs and improving efficiency. Li concludes his conference presentation with an exhortation to move quickly to reform the outmoded management system and improve product quality in order to meet the requirements of an increasingly market-based PRC economy.

Unfortunately, the factory managers in attendance at the conference do not actually understand what Li was getting at in his presentation. Instead, they decide to manufacture more "meeting robots" like Qiao the Younger. According to the managers, "There will be more and more meetings like this in the future, so this product will be embraced by the market."[39] However, as the post-Mao economic reforms transform managerial processes, the number of meetings shrinks. The factory managers discover that their "meeting robots" have not been selling well. At this juncture, Qiao the Younger falls ill. After a thorough examination and diagnosis, the engineers conclude that while the robot's hardware is working flawlessly, the robot himself is suffering from a psychiatric disorder. In the past, Qiao the Younger attended hundreds of meetings every month, but more recently there have been hardly any meetings. The drastic reduction has severely confused Qiao the Younger. Because this robot does not know how to respond to the altered situation at work, it has fallen ill. At the end of the narrative, the engineers decide to overhaul Qiao the Younger's programming in order to help the robot cope with its new circumstances.

Like many other works of thaw-era PRC fiction, this story critiques bureaucratic red tape in economic enterprises and calls for deepened systematic economic reforms. The story also reaffirms the main thesis of "Professor Shalom's Confusion": robots can only follow pre-set commands, and thus lack independent and critical thinking. Therefore, robots cannot readily supersede or replace humans in everyday interactions of an actual society.

At the surface level, "Qiao the Younger Fell Ill" is a satire of the excessive number and duration of meetings at many PRC enterprises and government bureaus. Symbolically, the illness of the robot Qiao the Younger implies many executives of state-owned enterprises (SOEs) and Party officials who had grown accustomed to endless meetings in the Mao era's state-planned economy have also fallen ill in response to major changes to their routine in the post-Mao reform era. The Deng-era supervisors of these executives and officials increasingly carry out performance reviews based on objective criteria such as productivity metrics and efficiency instead of the old Mao-era criteria of ideology and seniority that frequent meetings tended to reinforce. However, many of these holdovers from the Mao era are too poorly educated to handle the new job metrics of productivity and efficiency, and thus easily become confused and fall ill, like the robot in Xiao's story. The thorough modification of the pre-set commands in Qiao the Younger implies that these Party holdovers from the Mao era need to undertake remedial study and upskill in order to catch up with the Deng-era PRC's economic and social advances.

In addition, the story is a response to Deng-era government imperatives about science and technology contributing to economic advances and increases in overall prosperity. In December 1978, the Third Plenary Session of the Eleventh Central Committee summed up the Party's new emphasis on economic growth instead of Mao-style class struggle through its *bazi fangzhen*, literally "guiding principle in eight characters" – "readjustment, reform, rectification, and improvement" – so as to "guide economic reconstruction in line with [Deng Xiaoping's] Reform and Opening Up."[40] In "Qiao the Younger Fell Ill," we can see that the original design and subsequent modification of Qiao the Younger are related to the need to improve the factory's productivity. The robot's original design as a meeting attender stemmed from the need of factory engineers to focus on scientific research and development that could improve productivity instead of time-wasting administrative formalities. Following implementation of Deng's results-oriented policies that focus on raising productivity, the huge cutback on meetings requires Qiao the Younger to undergo a thorough modification of his approach to work at the factory. Therefore, the story illustrates the emphasis of the reform-era government on economic growth and prosperity through more effective management and advances in science and technology. The story also affirms that the Communist Party's leadership is indispensable to the country's economic reforms. The engineer Qiao Ming is both professionally competent and politically aligned with the proper Deng-era policies of focusing on raising productivity, but he lacks the authority to press for reform on his own initiative. It is only through the help from the reform-minded Party official Li that better managerial techniques and advances in technology improve productivity at the factory.

In her ground-breaking work *How We Became Posthuman*, Katherine Hayles argues that the posthuman condition has a "dual connotation of superseding the human and coming after it."[41] The "terror" that we often associate with the posthuman condition manifests itself "in a general intellectual sense" that the posthuman "displaces one definition of human with another"; and "in a more disturbingly literal sense" that the "human is displaced as the dominant [force] of life on the planet by intelligent machines."[42] Meanwhile, Hayles also argues that the "human being is first of all an embodied being, and the complexities of this embodiment mean that human awareness unfolds in ways very different from those of intelligence embodied in cybernetic machines."[43]

In Xiao's two stories, both the Cola III and Qiao the Younger are "perfected intelligent machines with human form," but they do not have memories of the past or personal identities.[44] They live solely in the present moment. Their existence is fragmented and isolated within a short period of history. "Professor Shalom's Confusion" point outs robots' inability to understand complex human emotional states and exhibit human empathy. In the latter part of "Qiao the Younger Fell Ill," the Chinese engineers and Professor Shalom all agree that Cola III robots have high cognitive skills, but they still fall far short of the complexities of human psychology and emotion. Robots follow the instructions that humans have given them, and respond with a sort of conditioned reflex. They do not have independent ideas or the ability to think critically, and cannot respond effectively to changing circumstances. They are only "read as a futuristic underclass, ... defined and devalued by their artificiality."[45] The robots' lack of human empathy and the autonomy to respond effectively to changing circumstances resonates with the author's belief that robots will not be able to supersede or replace humans in actually societal settings.

Xiao Jianheng was at the forefront of his peers who wrote thaw-era Chinese SF about complex issues of posthuman interactions and the likely future impact of science and technology on human society. These issues are not only reflected in the fiction discussed above, but also appear in his non-fiction essays about SF. Xiao offers most of his theories and conjectures about SF in his lengthy "On the Development of Chinese Science Fiction," which includes topics such as Xiao's comparison of the history of SF in the West and in China, and the temporal distance between SF and the history of science. Xiao astutely recommended that PRC SF writers avoid the false dilemma of defining SF as either scientific or literary; he viewed SF as a blend of both. He also called for SF writers to avoid excessively utilitarian views of SF as merely a handmaiden for science popularization or merely a tool for exploring technical issues. He also argued that since science and technology are inseparable from modern life, SF should bring both natural science and social science within its orbit. While pondering future development in PRC SF, Xiao urged his peers to write more SF about science-related crises such as human-induced climate change and ecological destruction.[46] His concerns about environmental degradation and the impact of industrial development on nature and human society have indeed become major themes of Chinese SF in the new millennium. Some notable examples are Liu Cixin's *The Underground Fire* (*Di huo*, 2000), *Earth Canon* (*Diqiu dapao*, 2003), and *Round Soap Bubbles* (*Yuanyuan de feizao pao*, 2004); Xing He's *Mountains and Rivers* (*Shanshan shuishui*, 2002); and Tianyi Jushi's *The Sky Is Tilting to the Northwest* (*Tian qing xibei*, 2003).

6 Tech-SF and the Four Modernizations

This chapter focuses on long-neglected thaw-era SF narratives that helped lay the groundwork for an internationally renowned body of Chinese hard SF during the New Wave. This type of SF aimed to popularize scientific and technological knowledge among juvenile readers in order to spark their interest in science, technology, and other realms of knowledge underpinning the Four Modernizations. In addition, many of these PRC authors used fiction to illustrate their assumptions about science or about technological innovations. The globally renowned New Wave SF novelist Liu Cixin dubbed this sort of writing "tech-SF" (*jishu kehuan*) and "invention-SF" (*faming kehuan*), for this subgenre of SF focuses on technological innovations and inventions. Liu regards it as a type of "uniquely made-in-China SF."[1] He argues that these PRC writings share similarities with the works of Jules Verne and John Campbell (1910–71) in their focus on high-tech inventions and gadgetry. This chapter surveys the most prominent technological innovations highlighted by this corpus of SF and explores reasons for its emergence and subsequent decline.

Tech-SF provided a literary space to echo the party-state's reaffirmation of the important role of science and technology in achieving the country's Four Modernizations by the end of the twentieth century. The concept of the Four Modernizations was first formulated by Premier Zhou Enlai (1898–1976) at the Conference on Science and Technology Work in Shanghai on 29 January 1963. According to Zhou Enlai, "We will achieve the modernizations of industry, agriculture, national defence, and science and technology … and build our country into a powerful socialist nation."[2] Zhou's talk was published two days afterward in the state-run *People's Daily*. After the Cultural Revolution ended in 1976, paramount leaders of the party-state such as Hua Guofeng (1921–2008) and Deng Xiaoping revived the long-dormant policy of the Four Modernizations by advocating it on several occasions. Hua Guofeng, leader of the party-state from September 1976 until December 1978, proclaimed that the Four Modernizations would enable the PRC to become a powerful socialist country before the end of the twentieth century during his speech at the CCP's Fifth National Congress in the early spring of 1978. The State Council consequently held lengthy meetings about how to accelerate implementation of the Four Modernizations during July and September 1978. Deng Xiaoping announced his decision to shift the Communist Party's main focus from the Mao era's emphasis on class struggle to the reform-and-opening era's pursuit of modernization and economic prosperity at the Third Plenum of the Eleventh Central Committee in December 1978.[3]

Many SF writers enthusiastically responded to Dengist modernization and opening to the world. For example, Xiao Jianheng said to his peers on the literary scene, "Today at this new historical juncture when [the Party] announced its accelerated implementation of the Four Modernizations and renewed focus upon science, our primary task is to foster creative SF writing."[4] Similarly, in "The Four Questions about Science Fiction," Huang Yi claimed that PRC SF had shouldered its responsibility of contributing to the Four Modernizations. He suggested how imaginative PRC SF writers might do their part to promote their country's modernization: "Some might fly to Sagittarius and conjure a vision of the vast and mysterious universe; others might depict artificial intelligence and multifunctional robots; and some might combine laser technology with genetics and cryonics into their SF narratives."[5] He argued that even though most SF writers did not personally take part in scientific research or technological innovations, their mind-expanding SF writings could inspire young people to enter career paths in science and technology.[6]

Tech-SF thus became closely associated with advances in science and technology, including newfangled gadgetry. These tech-SF narratives not only celebrate scientific and technological progress, but also emphasize their function in the accelerated development of a modernized and powerful China. These stories frequently celebrate increasing productivity in agriculture, manufacturing, and military technology. The narratives about agricultural modernization range from marine aquaculture and high-tech pastures to plant and animal breeding. Tech-SF about manufacturing illustrates how computers and other high-tech equipment improve production and management while enhancing environmental protection. Tech-SF about the military covers topics such as high-tech counter-intelligence and border security.

Many works of tech-SF combine bionics with advanced electronics. For example, Wang Bao'an's "Pursuit in the Desert" ("Shamo zhuizong," 1979) describes kangaroos implanted with electronic devices that can detect the approach of incoming enemy aircraft. In Zheng Wenguang's "The Shark Scouts," scientists transplant an electronic monitor into the eyes of sharks, so that sharks can guard against foreign encroachments in territorial waters. In Ye Yonglie's "A Strange Bee" ("Yizhi qiguai de mifeng," 1978), beekeepers use robotic bees to guard their hives. Another story by Ye entitled "Sea Horse" ("Hai ma," 1978) portrays the implanting of electronic gills in horses, cows, and sheep so that they can graze on seaweed on the ocean floor. In Ye's "The Secret of Gecko Men" ("Feiyan zoubi de mimi," 1979), firefighters wear gecko-like bionic suits at work so that they can climb up the walls of tall buildings. In both Wang Yafa's "The Orange Helmet" ("Cheng huang se de toukui," 1978) and Xin Tianweng's "The Strange Bird" ("Guai niao," 1978), artificial gills facilitate underwater photography, while artificial wings enable humans to excel at aerial photography. In Chu Fengge's "The Magic Lamp" ("Shenqi de deng," 1979), a firefly's cold luminescence inspires a technician to design a lamp that also produces practically no heat. Lu Ke's "A Blind Man's Diary" ("Yige mangren de shouji," 1979) portrays a pair of special eyeglasses that use bat-like echo location sonar and enable a blind man to walk without the aid of a cane or a seeing-eye dog.

A number of tech-SF narratives portray sonar devices with applications in agriculture and aquaculture. Xiao Jianheng's "Secret in a Carrot Field" ("Huluobo di li de mimi," 1978) tells of a sonar device that broadcasts sound waves over a field of carrots, speeding their growth cycle. Zhao Yuqiu's "Fishery" ("Mu yu," 1980) describes the management of an ocean fishery with the aid of sonar technology. Other sonar devices help zoologists and mining engineers do their jobs more efficiently in several tech-SF works. Radio-tracking receivers enable biologists to follow radio-collared brown bears in Deng Gangzhou's "Strange Radio Wave" ("Qiguai de dianbo," 1978). Ji Hong and Miao Shi's "Remote Sensing at Crystal Mountain" ("Yuan tan shuijing shan," 1978) portrays the utilization of remote sensing technology to detect mineral deposits underground. In Wei Liao and Zhang Yiwu's "A Report on the Big Earthquake at Tangshan in 2001" ("Er ling ling yi nian Tangshan da dizhen baogao," 1978), scientists predict earthquakes by detecting variations in gravitational forces. They also sometimes prevent earthquakes by relieving pressure on seismic faults through underground detonations of small-scale nuclear bombs. Other tech-SF stories describe medical applications of sonic waves. Stories that relate the use of sonic instruments to monitor cardiovascular patients include Dai Shan and Wang Jinhai's "The Secret of the Eagle Brand Watch" ("Ying pai shoubiao de mimi," 1979), Chen Ripeng's "The Third Button" ("Di san ke niukou," 1978), Zheng Yuanjie's "Uncle's Watch" ("Jiujiu de shoubiao," 1978), and Liu Husheng's "The Mysterious Earrings" ("Shenmi de erhuan," 1979). Wang Yafa's "The Magic Pillow" ("Mo zhen," 1979) describes how a sonic device imbedded within a pillow helps alleviate insomnia.

Another popular subject in tech-SF is the invention of new high-tech materials. For example, Wei Yahua's "The Tumult of the Flying Blanket" ("Feitan de fengbo," 1979) features a superconductor with aerospace applications. In Xu Jie's "The Architects on a Coral Island" ("Shanhu dao shang de jianzhushi," 1978), architects transform coral into construction materials. Jia You's "Grow a House" ("Zhong fangzi," 1978) features a synthetic material that can generate construction materials through photosynthesis. Wang Yafa's "Tumult in a Small Town" ("Xiaocheng fengbo," 1979) portrays an exterior paint that helps protect buildings from earthquakes. Jiang Lai's "A Sky Full of Wind-blown Red Leaves" ("Hongye mantian fei," 1979) features synthetic fabrics that take the place of traditional fabrics containing natural fibres. In both Shi Lin's "An Animated Comic Book" ("Yiben donghua xiaorenshu," 1978) and Miao Shi's "The Magic Picture Book" ("Tuhua shang de qiji," 1978), scientists paint 3D comic books with special high-tech chemicals.

Induced precipitation is another topic that often appears in tech-SF. In these narratives, the demand for rainfall comes mainly from agriculture. For example, Xie Shijun's "Aerospace Precipitation" ("Hangtian boyu," 1979) portrays the inducement of rainfall to reduce droughts in northern China. Xie's scientists manufacture bombs out of a type of soil-based nitrogen. They next trigger the launch of rockets that deliver these bombs for explosion in drought-stricken regions. Nitrogen released from these explosions mixes with moist air to produce rainfall. The extra nitrogen in the induced rainfall also acts like a fertilizer to stimulate plant growth. In Wang Yafa's "An Interesting Incident outside the Sports Field" ("Qiuchang wai de quwen," 1979), scientists seed clouds with dry ice and silver iodide in order to induce precipitation. They also generate ultrasound waves in order to catalyze rainfall.

Tech-SF and Life Sciences

The 1970s witnessed breakthroughs in genetic engineering worldwide. As early as 1953, American and British scientists announced their discovery of the double-helix structure and information-coding function of the DNA molecule. The 1970s were especially notable for breakthroughs in genetic engineering. For example, the first recombinant DNA molecules were created by Paul Berg in 1972; the first transgenic organism was created by Herbert Boyer and Stanley Cohen in 1973; and the first transgenic animal was created by Rudolf Jaenisch in 1974.[7] PRC scientists began to participate in worldwide research on genetic engineering during the late 1970s. In February 1977, the Chinese Academy of Sciences convened its preliminary working meeting on genetic engineering, and drew up research plans for the next three years up through 1980. At the end of the same year, the academy held a forum on genetic engineering research and drew up five- and ten-year research plans. Two more genetic engineering conferences were convened in Beijing by the end of 1980.[8] Meanwhile, many Western research monographs and articles on genetic engineering, molecular science, and biology were translated into Chinese. For example, between 1977 and 1980 the Chinese Science Press translated and published R.H. Burdon's *RNA Biosynthesis*, Alan E. Smith's *Protein Biosynthesis*, C. Sybesma's *An Introduction to Biophysics*, and C.A. Knight's *Molecular Virology*.[9] PRC authors in the life sciences also published compilations of Western research on genetic engineering. Chinese translations of these Western academic books and articles not only provided valuable research materials for academic researchers and textbooks for college students, they also popularized biological knowledge and genetic technologies among lay readers, including SF writers.

Worldwide advances in molecular science and genetic engineering provided PRC writers with a hard science frontier of anticipated advances. The scientific possibilities for genetic engineering made their way into Chinese SF in the late 1970s. These narratives presented some of the most detailed and compelling thought experiments in genetic engineering, cryonics, organ reconstruction, brainwaves, and memory. In many narratives, the quest to ferret out class enemies or foreign spies gave way to scientific exploration of the genome in the life sciences. The main adversary changed from foreign geopolitical foes to the enemy within – cancer, bio-weaponry, and genetic manipulation.

Genetically engineering animals in SF can involve the creation of new species, the extension of the human lifespan, raising human IQs, and gaining more control over the mechanisms of human memory. Several PRC SF stories portray the creation of new animal species through genetic engineering or interbreeding, such as Yang Nan's "The Rare Animal Veterinary Hospital" ("Zhengui dongwu baojian yiyuan," 1978), Yuan Li and Lü Zhenhua's "Eggs" ("Dan," 1978), Ji Hong and Miao Shi's "The Fabricator of Rare Animals" ("Zhenqi dongwu de chuangzao zhe," 1978), Xin Bao's "Cats That Grow Wings" ("Zhang chibang de mao," 1979), and He Bin's "Sheep Coloured by DNA" ("DNA caise yang," 1979). Ji Hong highlights the technology of animal cloning in "The Missing Snow Leopard" ("Shizong de xuebao," 1979).

Medical applications of genetic engineering and the manipulation of DNA also appeared in many tech-SF narratives. Zhou Yongnian, Zhang Fengjiang, and Jia Wanchao co-authored "The Last Cancer Patient" ("Zuihou yige aizheng huanzhe," 1980). The medical researchers in this story discover a chemical in shark cells called TATA, which can repair the damaged human DNA and even cure some cancers. After analysing the molecular structure of TATA, these scientists discover how to synthesize it and thus facilitate its use in treating cancer in humans. Similarly, scientists in Lu Zhaowen's "The Sweet Lily" ("Tiantian de shuilian," 1981) discover how to improve the results of cosmetic surgery by harnessing leprosy bacteria and cancerous cells. In Huang Tiange's "A Dumb Girl Becomes Smart" ("Dai guniang bian congming le," 1978), scientists are able to raise a person's IQ by editing genes in some of her brain cells. Three of He Bin's stories published in 1979 portray extrasensory communication through high-tech manipulation of brainwaves, along with the extension of the human lifespan through newly created genes: "The Tragedy of the T Factor" ("T yinzi de beiju"), "The Mental Computer SJ-1" ("SJ-1"), and "The Dolphin Brainwave Longevity Machine" ("H-N-Y"). Ma Guangfu's "The Fifth Corpse" ("Di wu hao sishi," 1979) depicts the transplantation of brain cells from a mathematician into the brain of his granddaughter so that she will be able to retrieve many of her grandfather's memories. In Leng Zhaohe's "Before Leaving for Abroad" ("Chuguo zhiqian," 1979), scientists synthesize a gene that helps patients with a memory deficit form more lasting memories in their brains.

High-tech suspended animation or cryonics also emerged as an important variety of post-Mao tech-SF narratives about the life sciences. At least six PRC stories featuring cryonics came out in 1979 alone. These narratives turn to the use of cryonics or suspended animation mostly as a solution to the problem of the vast distance and time periods involved in interplanetary space travel; astronauts must undergo a sort of hibernation aboard the spaceship in order to conserve oxygen, water, and fuel during most of the long journey. In Deng Xiaoqiu's "News from Halley's Comet" ("Halei huixing dailai de xinwen"), scientists formulate a cryonic agent for inducing suspended animation with the aid of an anticoagulant they extracted from an insect that lives in Antarctica. Scientists also place a Pluto-bound astronaut into suspended animation through cryonics in Ye Yonglie and Wen Pianjing's "An Astronaut

Flying to Pluto" ("Fei xiang mingwangxing de ren," 1979). Three stories portray the use of cryonics to place cancer patients in suspended animation until a future cure for their types of cancer eventually emerges: Ye Yonglie's "A Series of Strange Incidents" ("Guaishi lianpian," 1979), Zhang Xiaotian's "Coming Back, Luolan" ("Huilai ba, Luolan," 1979), and Zhou Baoqing's "Zhao Lan and Her Parents" ("Zhao Lan he ta de shuangqin," 1979).

Many Chinese writers who were thinking about forthcoming breakthroughs in plant biology created visions of an agricultural utopia. As a high-tech outgrowth of traditional plant breeding, genetic engineering has greatly increased the yield and productivity of grain, vegetables, and fruit crops. In PRC tech-SF, apples, lychees, pears, and grapes often grow on the same fruit tree; genetically engineered hyacinths are planted in lakes to purify the polluted water; rice paddies spread out in all directions as though they were golden carpets extending to the horizon. In 1979, Guangdong Science and Technology Press published a collection of SF short stories entitled *Songs about Life: A Collection of Science Fiction Stories*, co-authored by Zhang Yiwu and Wei Liao. This volume includes eight stories about genetic engineering technologies used in animal breeding, horticulture, and other agricultural disciplines. In the preface to the collection, the two authors indicate that these stories were written to echo the coming of the "springtime of science" in China, a metaphor for the PRC central government's affirmation in late 1978 that science and technology amount to advanced productive forces.[10]

In this collection, "The Magic Orchard" ("Mo yuan"), "The Blue Encirclement" ("Lanse de baowei quan"), and "A Golden Carpet Extending to the Horizon" ("Jin ditan pu shang le tian") are about genetically engineered plants. In addition to the stories in this collection, many similar tales were published in popular science magazines and SF journals, such as Wang Jinhai's "The Jade Island" ("Feicui dao," 1978), Hu Yonghuai's "The Sweet Season" ("Tianmi de jijie," 1979), Lu Zhaowen's "The Sweet Lily," and Jin Tao's "The King Lichen" ("Diyi zhi wang," 1981).

Both "A Golden Carpet Extending to the Horizon" and "The Magic Orchard" reveal how increased productivity in the growing of grains, fruit, and vegetables results from advances in plant breeding and genetic engineering. In 1978, the PRC government began to implement nationwide reforms to improve efficiency in agricultural production. As the government began to establish and develop an increasingly market-based economy in rural areas, farmers diversified into livestock, aquaculture, and fruit and vegetable production while simultaneously increasing the tonnage of grain harvests. Studies show that post-Mao China's growth in agricultural productivity has had a lot to do with new varieties of technology and niche specialization that utilize resources more efficiently.[11]

"A Golden Carpet Extending to the Horizon" is narrated by a young girl named Little Ling who goes to a gallery with her grandfather, a plant biologist. The first painting they see is a portrait of former Premier Zhou Enlai standing in a paddy while brandishing a sheaf of golden rice. Her grandfather then recalls that Premier Zhou advocated the policy of the Four Modernizations twenty years previously. When looking at a painting of an orchard, Little Ling's grandfather envisions that he and his colleagues will plant hybrid trees that produce watermelons, beans, and various types of fruit. Returning from the gallery, Little Ling learns that her grandfather and other scientists have been experimenting with genetically engineering rice in order to generate a larger yield. The scientists use gene splicing to extract genetic nitrogen-fixing functionality from legumes such as beans and peas and transmit this functionality to rice at the microscopic level. In this way, the roots of the genetically engineered rice gain the ability to fix nitrogen from the air, and thus can fertilize themselves with nitrogen in the manner of nitrogen-fixing legumes. Upon the success of their experiment, the scientists envision that this technology could be broadly utilized throughout China. Genetically engineered rice paddies would thus spread all the way from the country's frigid northeastern border provinces to the humid climes of southern China.[12]

The major source of inspiration for the fictional experiment of nitrogen-fixing rice consists of research on the nitrogen-fixing corn and hybrid rice that had been pursued by British and Chinese agricultural scientists during the 1970s. Ever since 1974, English scientists had been using innovative techniques to penetrate the cell walls in plants and combine the cells of different species. For example, their experiments included fusing soybeans with corn to produce a nitrogen-fixing variety of corn. The soybean's nitrogen-fixing abilities would enable the corn to grow rapidly without need for artificial fertilizer.[13] The Chinese agronomist Yuan Longping (b. 1930) and his colleagues developed the PRC's first genetically engineered varieties of hybrid rice in the 1970s. This strain of rice, already growing in popularity among PRC farmers by 1976, was perhaps the most important breakthrough in PRC agricultural technology of the mid- to late 1970s. Memories of the Great Famine in rural areas of the PRC from 1959 to 1962 still haunted the PRC villagers who had survived it, for over thirty million rural Chinese had died of starvation or malnutrition-related illnesses during that period.[14] Yuan's successful experiment thus affected the lives of ordinary rural Chinese people. Therefore, alleviating food shortages through genetic engineering became a timely and popular theme in Chinese SF. In "Golden Carpet," the scientists view their botanical experiments as having successfully completed the mission that the party-state assigned them. They associate their engineered increases in rice yields with laying down a solid material foundation for their country's socialist construction.

"The Magic Orchard" explores how scientists use recombinant DNA technology to create new species. Employing this new technique that was developed in the early 1970s,[15] scientists cut out portions of DNA from two different species and inserted them into a host organism in order to produce new genetic combinations. For the first time, in 1975 scientists assembled a complex strand of DNA using about 600 units of nucleic acid.[16] In "The Magic Orchard," the author makes a much bolder extrapolation about how Chinese scientists would eventually use these technologies to create new plant species or animal-plant hybrids. The story starts with young Lulu's dream of wandering in an orchard in which a single tree bears several types of fruit such as lychees, apples, pears, and grapes (see figure 6.1). In reality, Lulu and his good friend Kunkun engage in plant-breeding experiments in their school's botanical garden. One day they find their plants have been smashed by a green-haired monster. They follow the monster to the genetic engineering centre, where they see peanuts and beef growing on the same tree. They also find more green-haired monsters in the genetic engineering centre. They are so frightened by what they have seen that they check themselves into a local hospital and take to sickbeds. The genetic scientist Professor Zhao comes to the hospital and explains to them that these hybrid vegetable and animal species are all products of genetic engineering. For example, local scientists transfer the desired portions of DNA from a cow into a pig so that the genetically engineered pig can grow as big as a cow. Similarly, local scientists transfer the plant chlorophyll DNA into a chicken in order to create a new species of chicken that can manufacture its own nutrients from sunshine through photosynthesis; they also recombine DNA strands from a cow and an apple in order to create a new hybrid species of beef-tree.

Though the two young boys call the hybrid green-haired creature a "monster" and express their fear of this new species, Professor Zhao justifies the validity of his scientific experimentation by linking it to a larger yield of agricultural products. He claims that the technology of genetic engineering will provide a sufficient supply of material resources for the world's expanding human population. He says, "Genetic engineering is a new tool that enables human intervention in the genetic information of microbes, plants, and animals, thereby benefitting

Figure 6.1. A fruit tree with a wide variety of fruit growing on it became a popular motif in PRC SF narratives and animated films during the post-Mao thaw. This is an image from the film *Dingding Fights the Monkey King* (1980).

research on plant and animal breeding."[17] He also propagates his evidence-based prediction that genetically engineered food would prove to be safe and healthy for human consumption. Professor Zhao goes so far as to say, "Our great socialist China is creating the newest and most beautiful scientific fantasies."[18]

The obliviousness to ethical concerns and seemingly indiscriminate approach to genetic engineering appeared in many other SF narratives during this period. Liu Cixin has noted that this general outlook has been common in PRC tech-SF: many narratives throw caution to the winds in their preoccupation with twisting nature aggressively to suit human ends, focusing entirely on the wonders of future technological wizardry.[19] Because of this lack of ethical concern for non-human animals and nature in general, many stories depict scientists' creation of outlandish new hybrid monstrosities, as in "The Magic Orchard." A few relatively sober-minded authors and critics were well aware of this issue, however. For example, in "Ducks Growing on the Tree: Why We

Imagine," Xiao Jianheng confirmed that genetic engineering technology had expanded the subject matter of SF, but some writers had made illogical or unscientific assumptions about genetic engineering in their works. In one story, scientists grow ducks on a tree through a futuristic technology of animal-plant interbreeding. Scientists undergo all sorts of hardships in order to create a new tree species on which ducks can grow – only to discover that it is too difficult to collect duck eggs from the high branches. Xiao asked, Does SF function to popularize scientific viewpoints and knowledge, or merely to allure readers with the notion that science is merely a set of magic tricks, through which scientists can present us with anything we would like to see? He argued that if SF writers wanted to create something new in their fiction, they should tell their readers what purpose it served. He emphasized that scientific and technical innovations should aim to solve practical problems, and that scientific and technical fantasies should be cognitively grounded instead of merely fanciful.[20] Xiao's caution did not, however, prevent SF writers from spinning yarns about outlandish hybrids of plant and animal species in their works.

While these two stories focus on using genetic technology to improve agricultural productivity, two other narratives, "The Blue Encirclement" and "The King Lichen," touch upon ecology – the interconnectedness of organisms and their natural environment.[21] They portray how genetic engineering has reduced industrial pollution and waste. Though the technology of genetic engineering in the two narratives soon spins out of control and results in unexpected and often unwelcome consequences, they end with the scientists finding solutions that limit the damage from unintended consequences of genetic engineering. Hence, the narratives echo overly optimistic views about scientific and technological progress that were prevalent in PRC SF at that time. The two stories focus on problem solving and follow the pattern of presenting a problem, experimenting with a possible solution, encountering unwelcome consequences, and final resolution.

"The Blue Encirclement" opens with the description of water pollution caused by a food processing factory. The local municipal government shuts down the factory and urges the factory leader, Wang, to solve the problem. Wang's daughter is a graduate student in plant biology. She presents her father with genetically engineered hyacinth seeds, and suggests planting them in the polluted lake to purify the water. The seeds turn out to have originated from Mars. Scientists had taken the seeds to Mars in order to engineer the genes of hyacinth chloroplasts in order to improve the hyacinth's efficiency in photosynthesis. The genetically engineered hyacinth can absorb not only the red portion of the spectrum of sunlight, but also ultraviolet and infrared light. Unlike ordinary plant leaves, their leaves can thus undergo photosynthesis day and night. The scientists further engineer the hyacinths so that they can thrive even in polluted water and safely assimilate heavy metals, such as mercury, lead, and silver. The scientists thereupon ship the genetically engineered hyacinth seeds back to Earth, and ask Wang's daughter to experiment with them. But, the growth of these new hyacinths soon gets out of hand. They not only become an invasive and over-expansive species in the lake, but also block the city's sewer system after Wang's wife spills new seeds down her kitchen drain. In order to halt the invasive spread of the hyacinths, the scientists are able to stunt their growth and kill them by employing an A001 microwave device. One group of scientists can then dry the dead hyacinths and process them into a biofuel, while other scientists extract heavy metals from the dehydrated hyacinth plants and dispose of them safely. In this way, scientists solve the problem of water pollution in the lake.

"The King Lichen" explores how the genetic trait of symbiotic mutualism is used to break down construction waste into a safer end product. In the narrative, the young Ma Xiaoha is kicking a soccer ball in a narrow lane on his way home from school. The ball hits a passing scientist and breaks the bottle that the scientist has been carrying. The liquid inside the bottle then spills onto the soccer ball. Xiaoha becomes frightened and runs away with the contaminated ball. The next morning, cracks appear in the floor and ceiling of Xiaoha's apartment. Soon they spread throughout the entire building. At this crucial juncture, Professor Liu, whom Xiaoha encountered the previous day, comes to Xiaoha's apartment and finds the ball. He explains that the liquid that spilled onto the football contains lichen spores. Professor Liu has been experimenting with genetically engineering some lichen. Lichen is a photosynthetic algae living inside a durable fungus and supplying food for both while under the physical protection of the fungus. In addition, lichen can produce a special acid to decompose rock. Scientists have genetically engineered the lichen to produce more corrosive acid. The genetically engineered lichen acid can rapidly corrode and break down rocks, bricks, and concrete. Since lichen acid cannot corrode plastic or rubber, scientists can use them as corrosion inhibitors. Using this method, Professor Liu and his colleagues take measures to prevent the apartment building from suffering further corrosion. Professor Liu also associates his experiments with the huge and deadly Tangshan earthquake of 1976. He says his recollection of tons of debris in Tangshan following that earthquake motivated him to find an effective solution to the problem. At the end of the narrative, he envisions that genetically engineered lichen acid will soon be used in the construction industry to aid in the demolition of old buildings and clean up industrial waste.

Near-Future and Mid-Future Temporal Settings

The temporal settings of these four botanical genetic engineering narratives are all in contemporary China. Each illustrates the practical function of technical innovation in the further development of China's modernization. A near-future or mid-future setting is a major characteristic of tech-SF. During the 1980s, PRC SF writers and critics often discussed the gap between SF's exciting vision of future advances in science and technology and the present-day mundane realities of science and technology. For example, Ye Yonglie tried to distinguish amongst SF set in the near-future, the mid-future, and the distant future. Near-future SF refers to narratives in which the scientific and technological advances portrayed in fiction could actually be achieved in real life within the next ten years. In mid-future SF, the scientific and technological advances could be achieved by the end of the twenty-first century. Finally, distant-future SF portrays truly amazing scientific and technological advances that would require hundreds or even thousands of years to accomplish. He further argued that most thaw-era PRC SF was conjured in a near-future setting.[22] Ye's argument corresponds with thaw-era tech-SF. The technological advances that most tech-SF narratives portray are based on present-day technology; the narrator usually suggests that the technological advances portrayed in the work would actually be achieved within the reader's lifetime. The critic Yan Hui claims that near-future SF has the advantage of stimulating youthful readers' curiosity and kindling their imagination.[23]

Xiao Jianheng provided another reason that near-future SF prevailed in the 1980s, tracing the tradition back to the 1950s and 1960s. From the late 1950s to the early 1960s, one major function of SF was to reveal how science and technology would help increase agricultural productivity. Consequently, SF authors in the 1960s usually set their narratives in the near future in order to link future advances in technology more closely with present-day realities and thus make them appear to be more achievable. In the late 1970s, the PRC government's advocacy of accelerating the Four Modernizations similarly favoured the near-future for the setting of tech-SF.[24]

Corresponding to the settings of near future, mid-future, and distant future, the technological ideas in tech-SF are extension, breakthrough, and visionary when contrasting with technology that exists at the time of writing. In the first category of near-future extension, the technological innovations depicted in the narratives are merely an extension of existing technology, so the innovations are relatively plausible and achievable in the near future.[25] Some examples are the types of genetic engineering portrayed in "The Jade Island" and "A Golden Carpet Extending to the Horizon." Another example of near-future extension is Wan Huankui's short-short story (*weixing xiaoshuo*) "The Girlfriend Who Blows Smoke Rings" ("Tu yanquan de nüyou," 1982),[26] which depicts a new type of chimney that blows smoke rings into the upper atmosphere and reduces air pollution near ground level. Almost three decades later, when Liu Cixin commented on this story, he claimed that he actually observed this technology in action at a geothermal power plant in Japan during the 1990s. Liu further argued that many varieties of futuristic technology depicted in tech-SF could be achieved in reality if scientists and engineers had larger budgets to work with.[27]

Some tech-SF writers who focus on mid-future developments write about bold breakthroughs in technology that exists at the time of writing. These futuristic breakthroughs may not be readily achievable with current technology, but writers' visions might inspire one or two scientists to achieve breakthroughs of the sort portrayed in "The Blue Encirclement" and "The King Lichen." Another example is "The Sweet Lily," in which there is novel application of genetic engineering to cosmetic surgery.[28] In this narrative, a stage-performer suffers from facial disfiguration at birth. Her cosmetic surgeon injects her face with an experimental solution of leprous bacteria and cancer cells. After an initial failure, the injections change the contours of her face to a more normal and attractive appearance, and she becomes more sought after for performances on stage. This approach to mid-future breakthrough of technological advances might eventually inspire cosmetic surgeons to apply genetic engineering to their medical practice.

The third tech-SF category of technological advances in the distant future is visionary and will not likely be realized in the foreseeable future. One example is Wang Qi's short story "Rose and Sword" ("Meigui yu baojian," 1978), in which astronauts are collecting mineral specimens and conducting a geographical survey on an alien planet named "N." The idea of mining minerals on an alien planet is visionary, and not likely to occur in even a mid-future. There are far fewer tech-SF narratives set in the distant future than in the near future or a mid-future.

Simple Narrative Frameworks and Complicated Technical Descriptions

Many of the tech-SF narratives about genetic engineering discussed above display another important characteristic of tech-SF: they contain the sort of simple narrative framework frequently found in juvenile literature, but the technical descriptions therein are complex enough to interest adult readers as well. PRC tech-SF narratives are normally short stories of three to five thousand words. Some of them are even shorter. Plot development in the four botanical genetic engineering narratives typically follows a general formula that the Chinese SF literary critic Dingbo Wu has aptly summarized. The storyline typically features one or more non-scientists, most commonly children, who encounter a mystery or witness some phenomena in a workplace such as a research institute, factory, hospital, or farm. Scientists then clear up the mystery for the non-scientists with a rational explanation. The two-dimensional scientists typically brim with patriotism, self-sacrifice, and optimism, and the technical innovations in the story are the well-deserved results of the scientists' aspirations and wisdom.[29]

The simple narrative framework and straightforward approach to characterization have much to do with the utilitarian goal of PRC SF to popularize science and technology, as well as its common categorization as juvenile literature, especially during the Mao era. As Dingbo Wu has pointed out, "In China, science fiction's main function has been utilitarian rather than aesthetic."[30] Most PRC SF writers had avoided any topic or plot they thought unsuitable for juvenile readers, such as those found in romances, whodunnits, and crime novels. Some critics argued that juvenile readers were not looking for sensational yarns, themes of violence or sex, or other types of stimulation in SF. Instead, they were searching for scientific knowledge and vision in SF to find how they might better understand how to contribute to advancing the Four Modernizations.[31] The critic Zhou Jun criticized some SF works written for juvenile readers as having "dramatized such unseemly incidents as robbery and murder" instead of properly focusing on science and technology.[32] In light of these typical attitudes, it is not surprising that most PRC tech-SF displays a simple narrative framework and stereotypical characterization. However, the situation started to change during the late 1970s. Some SF writers, such as Zheng Wenguang, Ye Yonglie, and Tong Enzheng, started to improve the literary quality of their works and make the plot more interesting by borrowing narrative devices from detective fiction, tales of romantic love, and crime novels. They wrote not only for juvenile readers, but also for adults, though PRC SF usually has remained anachronistically categorized as juvenile literature. This change was a natural result of the growth of the genre.

The narratives about genetic engineering and other tech-SF stories discussed in this chapter were written during this transitional period. Though they still feature simple narrative frameworks and two-dimensional characterization, the scientific and political messages embodied in them are not merely for younger readers, but also for adult consumption. Here simple narrative frameworks and underdeveloped characterization are offset by complicated technical descriptions. They read rather like a detailed technical project proposal that has been framed within a simplistic narrative plot. Many tech-SF writers had an educational background in science and engineering and worked in one or more science popularization associations, universities, or research institutes. These writers typically were experienced in writing popular science essays, but many were novices in creative writing. They offered detailed descriptions of scientific and technical innovations not only to popularize this knowledge among lay readers, but also to explore their own innovative technological ideas. In reality, they might not have been able to find a way to put some of their ideas into practice; SF was thus an effective venue for illustrating their more futuristic scientific explorations and technical innovations. Liu Cixin admiringly argues that the technological expertise of this old generation of tech-SF writers was far beyond that of the younger New Wave PRC SF writers.[33]

Tech-SF's detailed descriptions of technological innovations resonated with the "vividness" that prominent novelists advocated at the time. In "My Experience of Writing Science Fiction" ("Chuangzuo kexue huanxiang xiaoshuode tihui," 1979), Tong Enzheng emphasized the importance of vivid description of technical details in SF. In order to attract a vibrant readership, PRC SF must achieve a high level of verisimilitude, not mere realism. The technical ideas embodied in SF must also contain visionary features that defy readers' expectations. Encounters with unfamiliar phenomena can give the impression that the story is pure fantasy, so to convince readers that the technical ideas in the stories are not merely dazzling fantasies about a high-tech utopia, the author needs to pay close attention to technical details. For example, in order to help readers sense the verisimilitude of the a portrayal of space travel, the author must describe such details as the interior and exterior of the spaceship and what it feels like for the astronauts to move about in zero gravity. These elements add to the plausibility of the story and make the technical ideas and the depictions of advanced technology seem logical and feasible.[34]

Technological Supremacy and Faustian Optimism

The evolution of science and technology means the continued development of new tools for solving problems. All the stories discussed in this chapter extol new technology without really addressing the possible negative consequences of it; nor do the authors express ethical concerns about the creation of new hybrid species. The scientists in the narratives typically draw upon the Party's ideological rhetoric to justify their adventurous scientific experiments. Moreover, this one-sidedly optimistic approach to genetic engineering and the lack of moral concern about pitfalls are part of the revolutionary legacy from the Mao era. Though some PRC intellectuals and writers started to reflect on the downsides of Mao Zedong's radical policies during the three decades after his death in 1976, revolutionary fervour remained and was fuelled by widespread anxiety to catch up with more advanced neighbours after a decade of stagnation in scientific research and industrial and agricultural production. In this new socio-political atmosphere, Mao's rhetoric about the conquest of nature found expression in biology: humans could manipulate mutation and evolution through selective breeding, cloning, and genetic engineering. Chinese intellectuals had long been obsessed with industrialization and technological progress ever since Darwinian evolution and Spencer's notion of "the survival of the fittest" were introduced to China in the latter decades of the nineteenth century. When genetic engineering became prominent, the wonders of increasingly "fit" organisms became powerful motivators for PRC SF. Research in the life sciences soon became a new battlefield. A revolution-inspired belief that humanity must conquer nature encouraged literary and biological exploration of plant hybridity and the laboratory-based creation of entirely new species. Many other tech-SF narratives present a similarly optimistic view, suggesting that new advances in technology could solve our major problems once and for all.

Conclusion

The analysis in the sections above demonstrates that tech-SF prioritizes scientific and technological innovation while popularizing science and technology and allowing the author's vision of future technological innovations to unfold. Most tech-SF narratives are set in the near future or mid-future, and combine a simple narrative framework with complicated technical description. The science and technology depicted in the narratives involve an extension, breakthrough, or visionary exploration of technology at the time of writing. These works convey a strong belief in the supremacy of technology – an optimistic view that ecologically astute design and efficient use of technology can solve our major problems. At the same time, some more cautious tech-SF writers express serious misgivings about excessive emphasis on reshaping nature to suit unlimited growth in agricultural and industrial production.

The literary critic Mingwei Song identifies three utopian motifs in the development of Chinese SF: the rise of China, the country's development, and scientific and technological advances.[35] In the stories discussed in this chapter, these motifs are manifested through the success of PRC scientists in genetic engineering, their creation of hybrid plant and animal species, and technological innovation. The post-Mao preoccupation with advanced technology has been deeply entangled with the PRC agenda of achieving the Four Modernizations and intellectuals' aspiration to quickly catch up with neighbouring nations' technological advances. PRC scientists' advances in science and technology have also strengthened the utopian vision of a modernized China since the dawn of Deng Xiaoping's reform era. These tech-SF narratives also reveal the transition of PRC SF from a minor branch of juvenile literature to a major literary genre designed primarily for adult readers.

These characteristics made Chinese tech-SF a promising subgenre around 1980. However, tech-SF did not develop into a full-fledged subgenre. Liu Cixin regretfully compares the decline of tech-SF in 1983 to a "vanished creek," because most of these works have been consigned to oblivion.[36] He points out that his novella *The Underground Fire* (2000) amounts to his tribute to this type of SF.[37] In addition to political repression of Chinese SF in the wake of the "Campaign to Eliminate Spiritual Pollution" in 1983, several other factors contributed to the decline of the tech-SF.

As mentioned earlier in this chapter, most tech-SF writers were novice writers of fiction. Few of them even began to write fiction until the late 1970s. Some worked for local science popularization organizations, where writing fiction to popularize scientific and technological knowledge was but one of their job duties. Other authors were SF fans and wrote stories for sheer enjoyment in their spare time. Both types of tech-SF writers had considerably less experience in imaginative writing than the veteran writers who had begun to write SF during 1950s or the 1960s. The subgenre's imbalance between its modest literary quality and its strong focus on technological innovation reduces the readability of these works. This type of SF was soon eclipsed by works written by such veteran writers as Zheng Wenguang, Tong Enzheng, Xiao Jianheng, and Ye Yonglie, who typically embody their vision of technological advances through clear-cut characterization and an intriguing plot. In addition, these novice tech-SF writers exerted very little influence on the literary scene and lacked the networks of support that benefited veteran SF writers. During the heyday of thaw-era SF, the status of a tech-SF practitioner was that of a fledgling writer – in contrast to the lofty position of celebrated literatus occupied by such veteran novelists as Zheng Wenguang and Tong Enzheng. They had already accumulated cultural and political capital over decades at the same time that the amateur tech-SF writers were launching their short-lived careers in imaginative writing. The veterans also enjoyed prominent venues for their fiction, such as mainstream literary magazines with a highbrow readership. In contrast, tech-SF stories tended to get published only in local newspapers or middlebrow magazines that focused on juvenile literature or science popularization. Therefore, their works had much less influence on the literary scene than those of the prominent veteran writers, and appealed to few readers except for "tech-heads" and hard SF fans.

However, tech-SF has not vanished entirely from the PRC literary scene. Though it did not flourish in the PRC after the 1980s, the supremacy of technology and focus on technological advances in these narratives have continued to be prominent features of the hard SF written by a new and more famous generation of Chinese writers in the twenty-first century. Many of the technological themes in tech-SF have reappeared in contemporary PRC SF, such as genetic engineering, colonization of outer space, regeneration of defunct brains and other organs, and environmental protection. For example, in You Yi's short story "The Mysterious Signal" ("Shenmi de xinhao," 1979), scientists regenerate the basic function of a 2,000-year-old human brain with high-tech gadgetry resembling an oscilloscope. They also extract some of the information by using laser holographic technology. Liu Cixin revisited these themes in his novel *China 2185*.[38] It appears that Chinese SF has been an unbroken chain. Tech-SF has metamorphosed into an undercurrent within the larger tide of contemporary Chinese hard SF.

7 Fledgling Media Convergence: PRC SF from Print to Electronic Media

PRC SF has prominently engaged in transmedia (*kua meiti*) storytelling since the late 1970s when SF expanded its media venues from the print forms of journals and magazines, comics, and illustrated books to the electronic forms of radio and TV dramas, animation, and feature films. As the SF critic Zheng Jun has summed up the evolution of 1980s PRC SF, "At that time, the emergence of SF feature films, TV dramas, and radio dramas heralded the incipient transmedia characteristics of Chinese SF."[1] In 1980, the popular science writer Li Yuan pointed out the important role of audiovisual technology in education: "We are living in a world full of radio, television, movies, audio recordings, video, and various visual images.... Our educational experience has expanded from reading literary texts to viewing pictures and listening to audio recordings.... Modern visual and audio education will help people learn more about the world and faster than ever."[2] These statements by thaw era PRC cultural critics accentuate the importance of a multimedia or transmedia strategy in science popularization and SF.

In his seminal *Understanding Media: The Extensions of Man*, Marshall McLuhan points out that in the electronic age "we have already extended our senses and our nerves by the various media."[3] He further distinguishes a "hot medium" from a "cool medium,"[4] defining a hot medium as one that extends one single sense in "high definition" – "the state of being well filled with data."[5] Photography, radio programming, and movies belong to hot media. "Hot media do not leave so much to be filled in or completed by the audience," so they are low in audience or reader participation. In contrast, a cool medium is "one of low definition," such as telephone conversations, cartoons, and TV programming, because it gives "a meager amount of information," and "so much has to be filled in by the listeners" or audience.[6] Therefore, "cool media are high in participation or completion by the audience."[7] By adopting

McLuhan's metaphor of hot and cool media, we can view Chinese SF's transmedia practice as a fusion of hot and cool media. This combination promoted the SF genre nationwide by helping PRC SF reach a much broader audience, especially by including illiterates and rural residents without access to TV broadcasts or movie theatres. However, PRC SF's transmedia practice did not achieve the full-fledged "media convergence" that Henry Jenkins describes in *Convergence Culture: Where Old and New Media Collide*; nor did it reach the impressive level of media mix that the Japanese anime and book industry achieved from the 1960s to the 1980s, as presented in Marc Steinberg's *Anime's Media Mix*. Each type of PRC media focused more on its own internal consistency and specificity than on forming a transversal connectivity with other media. Nevertheless, Chinese SF during the post-Mao era still developped a kind of "continuous, serial consumption across media texts that characterizes the Japanese anime media mix" and Kadokawa business strategy in the 1980s.[8]

PRC SF during the post-Mao era engaged in a small-scale, fledgling, and yet significant media convergence that increased the visibility of the genre, promoted the consumption of SF artefacts, and extended the genre to a much broader audience than it had ever previously enjoyed in China. The following sections will first examine forms of media that PRC SF adapted to its own uses. Next, the characteristics of Chinese SF's transmedia practice will be analysed in light of Jenkins's and Steinberg's theories of media convergence and media mix.

Chinese SF in Print: Cartoons, Comics, and Illustrated Books

The New Shorter Oxford English Dictionary defines the cartoon as "an illustrative drawing in a newspaper or magazine, especially as a vehicle for political satire or humour; an amusing drawing with or without a caption."[9] It goes on to characterize the comic book as a book of cartoon strips.[10] Finally, it defines the graphic novel as "a full-length story in the form of a comic strip, published as a book."[11] In his seminal *Understanding Comics: The Invisible Art*, Scott McCloud provides a more detailed definition of the comic book, or "comics" for short: "Juxtaposed pictorial and other images in deliberate sequence, intended to convey information and/or to produce an aesthetic response in the viewer."[12]

Such definitions help us make distinctions between these forms of cultural expression. The cartoon is an image with a single panel, while comics or comic books consist of panels of images in a sequential storytelling format. In contrast with a comic book, a graphic novel is much longer and has a more complex plot. While comics can be serialized in installments within periodicals such as magazines or newspapers, a graphic novel is already complete as a book. The Chinese term *manhua* literarily means "impromptu brush strokes" and refers to either a single-panel or multi-panel cartoon. *Manhua shu* (*manhua* book) specifically denotes a comic book. The Chinese term *lianhuanhua* (literarily, "linked-picture book") often denotes a graphic novel of varying length, though it can also refer to a non-fictional illustrated book. In this discussion, *manhua* will be used to refer to either a single-panel or multi-panel cartoon on a single page, *manhua shu* for sequential-panel and multi-page comics, and *lianhuanhua* for either a graphic novel or an illustrated non-fiction book. In addition, the Chinese term *chahua* will be used to refer to an illustration within a section of text.

Illustrations, cartoons, comics, and illustrated books have been popular visual art forms in China since the early years of the twentieth century. Lu Xun was one of the earliest Chinese intellectuals to promote illustrations in China. In 1929, he introduced contemporary Japanese and Western woodblock print illustrations in his journal *Morning Flowers in the Garden of Art* (*Yiyuan zhaohua*). In 1931, he organized a workshop on modern woodblock print illustrations. Under his influence, fifteen Chinese woodblock print organizations formed over the following five years. For example, the Committee of Shanghai Woodblock Artists set up shop in 1936. Many woodblock illustrations at that time presented "positive proletarian imagery that celebrated labor."[13] Later, Communist artists in Mao Zedong's wartime capital of Yan'an adopted the format of the woodblock print to transform traditional *nianhua* (New Year celebratory painting) into a tool of political propaganda. For example, the *nianhua* print entitled *Brother and Sister Settle the Barren Frontier* (*Xiongmei kaihuang*) communicated the uplifting and celebratory spirit of many traditional woodblock prints, while incorporating artistic elements from local *yangge* (rice-sprout song performances).[14]

In 1918, Shen Bochen (1889–1920) launched China's first cartoon magazine *Shanghai Puck* (*Shanghai poke*). In the first issue, Shen emphasized that the goal of this cartoon magazine was "to reconcile the new with the old, and to satirize the low and vulgar" (*tiaohe xinjiu, zhenbian mosu*). Yet as a result of budgetary shortfalls, the magazine stayed in print for only four issues.[15]

Chinese cartoon magazines found their footing in the 1920s around the new term "cartoon" (*manhua*). The artist and essayist Feng Zikai (1898–1975) coined this neologism in 1925 when he published a collection of his own cartoons under the title of "Zikai's Cartoons" ("Zikai manhua") in *Literature Weekly*.[16] According to Robert Petersen, "Zikai manhua" is a "beautiful fusion of Song dynasty–style painting and contemporary elements in a series of cartoons."[17] The first successful Chinese magazine to focus exclusively on *manhua* was *Shanghai Sketch* (*Shanghai manhua*), with its inaugural issue in 1928. It introduced cartoon characters such as Mr. Wang in Ye Qianyu's (1907–95) serialized cartoons and Miss Bee in Liang Baibo's (ca. 1911–70) serialized cartoons. Zhang Leping (1910–92) published his *Sanmao* (literally, "three hairs") series in 1935 to depict the suffering of the waif Sanmao in Shanghai, reflecting a growing sense of class consciousness and social injustice in China during the 1930s. After the end of the Second World War, Zhang Leping restarted his career as a cartoonist with *Sanmao* sequels that eulogize China's Communist Party such as *Sanmao Joins the Army* (*Sanmao congjun*, 1946), *Sanmao Yesterday and Today* (*Sanmao jinxi*, 1959), and *Sanmao Welcomes Liberation* (*Sanmao ying jiefang*, 1961).[18]

Chinese SF writers and critics have long recognized the importance of incorporating visual art within science popularization writing and SF. In 1980, Li Yuan particularly emphasized the visual component of materials for instruction such as popular science tracts: "The visual dimension is an important aspect of popular science writing. Without a visual dimension, a piece of writing will neither attract readers nor be readily understood by them."[19] He used the Chinese term *kepu meishu* (science popularization art) to refer to graphic illustrations interspersed within popular science writings. He emphasized that *kepu meishu* "draws upon art to help introduce readers to science and technology"[20] and described it as including drawings, cartoons, and photographs. According to Li, *kepu meishu* should be scientific, accessible, and artistic. In other words, it should be scientifically accurate; its composition should lend itself to ease of understanding; and its style should be artistic and modern. Li further emphasized that *kepu meishu* should position itself at the forefront of its own era and popularize the latest scientific and technological advances.[21] *Kepu meishu* often appear as a single-panel illustration in a popular science essay, in which text fills most of the page, while the illustration plays a supplementary role. Li referred to these supplementary illustrations interspersed within popular science texts as "popular science illustrations" (*kepu chatu*). He recommended that popular science writers think often and carefully about what sort of illustrations would effectively underpin the main points they are advancing in the text. In this way, the text will fuse naturally and organically with the illustrations. In another type of illustrated popular science narrative, it is cartoons or photographs that dominate the page layout, while text serves a supplementary role as caption for this visual content. Li referred to this type of narrative as "illustrated popular science narratives" (*tujie kepu*). Arguing that these illustrated science narratives are of great educational value, he recommended that publishers solicit and print more books of this sort.[22]

The Chinese cartoonist Miao Yintang (1935–2017) resembles Li Yuan in having advocated the incorporation of more illustrations in popular science writing and SF. Around 1980, Miao Yintang coined the neologism "science *manhua*" (*kexue manhua*) to refer to cartoons, comics, and illustrated books that propagate science.[23] Miao published his science *manhua* "Keke Goes Hunting for Wolves" ("Keke dalang ji") in the PRC popular science magazine *Knowledge Is Power* (*Zhishi jiushi liliang*) in 1979. "Keke Goes Hunting for Wolves" consists of sequential panel comics, and features a young protagonist named Keke, who draws upon modern technological advances to more effectively hunt for wolves in the mountains. The Chinese character *ke* in his name also means "science," so Keke refers to a person who achieves remarkable feats by drawing upon science and technology (see figure 7.1). Miao subsequently created and published sequels of science *manhua* that feature the adventures of Keke. Miao also edited a regular column in the magazine entitled "Knowledge and Humour."[24]

In addition to illustrating science *manhua*, Miao wrote essays about the history of *manhua* in China. Moreover, he promoted this art form among popular science authors and SF writers. Miao argued that *manhua* often functioned as social or political satire when it first gained prominence in China during the 1920s and 1930s. After the founding of PRC, social or political satire in *manhua* largely gave way to didactic and educational functions. In particular, popular science magazines started to adopt *manhua*-style illustrations in popular science essays during the 1950s and 1960s. During the post-Mao era, even more popular science magazines adopted *manhua*-style illustrations, increasingly including columns featuring science *manhua* within each issue. In 1981, China's Popular Science Writers Association hosted an exhibition of Chinese popular science illustrations and *manhua*. Since about that time, *manhua* artists have included popular science as a key field for their artistic creation. Miao emphasized that the PRC of the reform era accelerated the country's modernization in keeping with the elevation of science as a primary engine of production. Therefore, *manhua* has in turn adapted to the needs of the new era and expanded its purview to disseminate advances in science and technology.

Miao Yintang also commented on the communicative prowess of *manhua*. Because the concision and vividness of *manhua* make it accessible to readers of all levels of ability, it is an efficient vehicle for conveying information and knowledge to the broad populace. He argued that

Figure 7.1. Miao Yintang's science *manhua* "Keke Goes Hunting for Wolves" (1979).

there is a synergy between science and *manhua* because both endeavours require creativity and wisdom. Miao insisted that science *manhua* must be scientific in spirit, and thus cannot properly undermine or marginalize science. The content of science *manhua* revolves around scientific knowledge, science fantasy, and news related to science and technology. Some science *manhua* support scientific thinking by satirizing unscientific ideologies and superstitions.[25]

Ye Yonglie resembles Miao Yintang in calling attention to the synergy between *manhua* and science. Ye argued that *manhua*'s "hyperbole and artistic style" enables it to "vividly popularize scientific knowledge."[26] Ye referred to Zhang Leping's post-Mao *Sanmao* cartoons as an example of such science popularization. In 1978, Zhang Leping undertook a new serialization of *Sanmao* cartoons entitled *Sanmao Loves Science* (*Sanmao ai kexue*) in the magazine *Children's Time*. This *manhua* serialization introduced the magazine's youthful readership to eight scientific and technological advances such as genetic engineering and solar energy generation.[27]

SF illustrations that had appeared mainly in popular science essays and magazines from the 1950s through the 1970s began to cross over into *lianhuanhua* by the late 1970s. While science illustrations and science *manhua* continued to appear mainly in popular science narratives, *lianhuanhua* soon became a prominent visual vehicle for SF. Some *lianhuanhua* originally appeared piecemeal through serialization and only later were brought together and published as a book; others appeared in book form from the outset. The history of printing illustrated storybooks goes back over a millennium in China; a key development was the fourteenth-century rise of an aesthetic approach in woodblock printing known as *shangtu xiawen* (illustrations above and text below). With the nineteenth-century introduction of lithography to China from the West, lithographic illustrated storybooks emerged in China by the late 1890s. The term *lianhuanhua* was coined in 1925 with the publication of an illustrated version of the famous Ming dynasty novel of statecraft *Romance of the Three Kingdoms*. The emphasis was on the drawings, with minimal text provided at the bottom or side of the page to recount the story. From that point on, the term *lianhuanhua* entered common use as a moniker of the new genre.[28] *Lianhuanhua* is a synergetic art form that combines prose with pictorial representation. In the 1940s, the Chinese Communist Party started to make aesthetic changes to this artistic genre in Yan'an, and promoted this sort of Chinese Communist–style didactic graphic narrative as the "new" *lianhuanhua*. It became a key tool of propaganda for indoctrinating the populace in Communist ideology. Mi Gu's (1918–86) *Young Erhei Gets Married* (*Xiao Erhei jiehun*, 1950), adapted from Zhao Shuli's 1943 short story of the same title, is a representative work of the "new" *lianhuanhua*, not only because it promotes the common theme of new-style marriage by choice instead of a traditional arranged marriage, but also because it utilizes a realist style of illustration. "Shadows done with crosshatching were eliminated and there was an emphasis on contour and a minimum of decoration.… The figures were realistically rendered but often had a flat quality with open space reminiscent of classical Chinese painting."[29] This artistic style became a model for future *lianhuanhua* in Mao-era China. For example, Han Heping and Ding Binzeng co-drew the *lihuanhua* version of *Railway Guerillas* (*Tiedao youjidui*) by adopting the bulk of Mi Gu's realistic style. *Railway Guerillas* comprises ten volumes that came out between 1954 and 1962 and remains "one of the most successful *lianhuanhua* publications."[30]

After mostly disappearing from bookstore shelves during the Cultural Revolution, *lianhuanhua* became popular with PRC readers once again during the post-Mao era as inexpensive large print runs became available. The pocket-size *lianhuanhua* is also called *xiaoren shu*, literarily "kid's book." Though the target readership of *xiaoren shu* has been youth, these editions have been bought and read by adult readers as well. During the "reading fever" of the post-Mao cultural thaw, many classics of Chinese and foreign literature were adapted to *lianhuanhua* versions, such as *Journey to the West*, SF novels by Jules Verne, and Arthur Conan Doyle's Sherlock Holmes series.

By the late 1970s, the ingredients were there for the emergence of SF *lianhuanhua*. Talented writers and artists looked for ways to free up the form and find a readership for relatively mature narratives. A fairly sophisticated adult readership was well-grounded in prose SF and had become familiar with the more artistically adventurous narratives of Verne and Conan Doyle. Since the target readership increasingly included adults, more sophistication in content and style was required. One likely source for sophisticated content that could be expressed in visually prominent graphical style was fantasy and SF. The artistic and commercial success of *lianhuanhua* adapted from Chinese and foreign literary classics around 1980 helped create a group of adult graphic novel readers with high expectations for such a narrative. As market-based incentives for PRC publishers increased during the post-Mao cultural thaw, these publishers increasingly viewed SF *lianhuanhua* as a profitable niche, reacting quickly to adapt SF narratives to the *lianhuanhua* format.

SF *lianhuanhua* became an increasingly common vehicle for PRC SF narratives because it was commercially successful as entertainment fiction. For example, the key transitional work – artistically and in its unprecedented commercial success as a trade item – was Ye Yonglie's Jin Ming series. After initial serialization of a Jin Ming narrative in a periodical, it was published as either a book or a *lianhuanhua*. According to Ye, the print run of each narrative in the series was no fewer than 200,000 copies, while the total print run of the Jin Ming *lianhuanhua* books exceeded seven million copies.[31] The most renowned *lianhuanhua* series was published by the Guangzhou Sub-branch of the Popular Science Publishing House. It adapted thirteen narratives into *lianhuanhua* volumes under the moniker of the Scientific Holmes Series. The front cover of each volume usually foregrounds Jin Ming in his uniform of a PSB officer, with his sidekick and other main characters arrayed behind. This pictorial configuration highlights the key role that Jin plays in each narrative in the series. *Black Shadow in Ghost Mountain* was the first Jin Ming narrative to come out as an illustrated book, published in December 1981. On the back cover a paragraph introduces the Jin Ming series, the author, major characteristics of the SF thriller, and a summary of the narrative. The editor lavishes praise upon the Scientific Holmes Series, insisting that it is more realistic and up-to-date than Conan Doyle's Sherlock Holmes series. The editor concludes by announcing plans for ten more volumes in the series from December 1981 to June 1982 and urges readers to be on the lookout for updated news about these forthcoming volumes so as to not miss an opportunity to purchase them while they are still in stock.

On the basis of Ye's own estimate, the print run of *lianhuanhua* adapted from his SF narratives was about twenty-one million copies, which encompassed seventy-nine different *lianhuanhua* versions of his SF narratives. Most of these *lianhuanhua* were published between 1980 and 1983. Ye noted that the figure of twenty-one million is actually too low because it does not include his *lianhuanhua* volumes that lack information about its total print run on the back cover. Ye went on to quip, "I would have become a millionaire if only those publishers had paid me royalties, given the fact that each volume had a total print run of several hundred thousand copies."[32]

Ye's remark reveals a problem that many PRC writers and artists encountered – few publishers paid royalties to authors whose narratives they adapted into *lianhuanhua* volumes. In 1977, the Chinese National Publication Bureau issued a regulation to overturn the widespread practice during the Cultural Revolution of refusing to pay authors any remuneration whatsoever.[33] But the PRC copyright law did not go into effect until 1990, so many publishers adapted narratives as *lianhuanhua* volumes without notifying the authors, let alone paying them royalties. According to Ye, the only exception was the Guangzhou branch of Popular Science Publishing, which sent him one hundred complimentary copies of *lianghuanhua* volumes that it had adapted from his Jin Ming series. However, as with other publishers, it paid him no remuneration or royalties at all.[34]

Ye Yonglie argued that a few typical features of his SF narratives lend them to adaptation into *lianhuanhua* volumes: plot twists, well-defined beginnings and ends, vivid imagery, and frequent changes in setting. These features also give illustrators much creative leeway while moving from text to drawings. Ye explained that his storytelling skill is the major reason his SF narratives were in greater demand by publishers of *lianhuanhua* volumes than were narratives of other PRC SF writers in his day. Ye recalled that when one of his SF stories was serialized in the *Yangtse River Daily*, readers lined up each morning at newspaper stands for the latest instalment. He carefully ended each episode on a high note of suspense to lure readers into the next instalment. He also pointed out that his narratives are often rich in the sort of visual imagery that films rely on to advance a narrative. Moreover, his SF narratives often draw upon features of traditional Ming-Qing novels such as twisting plot, chapters that end on a note of high suspense, and frequent changes in setting.[35]

Ye pointed to two additional factors responsible for the popularity of SF *lianhuanhua* volumes: "beautiful drawings and low prices."[36] In the late 1970s and early 1980s, readers paid only two to five cents to rent a volume of *lianhuanhua* or *xiaoren shu* at a street-side book rental stall. They could finish reading an entire volume within half an hour. The *lianhuanhua*'s low cost for rental or purchase and modest demands on the reader's time attracted both juvenile and adult readers.[37]

The generally high quality of illustrations in *lianhuanhua* volumes also attracted many readers. Sun Xiongfei (b. 1943) was a visual artist who illustrated many of Ye's SF works. Sun was working as both a painter and screenwriter at the Shanghai Film Studio during the *lianhuanhua* craze. Starting around 1976, his paintings won awards at visual art contests. Impressed by Sun's talent, Ye invited Sun to illustrate some of his SF works, and commented to a friend as follows, "Sun draws his illustrations quickly and skilfully. I am very satisfied with his work."[38] When some of Ye's full-length novels were serialized in newspapers, the editor often required Ye to supply an illustration with each instalment. Under these circumstances, Sun made a daily bicycle ride to Ye's home, where he read Ye's latest instalment and then drew an illustration. Eventually, Sun drew all the illustrations for seven *lianhuanhua* volumes that had been adapted from Ye's SF narratives (see figure 7.2). Each volume ran to over a hundred pages in length. Ye noted that even if one of Sun's illustrations consisted of just a few brushstrokes, it was invariably "vivid and lifelike."[39]

Although the front covers of these volumes sport full-colour illustrations, the inside pages of Sun's *lianhuanhua* and those of many other painters are illustrated entirely with black-and-white line drawings in a time-honoured layout and style reminiscent of *Young Erhei Gets Married* and *Railway Guerillas*. Instead of using a combination of speech balloons and thought balloons as in popular Western graphic narratives, *lianhuanhua* utilize captions at the bottom or side of the illustration (see figure 7.3). Even a reader who is mostly or entirely illiterate can still grasp the gist of the narrative by merely looking at the illustrations. SF *lianhuanhua* thus helped make SF accessible even to illiterates.

In addition, *lianhuanhua* helped spread thaw-era PRC SF fiction to relatively remote rural areas where TV and films were not yet

Figure 7.2. Front cover of *Secret Column* (*Mimi Zongdui*, 1982) drawn by Sun Xiongfei.

Figure 7.3. Page 14 of the *lianhuanhua* version of *Black Shadow in Ghost Mountain* (1981) drawn by Zhang Weijian.

available – functioning as a sort of still version of TV and film. McLuhan has emphasized the participational quality of the cartoon and comic book: "The modern comic strip and comic book provided very little data about any particular moment in time, or aspect in space, of an object. The viewer, or reader, is compelled to participate in completing and interpreting the few hints provided by the bounding lines."[40] A TV image resembles a cartoon image in the way it has a "very low degree of data about objects, and the resulting high degree of participation by the viewer in order to complete what is only hinted at in the mosaic mesh of dots."[41] He thereby argues that in the twentieth-century West, TV "was a real rival" of the comic book, and "TV hit the comic-book world so hard" because cartoon images and TV images "share a participational and do-it-yourself character."[42] That explains why "since the advent of TV, the comic book has gone into decline."[43] McLuhan's argument can explain why *lianhuanhua* volumes were so popular during the years before televisions became commonplace in PRC households.

As early as the 1950s and 1960s, *lianhuanhua* was already "used as a way to disseminate the message of the movie to rural areas where films were unavailable."[44] For example, Hua Sanchuan (1930–2004) illustrated the *lianhuanhua* version of *White-Haired Girl* (*Bai mao nü*) in 1965, basing his portrayal on the 1950 cinematic version of this Maoist narrative. This *lianhuanhua* volume spread the film's message of class-based oppression to underserved PRC rural audiences. Similarly, while the cinematic version of *Death Ray on a Coral Island* hit the box office in PRC urban areas in 1980, the *lianhuanhua* version circulated widely in the countryside. Though reading a *lianhuanhua* volume somewhat resembles watching a cinematic or TV narrative, it differs in that the reader can control the pace of reading by slowing down, speeding up, or pausing the narrative and then getting back to it later. Hence, *lianhuanhua* afford readers a flexibility of pace and intermittency that is lacking in TV and cinematic versions of a narrative. This might be another reason why SF *lianhuanhua* volumes were so popular when cinematic and TV versions of narratives were still limited mostly to urbanites in the PRC.

Chinese SF in Audiovisual Media: Radio Dramas, TV Dramas, and Films

The year 2019 was celebrated as "Year One [*yuannian*] of the Chinese SF film" soon after the release of the 3D movie *Wandering Earth* (*Liulang diqiu*). Frant Gwo directed this film, which he adapted from Liu Cixin's 2000 novella of the same title.[45] In the same year, two other notable PRC SF films came out: the comedy *Crazy Alien* (*Fengkuang de waixingren*), directed by Hao Ning, and *Shanghai Fortress* (*Shanghai baolei*), directed by Huatao Teng. With the successful box office of *Wandering Earth,* more and hot money was invested in Chinese SF films. It seems that SF films may well experience a boom throughout the 2020s. On the bandwagon of Chinese SF films, some old Chinese SF films resurfaced, including the first PRC SF film *Death Ray on a Coral Island* (1980). Tong Enzheng's short story "Death Ray on a Coral Island" is a representative work that has migrated across multiple forms of media, exemplifying Chinese SF's "transmedia" quality during the post-Mao era. According to the critic Zheng Jun, "The development of SF film, radio, and TV dramas reveals the promising transmedia quality of Chinese science fiction during the post-Mao era. The flow of SF texts through electronic media also reflects the Chinese people's aspiration to unfettered thought, and impelled society as a whole to focus more on science and the future."[46]

After winning the best short story award in 1978, "Death Ray on a Coral Island" was not only adapted into a *lianhuanhua* volume, but was also quickly recast as a radio play (*guangbo ju*) in the same year. The three radio presenters of this play were Qiu Yuefeng, Qiao Zhen and Yang Chengchun, each of whom was famous for having dubbed foreign movies in the Shanghai Dubbing Studio. Other SF writers' works were also adapted into radio plays, such as Ye Yonglie's *Xiao Lingtong Travels to the Future.* In addition to those radio dramas adapted from the works of such celebrated writers as Ye Yonglie and Tong Enzheng, there were also successful radio plays adapted from the SF works of relatively obscure writers. For example, one popular radio drama at that time was *A Green Cloned Horse* (*lüse kelong ma,* 1980), while nobody knew who had written the SF narrative upon which this radio play was based. Many PRC audiences first heard about genetic engineering while listening this drama. The drama's theme song, "Soar On, Spaceship of Science!" ("Feiben ba! Kexue de hangchuan") also became a hit of the time. The lyric says, "Soar on, spaceship of science! Brimming with our aspirations, you sally forth on wind and waves. Our hearts shall blossom with wisdom and sunshine."[47]

Some SF narratives bypassed radio altogether and were adapted into TV dramas, such as Wu Boze's novella *Invisible Man,* Zhang Fengjiang and Jia Wanchao's "The Last Cancer Patient," and Ye Yonglie's *The X-3 Case.* Yet since televisions were still a rarity in most PRC homes during the early thaw era, TV dramas failed to achieve the popularity of radio dramas and SF films at that time.

Prior to the debut of *Death Ray on a Coral Island,* PRC theatres screened two overseas SF films during the late 1970s. One was director Richard T. Heffron's American SF thriller *Futureworld* (1976), and the other was director Qi Fu's Hong Kong SF thriller *Life and Death* (*Shengsi bodou*, 1977) – the latter adapted from American SF novelist James E. Gunn's *The Immortals* (1964). Both films struck a chord with PRC filmgoers. For instance, the critic Zheng Jun claimed that he was so deeply impressed by his initial viewing of *Futureworld* that he returned to the cinema to watch it two more times. The enthusiastic PRC reception of these two overseas SF films encouraged the director Zhang Hongmei to adapt "Death Ray on a Coral Island" as a feature film. Zhang mentioned that the only SF film she ever watched prior to directing *Death Ray* was *Futureworld*. That was also the first time she had seen a robot appear in a film. Zhang was a quick learner, for she included a robot among the other characters in her own film. While the science consultants in the film crew emphasized adherence to scientific principles, Zhang insisted that the film focus more on vivid characterization and an intriguing plot. She further argued that since a feature film of this type was a fictional narrative, it should be viewed as neither solely for entertainment nor entirely educational.[48]

Constricted by the film's very low budget, Zhang and her crew lacked high-tech filming equipment. They also had no discretionary funds for travel abroad to learn about advanced film studios or shoot takes. Instead, they had to improvise and use their imagination to create special effects: they rendered the mushroom cloud of an atomic bomb explosion, for example, by filming loess soil dropped in a container full of water and then running the short take in reverse. Finally, all of the film's scenes set in foreign countries had to be borrowed from footage taken by a Hong Kong cinematographer.

In spite of difficult shooting conditions and a lack of up-to-date equipment, the film successfully portrayed futuristic scenes such as a scientific laboratory, a corridor under the ocean, an underwater elevator, and laser weapons. Such scenes offered sufficient novelty to attract unusually large audiences and strong box office ticket sales. Some critics claimed that the film's reddish burst of laser beams even set the stage for "a flash of miraculous light (*lingguang zhaxian*) – a new SF genre film in the PRC."[49] Aside from all the high-tech gadgetry and ultra-modern film sets, this film also introduced many PRC filmgoers to the conspicuous consumption of wealthy foreigners with scenes of a chic dance party, a fancy car chase, a private corporate jet, a tycoon's yacht, and luxurious houses.

In addition to *Death Ray*, another SF film that came out during the same period was *Shadow of a Ghost* (*Qianying*, 1981). It was adapted from the SF novella *Ghost in an Imperial Palace* (*Wangfu guaiying*, 1981), co-authored by Ji Hongxu and Ji Sanmeng. *Shadow of a Ghost*, showcasing a more realistic style than *Death Ray*, was promoted as a detective thriller. The boundary walls of an ancient imperial palace provide the rainy-night setting for ghost-like apparitions. Police officers and scientists investigate. A young scientist utilizes a device he has invented to study these apparitions on a rainy night, but the film ends with its failure to clarify what they actually are. Such an ending seems out of accord with the early-1980s mood of "looking forward" to the future and expressing optimism about the unlimited potential of technological progress. In contrast with *Death Ray*, *Shadow of a Ghost* performed poorly at the box office.

Death Ray and *Shadow of a Ghost* are the only two SF films that came out in the PRC during the early 1980s. There might have been more such thaw-era SF films if film directors and SF writers had adapted other SF narratives into films. For example, during the late 1970s Ye Yonglie was unable to drum up interest in a cinematic adaptation of *Xiao Lingtong Travels to the Future*, even though this 1978 blockbuster novel garnered a print run of three million copies, and a script by the novelist Liang Xiaosheng came out in 1979 in *Cinematic Scripts* (*Dianying chuangzuo*). The backward state of special effects at thaw-era PRC studios was a major stumbling block, however. The veteran film director Xie Tian summarized the difficulties that a PRC studio of that era faced with *Xiao Lingtong Travels to the Future*: "The levitating vehicle that Xiao Lingtong pilots would be difficult to render on the silver screen. The levitating vehicle has a transparent exterior, and can either fly through the sky above or plough through the waves below. The current state of special effects technology in China is not up to the task of making this film."[50] Facing the sort of shoestring budgets that were typical in PRC film studios during the thaw era, Xie concluded that it was not yet possible for directors like him to produce a film containing futuristic SF gadgetry. Having witnessed the success of high-tech special effects in the recent PRC SF film *Wandering Earth* three decades after the thaw Eea, Ye Yonglie could not help but sigh, "Back [in the thaw era] when the country was not yet affluent, making a high-tech SF film was merely a faraway and self-indulgent dream."[51]

After these modest beginnings, the genre of SF films disappeared from the PRC for a few years in the wake of the party-state's crackdown on "spiritual pollution." The situation began to improve slightly when Richard Donner's 1978 version of *Superman* received government approval for screening in the PRC in 1986. In the next year, Toshio Masuda's Japanese SF disaster film *Tokyo Blackout* (*Shuto shoshitsu*, 1987), also received government approval for screening in the PRC. Both films proved wildly popular among PRC filmgoers and achieved impressive ticket sales. Having noticed the startling success of these foreign SF films, PRC studios produced four homegrown SF films between 1986 and 1989. Wang Weiyi directed *Wildest Fantasy* (*Yixiang tiankai*, 1986), a comedy that joins disparate motifs of space aliens, *qigong*, and martial arts. Huang Jianxin's *Dislocation* (*Cuo wei*, 1987) features a scientist who creates a lookalike robot to attend boringly scripted workplace meetings in his stead so that he can focus more on substantive research projects – a darkly comical satire of overly bureaucratized state-owned enterprises. Weng Luming and Song Chong's *Wonder Boy* (*Pili Beibei*, 1988) portrays a wondrous boy whose body can generate a powerful electric current. Hu Qingsheng and Liu Yichuan's *The Head in the House* (*Xiongzhai meiren tou*, 1989) drew upon Alexander Belyaev's SF narrative *Professor Dowell's Head* (1925), merely switching the setting from Russia to China and transforming the narrative into a SF thriller. In contrast with *Death Ray*, these PRC SF films of the late 1980s seldom addressed issues in science and did not generate the enthusiastic reception among PRC filmgoers that *Death Ray* had garnered in 1980.[52]

In the 1990s, PRC studios produced four more SF films. Feng Xiaoning's *The Ozone Layer Vanishes* (*Daqiceng xiaoshi*, 1990) emerged as a landmark of the PRC eco-SF film. In it, three tankfuls of toxic chemicals spill during the chaos of a train robbery. The chemicals vaporize and destroy much of the upper atmosphere's ozone layer, endangering most life on Earth. The year 1990 also saw the release of the SF film *Magic Watch* (*Mo biao*, 1990). In it, young Kang Bosi buys a wristwatch that contains metal that has reached Earth from outer space. The strange powers of this watch transform Kang overnight into an adult, enabling him to take part in wondrous adventures. Zhang Zi'en's *Invisible PhD* (*Yinshen boshi*, 1991) is a mixed-genre detective SF film. In it, scientists invent a medicine that makes anyone who takes it invisible. Unfortunately, a thief steals it, becomes invisible after taking a dose, and commits a series of crimes with the aid of his invisibility. Finally, Li Guomin's *Revived Warrior* (*Zaisheng yongshi*, 1995) is another detective SF movie, but distinguishes itself from other films in this mixed genre by taking on the scientific theme of genetic engineering.

Animating Science and Technology

While SF films cater mainly to an adult audience, scientific animated films aim at a juvenile audience. With the advantage of conveying a message in a simple, linear, and easily understandable manner to youthful viewers, PRC animation from the 1950s to early 1980s was a propaganda tool that served the new Maoist order, promoting the construction of a new China, and educating young Communist successors of the future. During those three decades, PRC scientific animation (*kexue donghua*) popularized scientific knowledge and new technologies, promoted scientific thinking, and responded to the Communist Party's rhetoric about achieving the Four Modernizations by the end of the twentieth century. This discussion focuses on the scientific animated films that the Shanghai Animation Film Studio (SAFS) produced between 1957 and 1983.

Produced at several junctures in the history of PRC animation, these works differ drastically in their approach to the power of science and technology as well as the relations between characterization and science and technology. We can detect a trend in how protagonists from the earlier films tended to address and solve problems, while characters from films made during the post-Mao thaw era blissfully consume modern goods. In addition, scientific animation films of the 1950s and 1960s were usually set in the present day and realistic in orientation, dealing with familiar sciences and applied technologies, such as *The Little Inventor* (*Xiao faming jia*, 1958), *The Cuckoo Is Late* (*Buguniao jiao chi le*, 1959), and *Little Tadpoles Look for Mama* (*Xiao kedou zhao mama*, 1960). *The Little Inventor* is a puppet-based animated film that came out in 1958, which depicts how students use their knowledge to build a wind-powered automatic conveyor belt between two mountains so that they need no longer worry about a lengthy commute between home and school. *The Cuckoo Is Late* is a Chinese-style watercolour animation directed by Qian Jiajun (1916–2011), which came out in 1959. Even though the film echoes the central government's rural policy of double-cropping in the late-1950s Great Leap Forward, the film makes no overt references to this political movement. *Little Tadpoles Look for Mama* is an animated film famous for its melding of traditional Chinese watercolour painting with cinematic visuals. The scientific character of the film lies in how it popularizes the knowledge of the biological development of a frog from egg to tadpole to frog. Through a series of misunderstandings, the film also introduces its young audience to the physical features of aquatic creatures such as goldfish, crabs, turtles, and catfish. These three early scientific animated films contain subtle political propaganda and didacticism, and convey scientific and technological messages through a narrative strategy of focused problem solving. These scientific themes are based on known sciences and existing technologies, with bits and pieces of factual knowledge interspersed throughout. Their main functions are to popularize science and promote scientific thinking.[53]

In contrast, scientific animation films made during the post-Mao thaw focused more on possibilities, introducing the viewer to elements of SF and futurism, such as in *The Hens Move to a New Home* (*Muji banjia*, 1979),

Yuanyuan and the Robot (*Yuanyuan he jiqi ren*, 1980), and *Dingding Fights the Monkey King* (*Dingding zhan houwang*, 1980). These changes reveal the tension between an approach to science that reflects present-day developments and a vision of science that imagines the future. This tension has much to do with the Communist Party's changing rhetoric from building a socialist new China during the 1950s and 1960s to looking forward to achieving the Four Modernizations during the post-Mao thaw.

The development of scientific animation resonated with the growth of PRC scientific literature and arts, especially SF. Ye Yonglie defined the scientific animated film as a combination of the scientific fairy tale (*kexue tonghua*) and the sort of animation that popularizes science and technology for youthful viewers. He believed that such a film usually employs moral didacticism. Ye thought *Little Tadpoles Look for Mama* was an excellent scientific animated film because it combined features of didacticism, art, and science. These three features are also the main criteria for defining scientific literature and art.[54] In addition, Ye emphasized the "fairy tale" quality of scientific animated films. It appears that Ye used the term "fairy tale" to refer to fantastic elements in this type of film. Ye argued that scientific animated films should create an atmosphere of fantasy and transcend everyday life.[55] This emphasis on fantasy contrasts with the tenets of socialist realism that PRC scientific animated films officially observed during the 1950s and 1960s.

After production was suspended between 1965 to 1973, largely overlapping with the most chaotic years of Mao's Cultural Revolution, PRC animated filmmaking resumed production in 1973. The political and social atmosphere that characterized the post-Mao cultural thaw pushed scientific animated filmmaking in new directions: some writers presented a vision of a better future brought about by advanced science and technology, combining scientific principles with fantasy. Consequently, the typical subject matter shifted from agricultural technology and the biological and physical sciences in the 1950s and 1960s animation to space exploration and the Four Modernizations of industry, agriculture, national defence, and science and technology in the post-Mao animated films. Chinese animation manifested "a growing interest in science and technology, the creation of a myth of science, and a consequent passion for the science fiction genre," similar to what Laura Pontieri has observed about Soviet animation during the post-Stalin cultural thaw of the mid-1950s.[56] From the late 1970s through the early 1980s, the SAFS produced such scientific animated films as *A Strange Patient* (*Qiguai de binghao*, 1978), *Hens Move to a New Home* (1979), *A Strange Ball Game* (*Qiguai de qiusai*, 1979), *My Friend, Young Dolphin* (*Wode pengyou xiao haitun*, 1980), *Yuanyuan and the Robot* (1980), *Dingding*

Fights the Monkey King (1980), and *The Little Red Face and Little Blue Face* (*Xiao honglian he xiao lanlian*, 1982).

Works of SF or the scientific fairy tale provided the basis for some of these films. For example, *A Strange Patient* was adapted from Ye Yonglie's scientific fairy tale "The Patient of Unknown Background" ("Laili buming de bingren," 1978) about a cabbage worm, and *My Friend, Young Dolphin* was adapted from Liu Xingshi's SF short story of the same title in praise of a harmonious relationship between humankind and nature. A small portion of scientific animated films continued the 1950s tradition of popularizing knowledge, such as *The Little Red Face and the Little Blue Face*, a film that urges children to brush their teeth every evening before going to bed. A large portion of scientific animation during this period was closely related to the nation's modernization of industry, agriculture, national defence, and innovative technology. The science-related themes deal with computers, robots, artificial intelligence, electronics, aerospace technologies, satellites, and submarines. The following paragraphs analyse two short films to reveal how their science-related themes helped promote the central government's rhetoric about the Four Modernizations.

The short film *Yuanyuan and the Robot* is a puppet-based animated film made in 1980 to advocate the PRC's industrial modernization. The film's use of actual and model toys in puppet animation is a continuation of a staple in Chinese animation since the early 1930s. The film is like a miniature version of *Toy Story* (1995), which also features toys as the cast of characters, but it came out fifteen years earlier than its American counterpart. The film begins at a toy store that sports a table-top display of a robot and three dolls: Yuanyuan and his two friends. One day, after the store closes, Yuanyuan and his friends go outside to play a traditional Chinese game of shuttlecock. Yuanyuan accidentally kicks the shuttlecock into a maintenance hole. He decides to make a new one for his friends and asks the robot to help him catch a rooster. On their way to look for a rooster, the robot and Yuanyuan encounter minor incidents that showcase the robot's abilities: it can fly, trundle along as fast as a car, and even operate a crane.

The critics Wang Dazhi and Cao Ying argue that even though the robot adds a futuristic element to the film, the film has nothing to do with scientific fantasy. The robot is not fundamentally different from the other cartoon images except it flies higher, moves faster, and adds more fun.[57] Their argument is partially right about the function of the robot in the film, but the film provides far more futuristic and scientific elements than they have noted. For example, there is an atom logo on the robot's breast, which represents advances in physics. There is

Figure 7.4. Yuanyuan and the robot stand in front of a big poster, in *Yuanyuan and the Robot* (1980).

also a big poster on the roadside that portrays a boy (who looks like Yuanyuan) riding a rocket-powered spaceship (see figure 7.4). An observatory stands in the background when Yuanyuan and the robot converse. The poster and the observatory represent major achievements of the nation's aerospace industry and present an extrapolative vision of space exploration. In addition to the scientific content, the film also articulates a moral lesson. At the end of the film, Yuanyuan catches a rooster and is about to start plucking feathers to make a new shuttlecock, but his two friends force him to let the rooster go. In doing so, the film advocates humane values associated with compassion for life.

In addition to the scientific and moral messages, the film also presents urban and commercial elements. For example, the film presents images of a modernized city with highways, a huge viaduct, electric power plants, construction sites, and cranes lifting steel pipes. The space in which Yuanyuan and his friends play shuttlecock is a public commons surrounded by flower beds and trees. A toy store, a roadside fruit stand, balloons in a pedestrian's grip, and a truck loaded with cages of chickens all point to the commercial and consumerist culture that has re-emerged in mainland Chinese society by 1980. Though this imagery of urban life and commercialization has been commonplace in the animated films of other countries, such imagery was still relatively new in PRC scientific animated films. After all, early PRC scientific animated films from the 1950s and 1960s normally had a rural setting and emphasized agricultural production.

If we were to characterize *Yuanyuan and the Robot* as simply a "naive" or primitive robot story with limited scientific fantasy, then *Dingding Fights the Monkey King* could be considered the first PRC SF animated film, as the result of its skilful combination of classic Chinese narration with the genre of science fantasy. More importantly, it was released immediately before the Japanese animation series *Astro Boy* (or *Tetsuwan Atomu*) was imported to the PRC near the end of 1980 – and before foreign SF animation started to influence China's animation industry in aesthetic expression, thematic concerns, and technological methods. *Dingding Fights the Monkey King* was adapted from the comic strip *Young Sun and Old Sun* (*Xiao Sun he Lao Sun*) and directed by Hu Jinqing (1936–2019) in 1980. The film is a salute to the classic feature animated film *Uproar in Heaven* (1961–4) and follows its aesthetic style; the film also borrows such scientific motifs as chemistry equipment, geometry problems, and discussions of the power of knowledge from earlier SAFS productions.

The film starts with Dingding watching *Uproar in Heaven* on television. The animators use footage from the classic SAFS animated film for a few moments. Dingding turns off the TV before the film ends and goes back to doing his homework. The monkey king thereupon jumps out of the TV screen to ask Dingding why he turned off the TV in the middle of the show. The monkey king initially looks much as he did in *Uproar*, but he grows into a giant about eight minutes into the film. His echo-chamber voice sounds like revolutionary heroes from Mao-era films, and his large and muscular hands remind the audience of stock proletarian imagery in Cultural Revolution poster art. Dingding replies that it is time for him to do his homework, and further explains that doing homework helps learners gain knowledge, and that scientific knowledge is a powerful force. In the film, knowledge is symbolized by a golden key that will open the door to the future (see figure 7.5). The sparkling lights that shoot from the key of knowledge are common in SASF films from the 1950s and 1960s. The golden key metamorphoses into an atom logo that represents advances in modern physics at its first appearance in the film. The golden key has the same magic power as that of the monkey king's golden cudgel; when the monkey king challenges Dingding to a fight, he tells the boy to use his golden key as a weapon. Dingding accepts the challenge, and the key metamorphoses into a spaceship that takes him on a space journey, during which he sees satellites and other spacecraft in near-earth orbit. The golden key metamorphoses into a submarine that takes Dingding for wondrous underwater visits to an aquatic farm, a factory for processing seafood, and a gem mine on the ocean floor. The film also showcases how gene modification has been used in agricultural production to produce a fruit tree that has a wide variety of fruit growing on it. These were also common motifs in contemporary Chinese SF at that time.

In the face of these feats of modern science and technology, the once mighty monkey king now looks clumsy and perplexed. He keeps falling

Figure 7.5. Poster of the animated film *Dingding Fights the Monkey King* (1980).

into misfortune. For example, he accidentally slips and falls into the bottom of a large laboratory vat, and later almost becomes dissolved in a very large test tube. Afterwards, he compares this laboratory equipment to the Taoist official Tai Shang Lao Jun's kiln that manufactures pills for immortality. While on the ocean floor, the monkey king becomes netted with various fish, shunted along an automatic conveyer belt, and stuffed into a tin can that has not yet been sealed shut. After Dingding rescues the monkey king from the tin can, the monkey king chews on a glass bottle instead of drinking the beverage inside. As the plot develops, the image of the monkey king changes from that of an arrogant and imposing giant to a humble and bumbling pupil. Witnessing the power of the golden key, the monkey king asks Dingding to lend him the key. Dingding replies that the monkey king must undertake diligent study before he will be qualified to borrow the key. The monkey king thereupon begins to study under Dingding's instruction. This change in image depicts a deliberate shift in official discourse from the revolutionary, represented by the monkey king's hyperbolic initial rejection of scientific knowledge, to the post-revolutionary period's embrace of hard-won and objective scientific knowledge.

The end of the film presents an extrapolative vision of the monkey king travelling throughout the universe on the spaceship. The film stresses that knowledge is the key to opening a better future. The motif of the golden key also appears in the theme song: "The small golden key radiates and opens its golden wings to fly forward. Fear not hardship or difficulty, and treasure your time for study. We love science when we are young, and will contribute to the Four Modernizations once we've grown up."[58] The film endows scientific knowledge with magical power, which is much greater than that of the monkey king's golden cudgel. It affirms the message of the central government that science and technology are society's primary productive forces. While revolutionary fervour was once the key to production, the advancement of science is now the major factor in production.

The film also clearly promotes new modes of consumption. Dingding's room is not only equipped with chemistry laboratory equipment, but also contains a sofa, a television, and a modern desk. The food that Dingding enjoys is Western, such as a juice beverage, bread, and sausage. Canned meat and genetically modified fruits and vegetables are presented positively and compose part of Dingding's diet. The collage in these scenes with cans, bottles, and kaleidoscopic dancing fruit showcase the affluence of Dingding's material life.

Though containing futuristic and fantastic elements, the two films made during the post-Mao cultural thaw are set in the contemporary world in order to give youthful audiences hope that they may soon be living in a thoroughly modernized society. These films also reveal the PRC's rapid and extensive urbanization and the emergence of a new culture of consumerism during that period. The didactic stance of these films is new: good juvenile behaviour has risen to the status of a heroic act performed in the name of studying hard to obtain more scientific knowledge. The young audience has been charged with the responsibility of building up the country into a modernized industrial superpower.

The film critics Wang Dazhi and Liu Xiaowei have regretted that SAFS did not produce more SF animated films about robots and futuristic civilizations during the early 1980s; otherwise, they feel, the history of Chinese animation would have showcased a more memorable trajectory. As the result of large-scale imports of Japanese and Western SF animation during the 1980s, the market for scientific and SF animation was dominated by foreign television series such as *Astro Boy*, *The Transformers*, and *Mobile Suit Gundam*. There are reasons for the large-scale imports of foreign animation to the PRC, including growing popularity of television as a form of entertainment for PRC households, and the expanding number of local TV stations in the country. The demand for TV programs such as animation increased far beyond the domestic supply, so both CCTV and locally run PRC television stations imported a sizeable number of foreign animated films.[59]

Many other factors also contributed to dramatic changes in PRC animation production during the 1980s, including the switch from a Soviet-style centrally planned economy to an increasingly market-based economy; unprecedented foreign capital investment in the PRC animation industry; establishment of privately owned and joint-venture animation studios in PRC coastal urban areas; increased commercialization of the industry, along with decreased emphasis on its artistic heritage; and a shift from labour-intensive animation techniques to computerized digital animation. In addition to these factors, the 1983 political "Campaign to Eliminate Spiritual Pollution" in PRC literature and art was also a crucial reason that SAFS did not produce more scientific animated films during the early 1980s. In the face of unfavourable circumstances, PRC animation studios took self-protective measures, such as the temporary abandonment of producing new Chinese-style scientific and SF animated films.

Admittedly, scientific animated films comprise a modest portion of all PRC animated films produced from the late 1950s through the early 1980s – making them too few to be categorized separately from other animated films. Nonetheless, these science-related films popularized academic subjects in science and technology, helped incorporate science more fully into PRC popular culture as a whole, and contributed to the overall development of PRC scientific literature and art.

The Convergence of Fledgling Media

This chapter's exploration of SF-related media reveals that PRC SF media have expanded in scope from a reliance on the print format of *manhua* and *lianhuanhua* to the audiovisual spectrum of media – primarily radio, TV, and film. The frequent crossing of boundaries across this spectrum of media by PRC SF during the thaw era may be referred to as "transmedia practice," a conceptual framework that bears comparison with Jenkins's discussion of the U.S. "media convergence" and Steinberg's analysis of Japan's "media mix."[60] The post-Mao thaw era was pre-digital, dominated by two major categories of media: print media such as books, newspapers, and magazines; and audiovisual media such as radio, TV, and film. Consequently, the discussion here of PRC SF's transmedia practice includes print media and electronic analogue media while omitting digital media. Moreover, during this initial stage of the Reform and Opening policy in the PRC, TV remained a rare and luxurious commodity, even within urban households. Hardly any rural families in the PRC owned a TV at this stage. In addition, although Deng Xiaoping began to roll out economic reforms in late 1978, the PRC's private sector still remained far smaller than that of the state during the thaw era. These factors help us understand the constraints on PRC SF's transmedia practice.

By media convergence, Jenkins means "the flow of content across multiple media platforms, the cooperation between multiple media industries, and the migratory behavior of media audiences who will go almost anywhere in search of the kinds of entertainment experiences they want."[61] In his study of media convergence in the digital era, Jenkins focuses more on cultural aspects than on technological features of such convergence. Media convergence is not merely "a technological process bringing together multiple media functions within the same device."[62] For Jenkins, the most significant feature of media convergence is the media consumer's active participation: "The circulation of media content – across different media systems, competing media economies, and national borders – depends heavily on consumers' active participation."[63] Media convergence thus "represents a cultural shift as consumers are encouraged to seek out new information and make connections among dispersed media content."[64] It is a "participatory culture," which brings about "technological, industrial, cultural, and social changes."[65] Jenkins's media convergence comes across as a concept of comprehensive change in media configurations. It "alters the relationship between existing technologies, industries, markets, genres, and audience."[66] "Convergence refers to a process, not an endpoint."[67] Jenkins emphasizes both consumer participation and collaboration between producers of media.

The transmedia practice of PRC SF during the thaw era lacks much of the consumer participation described by Jenkins in contemporary American media convergence, such as consumers' appropriation of their favourite media content for their own entertainment, the circulation of media content through personalized communication (such as through social media), and media users who are willing and able to travel afar to consume their preferred media content. This is understandable, given the fact that during the thaw era there was very little personalized communication about media except for personal letters from consumers to editors and content providers, along with newsletters published by SF fan clubs and other voluntary associations. However, PRC SF transmedia did enjoy a certain amount of consumer participation, to the extent that "convergence occurs within the brains of individual consumers and through their social interactions with others."[68] PRC SF fans frequently bartered items back and forth within their collections of SF magazines, *lianhuanhua* volumes, and comic books, and sometimes travelled afar to meet other SF fans or SF content providers. Their participation in circulating SF media content was limited by the lack of digital media and social media at that time, and thus did not create a full-blown "participatory culture" of media consumers. However, PRC SF media consumers were far from mere "passive spectators" of media.[69]

While Jenkins emphasizes the participatory culture of media convergence, Steinberg focuses more on its commercial aspects. As Steinberg explains his take on media convergence in his seminal work *Anime's Media Mix*, "The term 'convergence' now refers to the ways in which particular texts are made to proliferate across media forms, from television to novel to comic to video games to toy."[70] "Media mix" is the typical Japanese term for media convergence, and specifically "for the cross-media serialization and circulation of entertainment franchises" – media mix "gained its current meaning in the late 1980s."[71] The actual phenomenon of media mix preceded the term itself by a couple of decades, for Japanese anime "in the 1960s as a system of interconnected media and commodity forms was a major turning point and inspiration for the development of what would later be called the media mix."[72] Steinberg first discusses the 1960s media mix strategy of the anime *Astro Boy* (*Tetsuwan Atomu*, 1963–6), and then turns to the media mix strategy of marketing by publisher Kadokawa Books in the 1970s. Steinberg attributes Japan's success in anime and the media mix strategy of marketing to factors such as the materiality and merchandising of popular anime protagonists, the prevalence of televisions in Japanese households, a corporate culture immersed in advertising know-how, and a shift in consumption from Fordism to post-Fordism.

Thaw-era PRC SF transmedia practice lacked Japan's cooperation among media producers, and it did not utilize 1980s Japan's "systematized practice of marketing."[73] For example, even though the subject matter of the thaw-era SF short story "Death Ray on a Coral Island" smoothly adapted to numerous forms of media such as *lianhuanhua*, radio dramas, and a feature film, the production staff of these media did not interact cooperatively with one another in the way we might expect from the sort of convergence culture that Jenkins describes. All of the types of media mentioned above functioned much as disparate silos that produced their own version of the story without cooperation or collaboration with the production staff in other forms of media, who remained similarly isolated.

In sharp contrast with this situation in thaw-era China, Jenkins has borrowed term of "collective intelligence" from French cyber theorist Pierre Lévy to describe cooperation between the production staff of different media outlets: "Collective intelligence can be seen as an alternative source of media power."[74] Instead of reaching out to cooperate with the production staff of other forms of media to create this sort of collective intelligence, thaw-era PRC SF media outlets focused on what Ithiel de Sola Pool describes as a pre-digital "one-to-one relationship" with the core subject matter and perhaps its original author.[75] Having neglected to develop their collective intelligence, thaw-era PRC SF media consequently failed to create a coherent marketing strategy. After all, Deng's economic reforms had barely begun at this juncture, so marketing was still in its infancy in the PRC, which had neither large-scale private film and anime studios such as Japan's Mushi Production, nor major private publishing houses such as Japan's Kadokawa Books.

State-owned PRC publishers and film studios thereupon focused mainly on working internally within their own media forms, hardly ever reaching out to establish external or transversal connectivity with the production staff of other types of media. They almost never engaged in the "relationality discourse" that Steinberg describes as underpinning contemporary Japan's media mix. This relationality discourse includes such relationships as between "the company brand and its individual products," and "the interrelation of different aspects of a single product or product line's marketing campaign."[76] Contrasting media renditions of *Death Ray on a Coral Island* thus remained isolated from one another, as none of the production staff developed a cooperative transversal marketing strategy with other forms of media to promote their products as a unitary or comprehensive brand.

Steinberg further argues that the shift of Japan's culture of consumption from Fordism to post-Fordism played a key role in the success of media mix from the 1960s to 1980s: "The anime media mix and its Kadokawa extension are exemplary of the shift to post-Fordist experiential commodities."[77] Consumer durables "were the mainstay of the Fordist era of production and consumption," and had formed the core of consumption in early postwar Japan.[78] Consumer durables such as automobiles and refrigerators garner appeal among consumers from their "fixity, permanence, and sheer physical presence."[79] Since the 1960s, the Japanese consumption and production had gradually shifted from Fordism to post-Fordism. "The salient characteristics of the post-Fordist commodity became flexibility, fluidization, miniaturization, and increased portability."[80] Post-Fordist commodities are often "experiential commodities" such as "films, video games, vacation packages, and fashions, whose value to the consumer lies in the experience they provide."[81] According to Steinberg, "The historical transition from Fordism to post-Fordism entailed not only a shift from one commodity type to another (i.e., durable to experiential), but also a shift from a singular, discrete commodity (the television, the car) to a series of media-commodities interrelated through the media mix strategy (the film-novel-song-advertisement media mix or character merchandising as a technology of connection)."[82]

In light of Steinberg's discussion of Fordism and post-Fordism, we can observe that the thaw-era PRC still remained at the Fordist stage of consuming mostly durable commodities. In the Fordist postwar Japan, the "Three Sacred Treasures" of the Shōwa thirties (1955–64) refer to the black-and-white television set, the washing machine, and the refrigerator; the subsequent "Three Cs" of the Shōwa forties (1965–74) were the colour TV, the air conditioner, and the car.[83] In contrast, Mao-era PRC consumers' concept of desirable durable commodities aimed at more basic and less luxurious commodities than those of their Japanese counterparts. For example, in the 1970s, the phrase *sanzhuan yixiang* typified an appropriate set of betrothal gifts for a newly married couple in the PRC. *Sanzhuan* literally means "three things that go around," and refers in practice to a wristwatch, a bicycle, and a sewing machine. *Yixiang* literally means "one thing that makes sound," and refers in practice to a radio. Moving forward to the significantly more prosperous 1980s, the phrase *si da jian* or "four big items" denoted a set of appropriate betrothal gifts for a newly married couple in the PRC: a TV, a washing machine, a refrigerator, and a cassette tape recorder.[84] Though Chinese people's consumption during the post-Mao era still focused primarily on commodities that had "features of durability, longevity, performance and utility,"[85] many SF narratives and films started to promote a more futuristic lifestyle and post-Fordist patterns of consumption. Relatively well-educated, urban Chinese people were most attracted to the latter sort of lifestyle and approach to the increased consumption of experiential and cultural commodities. This incipient consumption of experiential commodities helps explain the thaw-era growth in popularity of PRC SF in *lianhuanhua*, radio dramas, feature films, and animated films.

SF's transmedia practice gave rise to pop culture icons such as the "Scientific Holmes" Jin Ming, along with youthful standard-bearers of science such as Sanmao, Keke, and Xiao Lingtong. However, thaw-era PRC transmedia SF narratives were not associated with the "character merchandising" of pop culture icons, in sharp contrast with the pop culture scene in 1960s Japan. Character merchandising here means "the selling of rights to produce character goods based on proprietary characters, thereby gaining income in the form of royalties."[86] We thus do not see thaw-era PRC SF media engaging in relevant commercial practices such as distributing stickers of sponsors' brands, profit-sharing with toy manufacturers who use the images of iconic characters, and collaborating with advertisers who draw upon the images of iconic characters in their ads.

Animation and TV commercials have strongly buttressed character merchandising in Japan's media mix, and played an important role in introducing TV advertisements to the thaw era PRC. Steinberg argues that *Tetsuwan Atomu*'s 1963 broadcast marked "a shift in the relation between commodities and advertisement."[87] As early as the 1960s in Japan, "animated character became a central element of media forms, advertising, and consumption."[88] In contrast, the TV commercial was an entirely new concept for thaw-era PRC media. Along with overseas Chinese TV advertising such as in Hong Kong and Taiwan, Japan's anime series *Tetsuwan Atomu* played a key role in introducing TV advertisements to PRC tele-broadcasting during the thaw era.

The PRC state-owned Chinese Central TV network (CCTV), headquartered in Beijing, started to broadcast *Tetsuwan Atomu* in December 1980 through an intermediary named Han Qingyu, who was a PRC expatriate then living and working in Japan. Han's advertisement company, Xiangyang She (Sunflower Society), played a key role in enabling CCTV to rebroadcast *Tetsuwan Atomu* in dubbed Chinese. One of Han's old friends named Ruan Ruolin was serving as vice director of CCTV at that time. Han urged Ruan to have CCTV adopt the business model of "programs with attached advertisements" (*jiemu dai guanggao*) as a way of importing broadcasts of Japanese anime programming to the PRC. According to this business model, a corporate advertiser such as Casio would purchase the copyright for CCTV broadcasts of *Tetsuwan Atomu* to the PRC television audience. As part of the agreement, CCTV would broadcast a Casio commercial near the beginning of each episode in order to remunerate the corporate sponsor for having paid for the program's broadcasting rights in the PRC. In this way, CCTV did not need to pay copyright or royalties to broadcast *Tetsuwan Atomu* in dubbed Chinese form. As a result of the great popularity of *Tetsuwan Atomu* among PRC TV viewers, Casio electronic watches became an especially famous and top-selling commodity in the PRC. Other Japanese anime TV programs soon followed as rebroadcasts dubbed in Chinese on CCTV – invariably in the form of "programs with attached advertisements," such as *Ikkyū-san* (Monk Ikkyū, 1975–82) and *Hana no Ko Lunlun* (The Flower Child Lunlun, 1979–80).[89] Before *Tetsuwan Atomu* and overseas Chinese models of advertising brought advertising knowhow to the PRC, the character-based pop culture icons in PRC SF had existed in isolation from effective commercial promotion.

The lack of an advertising strategy for thaw-era SF is also reflected in the interconnections between a book and a film with the same title. For a given title in both cinematic and print form in Japan, Kadokawa Books used "the new film to advertise for the novel, thereby producing a synergetic relation between them" in the 1970s.[90] Kadokawa Books thus treated "films and novels as exchangeable, that is to say, as connected, communicating commodities, and as advertisements for each other."[91] "Film-as-advertisement became the model of the commodity form in the culturization of the commodity – the elevation of the commodified cultural form into the preeminent commodity form."[92] In contrast, the thaw-era PRC lacked this "culturalization of the commodity." The short story "Death Ray on a Coral Island" and its later cinematic adaptation did not establish any sort of connection in promotion and advertising. The book publishers and film studios still remained isolated in their own silos, focusing on their own local business practices instead of collaborating in marketing and promotion.

On the basis of comparisons with post-war Japan in particular, it can be argued that thaw-era PRC SF had at most a fledgling and largely undeveloped level of media convergence. It was fledgling because it did not achieve anything close to the level of media mix and convergence that Steinberg and Jenkins found in Japan and the United States, respectively. Several pieces of the jigsaw puzzle are missing from the picture of mature media convergence, such as active consumer participation in circulating the content; cooperation between the production staff of different forms of media; and the commodification of characters as pop culture icons through advertisement. These missing features result from several problems in the thaw-era PRC: backwardness in digital media technology; lack of advertising know-how; the mere beginning stages of marketizing the economy; and the paucity of post-Fordist patterns of consumption. In spite of these problems, the transmedia practice of PRC SF embodies a promising trend towards media convergence: "the continuous, serial consumption across media texts."[93]

Steinberg points to the significant impact of media mix on the literary text: "Within the model of the anime media mix established by *Tetsuwan Atomu* and extended into film and literature by Kadokawa Books, the unity of a 'work' as previously conceived was broken down into multiple, serialized fragments."[94] Film and television theorist John Ellis similarly stresses the episodic or segmented nature of TV programming: "TV offers relatively discrete segments: small sequential unities of images and sounds whose maximum duration seems to be about five minutes."[95] In contrast, Raymond Williams proposes "the concept of flow to explain the organization (by the broadcasting agency) and the experience (by the TV viewer) of television as a continuous succession or flow of more or less tightly connected sequences of image and sound, as the flow of ad segments and program segments, and as the flow of larger units within the daily schedule of programs as represented in the TV listings of the newspaper."[96] Steinberg links Raymond Williams's conception of flow with John Ellis's concept of segment by arguing that "the logic of continuity between segments is provided by the serial or series forms, which work to manage the intervals between segments, thus giving rise to the experience of flow."[97]

Even though Steinberg, Ellis, and Williams all discuss the impact of TV on literary texts, their arguments shed light on the impact of transmedia on literary texts. Through transmedia linkages, PRC SF expanded "from a model of the text as a relatively self-enclosed entity to the text as a transmedia fragment."[98] Multiple levels of iteration of the text through different media can break the text into segments, but can also be experienced as an integral unit. Transmedia practice enables the SF contents to flow across different forms of media as both a segmentation and an integral unit. For example, the unity of the short story "Death Ray on a Coral Island" was broken down into multiple and serialized fragments of prose narrative, illustrated books, radio dramas, and a film. The fragmentation and flow across multiple media texts transport the narrative into spaces that had formerly been beyond the reach of the original short story. In this way, the SF characters and subject matter found their way into people's consciousness through media fragments and flow. In another example, daily serialization in newspapers and serial *lihuanhua* volumes of the Jin Ming series expanded the narrative world of detective Jin Ming and kept it refreshingly new for the reader. The characters in SF narratives migrated across radio dramas and films, and encouraged consumption of the original work of fiction as well as other SF narratives by the same author.

Because of this continuous and serial consumption of PRC SF across different forms of media, PRC SF has achieved a fledgling level of media convergence within its own genre. This multimedia flow of content attracted popular attention to the genre of SF, thereby increasing its visibility. Even though the production staff of different forms of media did not collaborate in marketing the same title across different forms of media, all media formats of consumption of a given SF title helped to grow the popularity of SF as a genre. This process has enabled PRC SF to transform from an overwhelmingly literary genre to a transmedia realm of popular culture.

8 Blooming, Contending, and Boundary-Breaking Even in a Genre of Government-Backed Literature

Previous chapters have offered a survey of the PRC SF scene and assessments of post-Mao SF works by the best-known veteran writers as well as the often overlooked tech-SF writers. This section of the book draws together key supporting arguments from previous chapters to substantiate my thesis that PRC SF of the post-Mao cultural thaw was a government-backed literature, and yet could be aptly characterized as blooming, contending, and boundary-breaking. On the one hand, thaw era SF showed great autonomy by redefining the genre during a transitional period that harkened back to the Hundred Flowers era of cultural blooming and contending. On the other hand, PRC SF during this period was a government-backed literature that helped to popularize and support government policies, while meshing adroitly with governmental rhetoric about strengthening the state through science and technology. In order to substantiate my thesis, I will clarify how post-Mao SF writers dealt with the troubling legacy of socialist realism, probe the connections between thaw-era SF and PRC SF from before and after the thaw era, and explore SF's resonance with contemporary mainstream literary trends. When addressing these issues, I will also relate my analyses to Darko Suvin's concept of "cognitive estrangement" in SF, and Rudolph Wagner's hypothesis of post-Mao Chinese SF as a variety of "lobby literature."[1]

The Legacy of Socialist Realism

Twentieth-century Chinese literature underwent alternate phases of embracing social realism at one juncture and socialist realism at another. During the first half of the twentieth century, many Chinese fiction writers "preferred a conscientious but technically unadventuresome social realism" that aimed to expose injustices and other social problems in a country riven by internecine conflicts – novelists including Mao Dun, Ba Jin, and Wu Zuxiang.[2] Leo Ou-Fan Lee indicates that "the concept of realism" took on "an ethical weight, a kind of patriotic pan-moralism, which tended to govern creative writing, especially in the 1930s.... The obsession with social reality served to perpetuate a new didacticism, which encouraged message-giving and literature's 'social effect.'"[3] In the wake of Mao Zedong's highly prescriptive Yan'an Talks of 1942, Chinese literary social realism changed course and instead emphasized "the correct attitude of the writer, the need for a popular language comprehensible to the masses, [and] the pre-requisite of 'extolling' and not 'exposing' revolutionary reality."[4] Exposure of the dark side of the socialist system under single-party Leninist rule hardly ever occurred in PRC literature of the 1950s and 1960s. Instead, as PRC writers mostly felt compelled to adopt the didactic Soviet style of socialist realism, "China's readers were left with rosy socialist realist formulas, leavened only by modified folk literary forms and dialect," such as in the fiction of Zhou Libo, Hao Ran, and Zhao Shuli.[5] During the Hundred Flowers phase of the late 1950s, a modest amount of "the engagé literature of social realism reappeared," such as Wang Meng's novella *The Young Newcomer in the Organization Department* (*Zuzhibu laile ge nianqingren*, 1956) and Liu Binyan's short story "On the Bridge Worksite" ("Zai qiaoliang gongdi shang," 1956).[6] After the Cultural Revolution came to an end in the latter half of 1976 following Mao's death, socialist realism dwindled over the next few years as more and more PRC writers gravitated towards the post-Mao revival of social realism. Kinkley points out that PRC society in the post-Mao era was groping for alternative trajectories to what they had endured under Mao's rule; serious and popular literature alike served partly as windows into society during this cultural thaw.[7] Readers of PRC fiction could thereby peek behind the facade of normalcy through such windows in order to observe curious socio-political actualities that had long been obscured.[8]

Shifts between socialist realism and social realism that occurred in mainstream PRC literature found an echo in PRC SF. During the 1950s and 1960s, PRC SF leaned overwhelmingly towards socialist realism. This Mao-era preference for socialist realism shrank but did not entirely disappear during the post-Mao cultural thaw. Meanwhile, the pre-Maoist modern tradition of social realism witnessed a major revival in PRC SF, much as mainstream thaw-era fiction adopted a more critical stance towards contemporary society and politics than anything written during the Mao era. By the 1990s, socialist realism dwindled ever further in the face of relatively vibrant New Wave PRC SF; at the same time, social realism continued to make its presence felt in such socially engaged SF as in Wang Jinkang's (b. 1948) *Ant Life* (*Yisheng*, 2007) and Han Song's (b. 1965) *My Fatherland Does Not Have a Dream* (*Wo de zuguo bu zuomeng*, 2002).

Some scholars have explored areas of overlap between socialist realist mainstream literature and socialist realist SF. In his study of Soviet SF, Leonid Heller argues that "the near-future science fiction [of the USSR] retains all the principal features [and] all the structural traits of socialist realist literature."[9] Soviet author Anatoly Britikov defines SF in the context of socialist realism: "If one studies the well-known characteristics of socialist realism – its fusion of romanticism and realism, the representation of life in its revolutionary development, the active socialist ideal – one realizes that, in principle, they present all the characteristics of a science fantasy."[10] Britikov's argument reveals the common characteristics of socialist realist literature and socialist SF in the Stalinist Soviet. Elana Gomel's study of Soviet SF during the post-Stalin thaw era expresses a similar view:

> In fact, the difference between Socialist Realism and Socialist sf becomes negligible at that time. Many of the ostensibly "realistic" texts of Stalinism are unabashedly utopian, not only in the sense of painting a picture of life in the USSR that has nothing in common with the sordid and violent reality, but also in their attempt to develop a new concept of character that reflects the ongoing project of creating the New Man. Sf, on the other hand … sets its sights on the very near future. The result of this convergence is the creation of a shared literary world that masks the horror of the Gulag in two senses: covering it up and yet also outlining its contours as a mask outlines the contours of the face.[11]

Though these scholars' comments focus on Soviet socialist SF, the close connection between socialist realism and socialist SF was also prominent in PRC SF during the Mao era. The PRC SF critic Wu Yan has argued that when examining the corpus of PRC SF, we have to acknowledge the strong influence that the former Soviet Union exerted upon it, both in Soviet literary thought and SF works themselves. As a result of this strong influence from Soviet literary thought and translations of Soviet SF into Chinese, Soviet notions about the "new socialist man" and the "inevitable" march to a "glorious" future under communism became staple ingredients of Mao-era SF narratives.[12] In their seminal studies of PRC SF of the 1950s and the post-Mao era respectively, Nicolai Volland and Rudolph Wagner both offer convincing proof of how strongly Soviet socialist realism influenced PRC SF.

In "Soviet Spaceships in Socialist China: Reading Soviet Russian Popular Literature in the 1950s," Volland claims that in the larger context of "learning from the Soviet Union," PRC translators and scholars introduced a substantial amount of Soviet literature into their country, including such classics of socialist realism as Nikolai Ostrovsky's (1904–36) *How the Steel Was Tempered*, Soviet treatises on literary theory, and genres of popular literature such as SF and adventure novels.[13] Even though "ideological and didactic concerns are central to the classics of socialist realism," popular fiction in the Soviet Union and other Warsaw Pact nations also tended to feature "action heroes and glimpses of a future with almost limitless possibilities."[14] Volland emphasizes that Soviet SF narratives "filled a gap left by the banning of both Chinese and Western pulp fiction after 1949," and "kindled the imagination through the projection of futuristic images like space stations and interplanetary travel, fearless anti-capitalist spymasters, and roaming borderland."[15] Soviet SF's "popular images of a technologically empowered future fueled by a superior morality and ideology" also frequently appeared in PRC SF of the 1950s, and continued through the early 1980s.[16] The preoccupation of PRC SF with scientific and technological minutiae also bear the mark of influence from Soviet SF. Volland adds that socialist realism "tied in nicely with the value systems and promises about a future socialist utopia that the CCP sought to disseminate through other channels."[17]

Wagner also argues that PRC popular fiction from the 1950s to the 1970s came under the strong influence of Stalin Era Soviet popular fiction, particularly with respect to an optimism and interest in scientific progress, as well as a fascination with high-tech gadgets and suspenseful narratives.[18] He explains how PRC SF from the 1950s through the 1970s tended to remain within a framework of socialist realism: "Gorki demanded that socialist literature combine 'active' romanticism with realism. After Mao Zedong's directive of 1958, Zhou Yang and Guo Moruo developed this into the Chinese version of socialist realism. Revolutionary romanticism is supposed to show the buds of the great future in the realities of today. Science-phantasy fiction is 'realistic' with its science element, and shows 'revolutionary romanticism' with its 'phantasy' component. Within this framework, there are differences of opinion both in theory and literary practice."[19] Theoretical disquisitions and literary works themselves both bore the stamp of socialist realism in PRC thaw-era SF. Treatises by Tong Enzheng, Xiao Jianheng, and Ye Yonglie discuss the complementary relationship between romanticism and realism in SF. For example, Xiao Jianheng defined SF "as a romantic literature within the doctrine of socialist realism" and ascribed the "pronounced romanticism" of SF to such popular classic novels as *Journey to the West*.[20] The PRC discourse of socialist realism helped convince many PRC SF writers to fall in line with the party-state's vision of an uncomplicated march in lockstep towards a glorious future. Many PRC readers of SF in turn bought into fantasies that a sort of scientific utopia would unfold within their own lifetimes. Many PRC SF narratives also eulogized the heroic collective subject, and relentlessly demonized "enemies," real and imagined.

Zheng Wenguang's *Flying toward Sagittarius* epitomizes the sort of socialist realist framework one can find in many post-Mao thaw SF narratives. Three young protagonists begin their involuntary space journey as a result of a conspiracy that the envious "Polar Bear" (Russia) has hatched. Because they learn as much as possible about how to make their space mission a success, they set themselves up for eventual rescue by other Chinese scientists. The novel thus eulogizes heroic collectivism while denouncing the plot of the adversarial country to thwart the PRC's space program. The novel also features youth-directed science popularization, suspense, and romantic love. These prominent characteristics of socialist realism are also evident in Tong Enzheng's revised vision of *Dense Fog over the Old Gorge*, the tech SF short story "A Golden Carpet Extending to the Horizon," and other works discussed in previous chapters.

Social Realism and SF's Resonance with Contemporary Literary Trends

Even though many SF works from the late 1970s to early 1980s bore the imprint of socialist realism, other SF narratives turned aside from socialist realism in order to address social problems such as bureaucratism, environmental degradation, and official corruption, while expressing pessimism about the prospects of science and technology. Wagner claims that such "pessimism is articulated in two scenarios: an eventual takeover by robots, and a terminal nuclear World War III."[21] These pessimistic concerns are reflected in such works as Xiao Jianheng's two robot stories "Professor Shalom's Confusion" and "Qiao the Younger Fell Ill," along with Zheng Wenguang's novel *Descendant of Mars*. Even in Zheng Wenguang's *Flying toward Sagittarius*, with its socialist realist framework and optimistic ending, one can detect the writer's concern about a future nuclear world war breaking out. Such features of social realism in PRC SF result from the genre's resonance with contemporary trends in mainstream PRC literature.

In Lee Yee's study of realism in Chinese literature around the 1980s, he uses the term "new realism" to refer to a spate of PRC fiction that emerged in the spring of 1979 and "revealed aspects of the reality of the Chinese experience previously suppressed in literature," such as "an economic system at a virtual halt, decreasing productivity in poorly managed factories, extreme poverty for those in the villages, administrative organizations riddled with corruption and materialism, and a bureaucracy unreceptive to the needs of its people."[22] These realist exposés of serious problems in PRC society found a vehicle in not only mainstream fiction, but in SF as well. For example, Tong Enzheng's "The First Defeat" reveals contemporary problems of decreasing productivity and poor managerial effectiveness. Xiao Jianheng's "Qiao the Younger Fell Ill" exposes a bureaucracy that routinely ignores the basic needs of the populace. In addition to exposing problems in PRC society, thaw-era SF narratives also celebrated humanistic values such as upholding the rule of law and drawing strength from China's cultural inheritance. By doing so, these SF narratives resonated with many contemporary works of fiction in the categories of "scar literature," "contemplative literature," and "roots-seeking literature." The discussion in chapter 2 of Zheng Wenguang's narratives *Star Labor Camp*, *Philosopher*, and "Destiny Nightclub" and in chapter 3 of Ye Yonglie's *Black Shadow* all illustrate how these novellas resonate with the thematic concerns frequently encountered in "scar literature" and "contemplative literature."

In addition, some post-Mao-thaw SF writers "extended their allotted time span in the other direction, the past."[23] Wagner notes that some PRC SF narratives deal with "the hidden wisdom of the Chinese ancestors, which is preserved in written records, as of astronomical observations."[24] For example, Tong Enzheng's "Song of the Stalagmites" portrays how ancient Chinese writers of poems and historical treatises recorded a variety of astronomical phenomena in detail. This effort of harkening to China's ancient past resembles the mid-1980s mainstream literary trend of "roots-seeking," which "indicates a historical endeavor, assessing what is happening now in the light of what happened in the past."[25]

In addition to resonating with contemporary trends in mainstream PRC fiction, some SF narratives assimilated elements from other popular genres such as love stories and detective fiction. In his study of Chinese love stories written between 1978 and 1981, Kam Louie argues that the prominence of a love interest in so many thaw-era short stories, poems, plays, and film scripts provides evidence of "a more liberal and individualistic trend that has typified Chinese thinking" at that historical juncture.[26] Those loves stories include such works as Zhang Jie's "Love Cannot Be Neglected" ("Ai shi buneng wangji de," 1979), Zhang Kangkang's "The Right to Love" ("Aide quanli," 1979), and Ru Zhijuan's

"The Love of Sons and Daughters" ("Ernü qing," 1980). While those love stories prioritize the value of "love above all else," they also reveal "recurrent problems such as the deforming pressures exerted on lovers by economic hardship and traditional morality."[27] Some love stories deal with more "unorthodox" aspects of love, such as couples with a large age difference, incestuous couples, and love triangles, as in Kong Jiesheng's "Across the River" ("Zai xiaohe nabian," 1979) and Chen Guokai's "What Should I Do" ("Wo yinggai zenme ban," 1979). However, most of these love stories stress the theme of "choosing the right person with the right political perspective."[28] The writers "emphasized love's political and moral aspects in their attempts to define it" as "a relationship between two people whose aim in life is to build socialism in China."[29] Similarly, many contemporary SF narratives also contain a love interest. For example, a young male scientist in Tong Enzheng's *Faraway Love* enters into a love relationship with a cloned alien woman. However, they decide to live apart from one another in response to the demands of their jobs and because "love is a feeling that not only concerns two people, but is strengthened by the love of work and society."[30] In Tong's "The First Defeat" and Zheng Wenguang's *Flying toward Sagittarius*, love also brings a couple together, but plays second fiddle to the overriding importance of industrial production and the country's space program.

In addition to overlapping with contemporary mainstream love stories, thaw-era SF also sometimes merged partially with contemporary crime fiction. The most prominent example is Ye Yonglie's Jin Ming series. Wagner observes that "the elements of suspense (*jingxian*) had its legitimacy only as a sugar-coating around the bitter but healthful pills of science which were administered to youth."[31] Ye Yonglie admitted, "I have sometimes grafted various techniques of the thriller onto my works of science fiction. Many thrillers focus upon drawing the reader in at once with an alarming incident near the very beginning."[32] Ye's Jin Ming narratives resonate with Deng Xiaoping's repeated insistence that "practice is the sole criterion for arriving at truth"; this positivist spirit would further buttress the widespread faith in scientific progress amongst the PRC populace.[33] And like most PRC post-Mao crime fiction, Ye's detective SF thrillers uphold aspirations to the rule of law in the PRC. Kinkley points out that "China since the thaw in the late 1970s has seen a renaissance of writing about crime and police procedure," and "delivers a strong message about China's need for more 'rule of law' and 'legal system.'"[34] "Rule of law" is "a slogan co-opted by the Deng Xiaoping regime to popularize everything it does in the legal sphere, reformist or retrograde."[35] It "indicates a commitment to a greater role for legal institutions in running society and is indeed linked to such populist sentiments as 'equality before the law,'" and "is also a basic legal spirit opposed to 'rule by men.'"[36] "Rule by men" refers to "China's traditional Confucian and revolutionary Maoist disdain for governing society by 'arbitrary' laws, when the state has available to it the more discriminating judgment of wise 'men.'"[37] The long-standing judicial practice of "rule by men" as portrayed in pre-modern Chinese detective fiction goes back to traditional Chinese "criminal-case" (*gong'an*) fiction, in which "a renowned wise judge (such as Bao, Di, or Peng) solves a difficult crime."[38] Kinkley indicates that the motif of *pingfan* (meaning "to reverse an unjust verdict") in *gong'an* fiction became very popular in post-Mao crime fiction. This thaw-era fascination with *pingfan* results from the fact that "so many trumped-up verdicts 'of the Gang of Four' have been reversed in real life" during this phase of the PRC's history.[39] Numerous thaw-era SF narratives such as *Black Shadow* and "Destiny Nightclub" discussed in chapters 2 and 3 touch upon the theme of reversing unjust verdicts.

In addition to sharing thematic concerns with mainstream fiction and genres of popular fiction, many post-Mao SF narratives dealt with ecological themes that mainstream writers rarely addressed. Tech-SF in particular tends to focus on themes related to ecology and the environment. As discussed in detail in chapter 6, tech-SF narratives often depict solutions to specific environmental problems. For example, "The Blue Encirclement" proposes a solution to water pollution; "The King Lichen" deals with industrial wastes and ecological impacts of construction. "The Girlfriend Who Blows Smoke Rings" proposes a way to eliminate air pollution. This deep concern about environmental issues eventually became a trademark motif of PRC New Wave SF, such as in Liu Cixin's novella *Underground Fire* (*Dihuo*, 2000) and Chen Qiufan's novel *Waste Tide* (*Huangchao*, 2013).

Government-Backed Literature

Wagner's treatise on PRC SF from 1978 to 1981 presents his hypothesis that it "operates as a lobby literature for the scientific community."[40] He insists that he intends nothing pejorative through his choice of terminology: "The term lobby literature is intended as a functional concept, without derogatory connotations."[41] Wagner attempts to substantiate his hypothesis by examining the portrayal in thaw-era SF of the workaday life of scientists, including laboratories and other workplaces, the conceptualizing and financing of scientific projects, and interpersonal relations. Wagner claims that thaw-era SF functioned as a lobby literature in two ways. On the one hand, it allegedly presented "the common aspirations" of the scientific community.[42] Most thaw-era SF writers were working scientists or writers engaged in science popularization, so they were "familiar with the interests and hopes of their peers" and used SF "to express, develop, and mold the common fantasy of their community."[43] On the other hand, thaw-era SF authors allegedly sought the attention of PRC officialdom by presenting "both demands and offers of compromise" from the scientific community.[44] The alleged "demands" included "a self-regulating science republic, with many improvements in the scientists' lives."[45] The alleged "offers of compromise" included "explicit support for the government's various policies, the promise of perfectly moral and patriotic behavior, and contributions to the international renown and defense of China."[46] Wagner's argument demonstrates that "literature may even represent group interests – not necessarily the homogenized interests of Mao's 'worker-peasant-soldier' 'vast majority,' but of groups newly self-conscious in post-Mao society."[47]

Wagner's hypothesis of lobby literature points to individualistic and self-promoting tendencies of thaw-era PRC SF writers, and thus has some basis in actuality. However, upon closer examination of the role of home-grown SF in the PRC party-state's Four Modernizations program, Wagner's hypothesis reveals itself as overblown. The thaw-era PRC government considered SF writers an important contingent of the voices promoting science and technology as advanced productive forces that were key to implementing the Four Modernizations. Therefore, thaw-era PRC SF actually functioned as a type of government-backed literature, whose writers were working more as in-house advocates of a key component of the central government's Four Modernizations agenda than as lobbyists or a group attempting to extract concessions from the government.

Many scholars have noticed the special status PRC SF enjoyed during the early years of the post-Mao era. Kinkley points out that SF enjoyed "more state sponsorship than the other genres, for it popularized scientific knowledge and prepared the way for the privileged role scientists must play in the Four Modernizations."[48] Even Wagner acknowledges that PRC SF "was reinstalled in the context of a renewed emphasis on science in the modernization of the country and a concomitant rehabilitation of the social status of scientists."[49] Thus there is considerable agreement that the PRC party-state favoured SF over other genres of literature during most of the thaw era.

The fervent promotion of science and technology by Deng Xiaoping and the party-state in general was purely pragmatic, as scientific progress was a linchpin of the Four Modernizations. Deng also sought to win the backing of scientists and other intellectuals in his intraparty policy wrangles with old-line Maoists. As for the perspective of thaw-era writers, they largely went along with the CCP's Marxist-Leninist dogma, while being especially appreciative of Deng Xiaoping's innovative ideological addenda, such as his assurance that the intelligentsia would henceforth be considered part of the working class and no longer part of the discredited old "bourgeoisie." Furthermore, even though many well-known PRC writers such as Wang Meng, Liu Binyan, and Zheng Wenguang had been persecuted for a considerable portion of the Mao era as the result of higher-ups' ideological nitpicking, they had still remained loyal to the CCP.

The close contacts of PRC writers with the nation's scientific community enabled them to portray scientific activity in highly appealing and individualized ways. Deng Xiaoping and the central government valued the viewpoints of these well-connected thaw-era SF writers and used them to help drum up popular support for the CCP's reform-era policies. At the same time, most of these SF writers were happy to compromise with the party-state when there were occasional bones of contention. Kam Louie thus notes that "writers sometimes acted as spokesmen for official policies" during the thaw era.[50] SF writers were especially good spokesmen because of the genre's target readership of intellectuals and educated youth. Although the audiences for SF *lianhuanhua*, radio dramas, and SF films came from all walks of life, the relatively elite readership of prose SF derived mainly from professional scientists and engineers, along with their students. SF writers made for a good fit with their target readership, thereby promoting the government's agenda of modernizing China through the assistance of a vitalized sector of science and technology.

The frequent evocation of thaw-era SF cognitive estrangement appeared to foretell a bright future for the PRC. Startled readers of SF often became more confident than ever that the PRC's revitalized scientific community during the new era of reform and opening would soon transform the country into a technologically advanced realm of material abundance. In his grounding-breaking *Metamorphoses of Science Fiction*, Darko Suvin argues for an understanding of SF as the "literature of cognitive estrangement."[51] He defines SF as "a literary genre whose necessary and sufficient conditions are the presence and interaction of estrangement and cognition, and whose main formal device is an imaginative framework alternative to the author's empirical environment."[52] In this definition, "concepts of science [are] for cognition, and fiction for estrangement."[53] Suvin also indicates that "significant modern science fiction, with deeper and more lasting sources of enjoyment, also presupposes more complex and wider cognitions: it discusses primarily the political, psychological, and anthropological use and effect of knowledge, of philosophy, and of science."[54] The framework of cognitive estrangement distinguishes the genre of SF from realist literature and more fanciful genres such as the fairy tale, mythology, and fantasy narratives. Estrangement signifies a break with the empirical world, but is simultaneously beyond the confines of reality through the assistance of a "novum" (strange newness).[55] This sort of estrangement often underpins the aesthetic framework of SF narrative.

Wagner discusses Suvin's concept of "estrangement" in the context of PRC SF in the early post-Mao era. He argues that estrangement "always implies a critical view of the present, by presenting a different future."[56] Wagner goes on to identify three ways that PRC SF evokes estrangement. One is the "extrapolation from the present," which mainly describes the "improved standards in Chinese science as a consequence of current science policies."[57] "Inversion" is another technique. One example is the "depiction in the SF of unlimited resources for scientific activities, and lack of controls, even though tight financial limits and political controls are imposed on present-day science."[58] The third technique is "negation," whereby SF narratives consciously avoid the portrayal of conspicuously negative phenomena in contemporary PRC society.[59]

Wagner's discussion of these three techniques for evoking estrangement appears to support his hypothesis that post-Mao thaw-era SF was a type of lobby literature. Meanwhile, we can also detect the cognitive aspects of the estrangement evoked by these techniques. In the first, the "extrapolation from the present," readers can indeed figure out that "improved standards in Chinese science" are "a consequence of current science policies."[60] Similar ideas that readers can identify in SF narratives also include the scientists' recently elevated social status and the need to humanize science. In most thaw-era SF narratives, scientists engage in heroic activities that deserve celebration. "Many of the [SF] writers were male intellectuals who tended to project their own images into the main characters.... Their social position rose dramatically after the Gang of Four fell. It must have been gratifying for the writers to be able to depict this historical change in their stories."[61] In addition, scientist protagonists often exude a spirit of patriotism. In such SF narratives as "Death Ray on a Coral Island," "Beta Wave," and *Black Shadow*, writers use the motif of "the confrontation of good and bad uses of science" to reveal the patriotic spirit of PRC scientists.[62] Patriotism is "a reliable guide in discovering hidden enemies, and inevitably leads Chinese scientists to China, the only place where discoveries and inventions can be put to positive use."[63] As shown in the above-mentioned three narratives, "the negative and even disastrous consequences might result from a scientific discovery if it ends up in the hands of imperialistic powers," such as Soviet Union and the United States.[64] Only "China's socialist system and promise not to become a hegemonic state ensure that science is free from such negative side effects."[65] Readers could easily link the improved social status of scientists and their patriotism in SF narratives to Deng Xiaoping's speech at the opening ceremony of the National Science Conference in 1978 about building a community of scientists and technologists who would be politically sound and professionally competent.

In addition, many thaw-era SF narratives attempted to humanize socialism and science. They frequently conveyed a confidence in gradual improvements in people's standard of living, and often portrayed a potent synthesis of ideology and science. Utopian motifs that had inspired many PRC SF writers during the 1950s and 1960s reappeared from time to time during the thaw era. This emphasis on humanizing social-technological progress in Chinese thaw-era SF is very similar to that in the Soviet post-Stalin SF. Csicsery-Ronay explains the instrumental significance of humanizing science and socialism to the Khrushchev leadership at that time:

> The emphasis was on "humanizing" social-technological progress, saving utopia from the mechanical laws of Marxist-Leninist history, and encouraging a sense of personal hope in the future. In this sense, sf served the purpose of the Thaw reforms perfectly. It encouraged the scientific intelligentsia and youth to imagine themselves as personally inhabiting the world they would construct – one adequate for them, replete with problems to be solved and obligations to be met. It encouraged a synthesis of personal and social heroism, and it humanized Socialism with a cheerful voice … the pain of the past would be relieved by their futures.[66]

Csicsery-Ronay's assertation reflects the close connection in the contemporary world between cognitive estrangement in SF on the one hand and socio-political realities on the other. Humanizing socialism and science in thaw-era SF texts is an assertion of socialist humanism's superiority to the inhumanity of Mao's Cultural Revolution and other purges.

The cognitive aspects of PRC SF linked contemporary Chinese society to the imagined future of a China benefiting from much more advanced science and technology. Cognitive estrangement envisions some historical cause-and-effect connections between the present and the future. This ability to inspire visions of a gloriously advanced future for China helped make thaw-era SF valuable to the PRC government and worthy of government backing.

Like Soviet post-Stalin thaw-era SF writers, thaw-era PRC SF writers had their own political sensibilities. "Party consciousness remained the guiding principle of approved literature."[67] PRC SF writers also understood the role that SF was playing in the political culture of their country. According to Ye Yonglie, "SF is one of the barometers of [China's] political climate. When the government calls for 'letting a hundred flowers bloom and a hundred schools contend' and advocates on behalf of science, works of science fantasy and science fiction flourish."[68] Most PRC SF writers were members of the Chinese Association for the Popularization of Science at one or another of the three levels – national, provincial, or county. Therefore, "none of the SF narratives could have been published without some sort of approval by officials on the 'outside.'"[69] The publication of thaw-era SF was subject to the approval of the bureaucratic apparatus under Deng Xiaoping, and was contingent upon this bureaucracy's judgment that the socio-political themes of this SF would support and not undermine the CCP's ideologies and policies. Whenever writers or other content creators demanded "excessive" creative freedom or otherwise appeared to undermine the CCP's authoritarian rule, the regime quickly and forcefully shifted to suppression. This explains why post-Mao SF sank to a low ebb on account of the party-state's heavy-handed "Campaign to Eliminate Spiritual Pollution" in 1983 and 1984.

Blooming, Contending, and Boundary-Breaking

The post-Mao cultural thaw functioned as an important period of transition for the genre of PRC SF. On the one hand, thaw-era SF inherited the legacy of Mao-era SF by undertaking a mission to popularize science and technology and often articulate aspects of socialist realism, even while adapting to the Communist Party's startling shift from Mao Zedong's failed policies in politics and economics. On the other hand, PRC SF from this period began to move beyond the traditional categorical boundaries of *kexue wenyi* and juvenile literature, thrived as an increasingly prominent popular genre of PRC literature, and paved the way for the development of the internationally renowned New Wave of PRC SF during the twenty-first century.

Thaw-era PRC SF shares the same traits of "blooming" and "contending" that Michael Duke has identified in PRC mainstream fiction during the same historical period.[70] Blooming refers to the "boom" or rapid growth in popularity of PRC SF during the thaw era. Never before had the PRC literary scene witnessed so many varieties of SF and such an abundance of it within a mere half decade. Its burgeoning readership and professional SF organizations set the stage for the emergence of SF fandom and more nuanced literary criticism and commentary in the PRC as well. As thaw-era SF accumulated more cultural capital, SF writers redefined the genre as sophisticated and serious enough in literary quality to receive major nationwide literary awards for the first time since the PRC's founding. Veteran SF writers such as Zheng Wenguang, Tong Enzheng, Ye Yonglie, and Xiao Jianheng had all been active during the Mao era prior to the Cultural Revolution and the post-Mao thaw era. They all wrote workmanlike SF during the early-to-mid Mao era (1949–65), and found their footing in the genre. After ten years of enforced dormancy during the Cultural Revolution, they had a chance to reflect on their old Mao-era SF and on the genre as a whole. When resuming their writing careers in the late 1970s, they showed more insight into the possibilities of the genre and were bolder about extending its imaginative boundaries beyond the limitations of their Mao-era SF writings. Aside from writing more creatively, veteran SF authors wrote more nuanced literary criticism about SF and engaged in theoretical explorations of the genre. Their critical writings laid a theoretical foundation for PRC SF in the thaw era and beyond. They nurtured and showcased up-and-coming PRC SF writers in edited anthologies, and supported the efforts of literary historians to re-introduce older works of Chinese SF and survey the contemporary SF scene. And thanks to Deng Xiaoping's economic reforms and the party-state's shift to favour market forces, these writers' royalties and other remuneration for their SF publications significantly increased. All told, thaw-era SF achieved commercial success for the first time since 1949, even though the transmedia practice of SF did not reach the level of the Japanese media mix or the media convergence in the West. In addition, even a sense of community developed as professional SF organizations and fandom clubs brought together writers, editors, readers, and researchers.

Thaw-era SF nonetheless had its share of contentiousness or "contending." Tensions between mainstream literary fiction and upstart SF continued to simmer. Rivalries sometimes flared up between SF writers and critics, as their views about SF as a genre clashed. Although a modest number of thaw-era SF stories and novellas came out in mainstream literary magazines and sometimes even won literary awards, many PRC writers and readers of mainstream literature continued to look askance at the entire genre of SF during this period. Overall, thaw-era

SF writers remained relatively isolated from mainstream literary authors. They formed their own community, joining SF-related associations instead of mainstream literary associations.

The spirit of contending amongst thaw-era SF writers surfaced with particular passion in debates among SF writers, editors, and popular science writers. For example, in 1979 the supplement of the influential state media outlet *China Youth Daily* published a series of opinion pieces entitled "Modest Discussions of Popular Science Writing." They broached such topics as the faulty understanding and over-simplified presentation of scientific ideas in some SF works, and the need to make popular science writing more interesting and entertaining. This newspaper series amounted to twenty-eight opinion pieces during its run of two-and-a-half years (April 1979–November 1981). These opinion pieces came out in an edited volume at the end of 1981. In his preface, Tao Shilong indicates the significance of the discussions: "The authors with various viewpoints freely expressed themselves, criticized one another, and also offered some self-criticisms. Though some of the authors' critiques are barbed, not a single one of these writers was subsequently banned from publishing or suffered ad-hominem attacks. This fact tells us that the era of 'shao shuo wei jia' (the less you say, the better) is now long-gone. An atmosphere of democratic repartee has instead emerged. This edited volume is a good start."[71]

Another factor worth noting was the rapidly increasing number of Chinese translations of non-Russian Western SF works during the early 1980s, which strongly influenced Chinese SF writers. During the cultural thaw, a withering of influence from old Soviet SF was accompanied by a burgeoning influence from Western SF. Thaw-era SF narratives adapted major themes in Western SF. For example, Xiao Jianheng responded to Asimov's *Three Laws* by writing robot stories that echoed Asimov's view that even advanced AI robots would not supersede or take the place of human beings. Ye Yonglie drew upon motifs from Japanese and European detective fiction when creating his new hybrid subgenre of the SF thriller. Zheng Wenguang found much of the inspiration for his Mars narratives from Western terraforming fiction. Tong Enzheng's participation in an international writing project helped to spur his fascination with composing SF about alien invasions. The thaw era was also the juncture at which writers and scholars such as Dingbo Wu, Ye Yonglie, and Tong Enzheng started to introduce PRC SF to Western readers and academic circles through translations, conferences, and scholarly articles. This post-Mao trend of bidirectional cultural and scholarly communication has internationalized PRC SF to unprecedented levels by the twenty-first century, with New Wave SF novelists such as Liu Cixin winning the Hugo Award as the world's top SF novelist for 2015.

This study of PRC SF during the post-Mao cultural thaw helps us better understand the contemporary wave of PRC SF that has gained global recognition, especially since the 2010s. Research findings in this book reveal that many of the characteristics usually associated with New Wave Chinese SF actually appeared in PRC SF as early as the thaw era; these features include a somewhat sceptical or even subversive political bent, a deep familiarity and engagement with the canon of Western SF, and a wide range of themes and narrative techniques.

Notes

1. The Field of Chinese Science Fiction, 1976–1983

1 Song, "Variations on Utopia in Contemporary Chinese Science Fiction," 90.
2 For a detailed discussion of the "Campaign to Eliminate Spiritual Pollution," see Gold, "Just in Time!" 947–74.
3 Gelder, *Popular Fiction*, 75.
4 Gelder, *Popular Fiction*, 75.
5 Gelder, *Popular Fiction*, 75.
6 Bourdieu, *Field of Cultural Production*, 29–73.
7 Johnson, "Editor's Introduction," 16.
8 Johnson, "Editor's Introduction 17.
9 Csicsery-Ronay, "Science Fiction and the Thaw," 337.
10 Csicsery-Ronay, "Science Fiction and the Thaw," 337.
11 Link, *Uses of Literature*, 15–36.
12 Link, *Uses of Literature*, 41.
13 Link, *Uses of Literature*, 41.
14 Link, *Uses of Literature*, 36–41.
15 Link, *Uses of Literature*, 5.
16 Johnson, "Editor's Introduction," 15.
17 Johnson, "Editor's Introduction," 15.
18 Johnson, "Editor's Introduction," 16.
19 Duke, *Blooming and Contending*, 29.
20 Duke, *Blooming and Contending*, 30.
21 Duke, *Blooming and Contending*, 44.
22 Duke, *Blooming and Contending*, 37.
23 Li Jingze, "Wo buxiang tanlun bashi niandai."
24 "Ershi shiji bashi niandai."
25 "Ershi shiji bashi niandai."
26 Link, *Uses of Literature*, 214–16.

27 Link, *Uses of Literature*, 215.
28 Link, *Uses of Literature*, 217.
29 World Bank Data, "Urban Population: China."
30 Duke, *Blooming and Contending*, 34.
31 Gelder, *Popular Fiction*, 40.
32 Johnson, "Editor's Introduction," 15.
33 Wu Dingbo, "Chinese Science Fiction," 264.
34 Wu Yan raised this insightful observation at the International Conference of Utopian and Science Fiction Studies, Beijing, 3–4 December 2016.
35 Zheng Wenguang, "Kexue wenyi zatan," 80.
36 Zheng Wenguang, "Kexue wenyi zatan," 81.
37 Link, *Uses of Literature*, 16.
38 Deng, "Deng Xiaoping zai quanguo kexue dahui kaimushi shang de jianghua."
39 Tang, "Wo yu kepu chuangzuo zazhi."
40 Tang, "Wo yu kepu chuangzuo zazhi."
41 Rao Zhonghua edited three volumes of *Zhongguo kehuan xiaoshuo daquan* [A compendium of Chinese science fiction], which were published in 1982. My calculation of the total number of SF stories published in 1978 is based on the stories included in these volumes.
42 Deng, "Zai zhongguo wenxue yishu gongzuozhe disici daibiao dahui shang de zhuci."
43 Link, *Uses of Literature*, 27.
44 Wu Dingbo, "Looking Backward," xxvi–xxviii.
45 Wu Dingbo, "Looking Backward," xxii.
46 The original Chinese text was published in *Renmin ribao* [People's daily], 16 November 1983, 1. I am using Thomas B. Gold's English translation. See Gold, "Just in Time!" 952.
47 Chu, "Xin shiqi tongsu wenxue xingqi xianxiang chongxi," 115.
48 Gold, "Just in Time!," 972.
49 Li Yang, "Kehuan shijie."
50 Gold, "Just in Time!" 962.
51 Wu Dingbo, "Looking Backward," xxvii.
52 Johnson, "Editor's Introduction," 7.
53 Gelder, *Popular Fiction*, 91.
54 Gelder, *Popular Fiction*, 90–6.
55 "Ershi shiji bashi niandai."
56 Chu, "Xin shiqi tongsu wenxue xingqi xianxiang chongxi," 114–21.
57 Ashley, *Science Fiction Rebels*, 239–45.
58 Ashley, *Science Fiction Rebels*, 240.
59 In a conversation with the author, 9 July 2020, Wu Yan indicated that, strictly speaking, it should be "the three magazines" instead of "the four

magazines," because *Kexue shidai* (Age of science) was a science popularization magazine in which there was only one small section for science fiction.

60 Ashley, *Science Fiction Rebels*, 240.
61 For the detailed history of this newspaper, see Zhang Xiyu, "Zhongguo diyi jia kehuan xiaoshuobao yaozhe shimo," 27–30.
62 Zhang Feng, "Zhongguo kehuan zazhi jijian shi."
63 Gelder, *Popular Fiction*, 92–3.
64 Wu Dingbo, "Chinese Science Fiction," 269.
65 Wu Dingbo, "Chinese Science Fiction," 269–70.
66 Gelder, *Popular Fiction*, 92.
67 Rao, *Zhongguo kehuan xiaoshuo daquan*, 1:4–8.
68 Gelder, *Popular Fiction*, 2.
69 Wu Dingbo, "Fandom in China," 134–6.
70 Liu Jian, "Ershi shiji jiushi niandai zhongguo kehuan aihaozhe zazhi zongshu."
71 Zhang Feng, "Shei shi xia yige Yao Haijun."
72 Zheng Jun, *Zhongguo kehuan zhi lu*.
73 Liu Jian, "Ershi shiji jiushi niandai zhongguo kehuan aihaozhe zazhi zongshu."
74 Liu Jian, "Ershi shiji jiushi niandai zhongguo kehuan aihaozhe zazhi zongshu."
75 Zhang Feng, "Shei shi xia yige Yao Haijun."
76 Johnson, "Editor's Introduction," 7.
77 Johnson, "Editor's Introduction," 7.
78 Gelder, *Popular Fiction*, 91.
79 Gelder, *Popular Fiction*, 97.
80 Wu Dingbo, "Chinese Science Fiction," 265.
81 Liu Cixin, "Shanhu dao shang de siguang."
82 Yao and Yang, "Kehuan Shijie sanshi nian."
83 Ye, "Rongyu fenzhi," 421–39.
84 Ye, "Rongyu fenzhi," 492.
85 Ye, "Rongyu fenzhi," 477.
86 Johnson, "Editor's Introduction," 9.
87 Johnson, "Editor's Introduction," 19–20.
88 The editor, Meiyun Liu, wrote an introductory essay about Zheng Wenguang entitled "The Father of Chinese Science Fiction" and published it in the first issue of *Asia 2000* (May 1981): 45–6, in Hong Kong to accompany the English translation of Zheng Wenguang's "The Mirror Image of the Earth." In October 1981, the Chinese SF writers Ye Yonglie and Chen Yu translated this essay into Chinese.Ever since Ye and Chen's translation came out, Zheng has been known as "the father of Chinese SF."

89 Gelder, *Popular Fiction*, 90. For Bourdieu's detailed discussion of economic capital, see his *Field of Cultural Production*, 29–37, and *Rules of Art*, 216–17.
90 Zheng Wenguang, "Bian hou ji," 341–2.
91 Wu Dingbo, "Chinese Science Fiction," 266.
92 Liu Cixin, "Shanhu dao shang de siguang."
93 Wu Dingbo, "Chinese Science Fiction," 267–8.
94 For detailed information of the remuneration of PRC writers from the 1950s to the late 1980s, see Wu Bin's "Xin Zhongguo chengli chuqi gaochou zhidu de zhiding yu xiugai"; and Zhou Lin's "Xin Zhongguo gaochou zhidu yanbian yu zuozhe diwei de bianhua."
95 Ye, "Rongyu feizhi," 421–3.
96 Li Qiang, "Naoti daogua yu woguo shichang jingji fazhan de liangge jieduan," 6.
97 Wang Defeng, "Wo suo jieshi de Ye Yonglie," 19.
98 Wang Yafa, "Huiyi Tong Enzheng."
99 Dong, "Liu Xingshi."
100 Gelder, *Popular Fiction*, 29.
101 Gelder, *Popular Fiction*, 13.
102 Bourdieu, *Rules of Art*, 218.
103 Gelder, *Popular Fiction*, 2.
104 Wagner, "Lobby Literature," 19.
105 Johnson, "Editor's Introduction," 6.
106 Johnson, "Editor's Introduction," 7.
107 Kinkley, *After Mao*, 11.

2. A Study of Zheng Wenguang's Mars Series

1 Part of this chapter was previously published in Li Hua, "'Are We, People from the Earth, so Terrible?'" Also see note 88 in chapter 1.
2 *Descendant of Mars* was completed in April 1983. Zheng was hospitalized and diagnosed with the life-threatening ailment of cerebral thrombosis soon after he finished the manuscript. Therefore, this novel turned out to be Zheng's last SF work. All translations from *Descendant of Mars* and Zheng's critical essays are my own.
3 Volland, "Comment on 'Let's Go to the Moon,'" 354.
4 For the translation of Soviet Russian SF and popular science works and their influence on Chinese SF and popular science, see Volland, "Soviet Spaceships in Socialist China."
5 Zheng Wenguang, "Tantan kexue huanxiang xiaoshuo," 21.
6 Chen, *Qinli zhongguo kehuan*, 74–5.
7 Chen, *Qinli zhongguo kehuan*, 74–5.

8 Volland, "Comment on 'Let's Go to the Moon,'" 354.
9 Chen, *Qinli zhongguo kehuan*, 74.
10 Volland, "Comment on 'Let's Go to the Moon,'" 356.
11 Chen, *Qinli zhongguo kehuan*, 75.
12 "The Second Moon" was serialized in four installations in *China Youth Daily* on 23, 25, 27, and 30 November 1954.
13 Volland, "Soviet Spaceships in Socialist China," 205.
14 Zheng Wenguang, "Tantan kexue huanxiang xiaoshuo," 22.
15 Volland, "Soviet Spaceships in Socialist China," 208.
16 Volland, "Soviet Spaceships in Socialist China," 208.
17 "Rending xi shengtian" originally appeared in Liu Guo's (1154–1206) *Collection from Long Zhou: Song of Xiangyang* (*Longzhou Ji: Xiangyang ge*), and argues that if people remain united and full of determination, their strength can exceed the powers of nature. In the late 1950s, Mao quoted this sentence in classical Chinese to emphasize his determination to reconstruct China in a new way. In her *Mao's War against Nature*, Shapiro explains how this particular sentence was promoted and used in Party propaganda for Mao's mass-mobilized migrations and campaigns in the 1950s and 1960s.
18 Zheng Wenguang, "Huoxing jianshe zhe Xia," 17.
19 Shapiro, *Mao's War against Nature*, 6.
20 Shapiro, *Mao's War against Nature*, 197.
21 Zheng Wenguang, "Tantan kexue huanxiang xiaoshuo," 21.
22 Zheng Wenguang, "Tantan kexue huanxiang xiaoshuo," 22.
23 Zheng Wenguang, "Tantan kexue huanxiang xiaoshuo," 21.
24 Zheng Wenguang, "Tantan kexue huanxiang xiaoshuo," 21.
25 Zheng Wenguang, "Tantan kexue huanxiang xiaoshuo," 22.
26 Volland, "Comment on 'Let's Go to the Moon,'" 356.
27 Volland, "Comment on 'Let's Go to the Moon,'" 356.
28 Rao, "Yongjiu de meili," 19.
29 Xiao, "Shi tan wo guo kexue huanxiang xiaoshuo de fazhan," 23.
30 Wu Yan, "Lun Zheng Wenguang de kehuan wenxue chaungzuo," 111–12.
31 Wu Yan, "Lun Zheng Wenguang de kehuan wenxue chaungzuo," 113.
32 Wu Yan, "Lun Zheng Wenguang de kehuan wenxue chaungzuo," 113.
33 Wu Yan, "Lun Zheng Wenguang de kehuan wenxue chaungzuo," 113–14.
34 Zheng Wenguang, "Kexue wenyi zatan," 89–91.
35 Zheng Wenguang, "Da Xianggang Kaijuan yuekan jizhe Lü Chen xiansheng wen," 139–47.
36 Zheng Wenguang, "Da Xianggang Kaijuan yuekan jizhe Lü Chen xiansheng wen," 139.
37 Zheng Wenguang, "Hou ji," 160.
38 Zheng Wenguang, "Hou ji," 160.

39 Zheng Wenguang, "Qian yan."
40 Zheng Wenguang, "Da Xianggang Kaijuan yuekan jizhe Lü Chen xiansheng wen," 144.
41 Zheng Wenguang, "Da Xianggang Kaijuan yuekan jizhe Lü Chen xiansheng wen," 145.
42 Zheng Wenguang, "Da Xianggang Kaijuan yuekan jizhe Lü Chen xiansheng wen," 146.
43 Zheng Wenguang, *Zhanshen de houyi*, 314.
44 Pak, *Terraforming*, 1.
45 Fogg, *Terraforming*, 90.
46 Zheng Wenguang, *Zhanshen de houyi*, 105.
47 Shapiro, *Mao's War against Nature*, 142.
48 Zheng Wenguang, *Zhanshen de houyi*, 93.
49 Zheng Wenguang, *Zhanshen de houyi*, 93.
50 Zheng Wenguang, *Zhanshen de houyi*, 135.
51 Pak, *Terraforming*, 56–97.
52 Bradbury, *Martian Chronicles*, 62.
53 Bradbury, *Martian Chronicles*, 273.
54 Pak, *Terraforming*, 65.
55 Pak, *Terraforming*, 62.
56 Konstanty Ciołkowski (1857–1935) was a Russian and Soviet rocket scientist and pioneer of the astronautic theory. He was the first author to coin the image of Earth as the "cradle" of humanity, which has to be left behind once the human race finally matures. This has been an influential ideological marker, not only in many Anglo-American SF stories, including classics such as Clarke's "The Sentinel" (1951), but also in many works of Chinese SF, such as La La's "The Radio Waves That Never Die" ("Yongbu xiaoshi de dianbo," 2007).
57 Zheng Wenguang, *Zhanshen de houyi*, 162.
58 Zheng Wenguang, *Zhanshen de houyi*, 187.
59 Pak, *Terraforming*, 71.
60 Zheng Wenguang, *Zhanshen de houyi*, 244.
61 Pak, *Terraforming*, 89.
62 Pak, *Terraforming*, 89.
63 Pak, *Terraforming*, 89.
64 Zheng Wenguang, *Zhanshen de houyi*, 294.
65 Quoted in Zheng Wenguang, *Zhanshen de houyi*, 294. I use the English translation of this sentence in Engels, "The Part Played by Labour in the Transition from Ape to Man."
66 Zheng Wenguang, *Zhanshen de houyi*, 165.
67 Zheng Wenguang, *Zhanshen de houyi*, 294.
68 Baukom, "Human Shore."

69 Chakrabarty, Dipesh. "The Climate of History."
70 Vermeulen, "'The Sea, Not the Ocean,'" 185.
71 Zheng Wenguang, *Zhanshen de houyi*, 297.
72 Zheng Wenguang, *Zhanshen de houyi*, 297.
73 Zheng Wenguang, *Zhanshen de houyi*, 123.
74 Zheng Wenguang, *Zhanshen de houyi*, 318.
75 Otto, "Kim Stanley Robinson's *Mars* Trilogy and the Leopoldian Land Ethic," 132.
76 Zheng Wenguang, "Xingxing ying," 33.
77 Chen, *Qinli zhongguo kehuan*, 128–31.
78 Zheng Wenguang, "Xu."
79 Zheng Wenguang, "The Mirror Image of the Earth," 132.
80 Zheng Wenguang, "The Mirror Image of the Earth," 132.

3. A Scientific Holmes in Post-Mao China: Ye Yonglie and His SF Thrillers

1 Wu Dingbo, "Looking Backward," xxiv.
2 According to Ye Yonglie, the Chinese term of *jingxian kexue huanxiang xiaoshu* (science fiction thriller) was first coined in March 1979, but he did not indicate who supposedly coined this term, or where was it first published (Ye Yonglie, "Jingxian kehuan xiaoshuo dayi," 63).
3 Ye, "Heng zao pipan," 545.
4 Ye, "Heng zao pipan," 543.
5 Ye, "Heng zao pipan," 563.
6 Ye, "Xu," 1.
7 Ye, *Lun kexue wenyi*, 102.
8 Ye, "Wo de kehuan qimeng."
9 Ye, "Heng zao pipan," 545.
10 Ye, "Heng zao pipan," 547.
11 Ye, "Heng zao pipan," 547.
12 Ye, "Jingxian kehuan xiaoshuo dayi," 64.
13 Glover, "Thriller," 136.
14 Glover, "Thriller," 137.
15 Ye, "Xu," 1.
16 Ye, "Jingxian kehuan xiaoshuo dayi," 64.
17 Ye, *Lun kexue wenyi*, 102.
18 Ye, *Lun kexue wenyi*, 101.
19 Ye, *Lun kexue wenyi*, 101.
20 Ye, "Xu," 2–3.
21 Ye, "Xu," 3.
22 Ye, "Jingxian kehuan xiaoshuo dayi," 66.
23 Seed, "Spy Fiction," 116.

24 Seed, "Spy Fiction," 117.
25 Ye, *Kexue fu er mo si*, 528.
26 Ye, *Kexue fu er mo si*, 533.
27 Ye, "Heng zao pipan," 546.
28 Ye, "Heng zao pipan," 547.
29 Ye, "Heng zao pipan," 533.
30 Ye, *Heiying*, 16.
31 Ye, "Jingxian kehuan xiaoshuo dayi," 66.
32 Ye, "Heng zao pipan," 546.
33 Ye, "Heng zao pipan," 539–40.
34 Ye, "Heng zao pipan," 540–1.
35 Ye, "Heng zao pipan," 541.
36 Zhao Shizhou, "Jingxian kehuan xiaoshuo zhiyi."
37 Ye, "Jingxian kehuan xiaoshuo dayi," 67.
38 Ye, *Lun kexue wenyi*, 102.
39 Ye, "Jingxian kehuan xiaoshuo dayi," 68.
40 Ye, "Jingxian kehuan xiaoshuo dayi," 67–9.
41 Zhao Shuli, a leading modern Chinese fiction writer, is commonly grouped with the *Shanyaodan* (potato) literary coterie. His specialty is the depiction of rural life and revolutionary changes in the northern Chinese countryside. His works include *Xiao Erhei jiehun* (Young Erhei's marriage, 1943), *Li Youcai banhua* (The rhymes of Li Youcai, 1943), and *San li wan* (Three-mile bay, 1955).
42 Ye, "Jingxian kehuan xiaoshuo dayi," 67–9.
43 Ye, "Heng zao pipan," 558.
44 Ye, "Heng zao pipan," 558.
45 Deng, "Deng Xiaoping zai quanguo kexue dahui kaimushi shang de jianghua."
46 Ye, "Heng zao pipan," 561.
47 Ye, *Heiying*, 166.
48 Ye, *Heiying*, 166.
49 Deng, "Deng Xiaoping zai quanguo kexue dahui kaimushi shang de jianghua."
50 Lu Xun, "Diary of a Madman," 12.
51 Link, *Uses of Literature*, 27.
52 Ye, "Heng zao pipan," 561.
53 Ye, "Heng zao pipan," 558.
54 Ye, "Heng zao pipan," 558.
55 Ye, "Heng zao pipan," 560.
56 Yang, "Bashi niandai de Ye Yonglie."
57 Wu Dingbo, "Looking Backward," xxvii.
58 Link, *Uses of Literature*, 22.

59 Yang, "Bashi niandai de Ye Yonglie."
60 Yang, "Bashi niandai de Ye Yonglie."

4. Tong Enzheng and the Motif of Alien Invasions

1 Wang Yafa, "Huiyi Tong Enzheng," 22.
2 *New Journey to the West* is his lone full-length novel, and it is a parody of the Chinese classic novel *Journey to the West*. Tong labelled his *New Journey to the West* a humorous novel and a pseudo-myth. See Tong, "Houji."
3 "My Understanding of Literature and Art about Science" was originally published in the sixth issue of *People's Literature* in 1979.
4 Tong, "Tantan wo dui kexue wenyi de renshi."
5 Lu Bing, "Linghun chuqiao de wenxue," 24.
6 Gordon, "Literary Science Fiction," 105.
7 Gordon, "Literary Science Fiction," 105.
8 Gordon, "Literary Science Fiction," 105.
9 Tong, "Chuangzuo kexue huanxiang xiaoshuo de tihui," 159.
10 Tong, "Chuangzuo kexue huanxiang xiaoshuo de tihui," 160–1.
11 Tong, "Chuangzuo kexue huanxiang xiaoshuo de tihui," 163–4.
12 Tong, "Chuangzuo kexue huanxiang xiaoshuo de tihui," 166–7.
13 Jones, "Icons of Science Fiction," 168.
14 Booker and Thomas, "Alien Invasion Narrative," 28.
15 Tong, "Wode jingli," 148.
16 Sima Qian, "Tianguan shu."
17 Tong, "Wuwan nian yiqian de keren," 186.
18 Zhao Yao, "Peiyang shehui zhuyi xinren yu dang de jiaoyu fangzhen de lishi tansuo."
19 Tong, "Wuwan nian yiqian de keren," 197.
20 Tong, "Wode jingli," 143–7.
21 Tong, "Wode jingli," 149.
22 Dong, "Tong Enzheng zhuan," January 4, 2007, http://www.360doc.com/content/07/0513/18/21434_498170.shtml (accessed April 3, 2017).
23 Tong, "Guanyu Shanhu dao," 57.
24 Tong, "Guanyu Shanhu dao," 57–8.
25 Dong, "Tong Enzheng zhuan."
26 Tong left China for the United States in 1991 as a visiting professor at the University of Pittsburgh. Then he taught in different universities and was a visiting scholar in Wesleyan University when he died in 1997.
27 Tong, "Yaoyuan de ai," 293.
28 Tong, "Yaoyuan de ai," 310.
29 Tong, "Yaoyuan de ai," 219.
30 Tong, "Yaoyuan de ai," 227.

31 Tong, "Yaoyuan de ai," 305.
32 *Han shu*, also known as *Qian Han shu*, is the work of Ban Gu (32–92). *Han shu* describes the history of the Western Han dynasty (206 BCE–23CE). It contains twelve imperial annals (*ben ji*), eight tables (*biao*), ten treatises (*zhi*), and seventy biographies and accounts (*lie zhuan*). "Yi wen zhi" is the bibliographical section of *Han shu*. For more about "Yi wen zhi" and *Han shu*, see Hulsewé, "Han shu."
33 Tong, "Shishun xing," 61.
34 *Huayang guo zhi* was compiled by Chang Qu (291–361) during the years of 348–54. It is a regional gazetteer about the history, geography, and people of early southwest China.
35 For more information about Du Guangting's account, see Verellen, "Evidential Miracles in Support of Taoism."
36 Tong, "Shicun xing," 66.
37 Jones, "Icons of Science Fiction," 169.
38 Jones, "Icons of Science Fiction," 169.
39 Jones, "Icons of Science Fiction," 169.
40 In her English adaptation of Tong's story, Hull alters the beginning of the narrative in order to fit more smoothly within the overall structure of the book.
41 Hull's adaptation deleted these sentences about the American government's sponsorship of the aliens.
42 Tong, "Middle Kingdom," 204.
43 Tong, "Middle Kingdom," 204.
44 Tong, "Middle Kingdom," 204.
45 Deng, "Deng Xiaoping zai quanguo kexue dahui kaimushi shang de jianghua."
46 Tong, "Middle Kingdom," 205.
47 Tong, "Middle Kingdom," 207.
48 Tong, "Wode jingli," 145–6.
49 Hollinger, "Science Fiction and Postmodernism," 243.
50 Jorgensen, "Postmodernism," 281.

5. Posthuman Conditions in Xiao Jianheng's SF Narratives

1 Milburn, "Posthumanism," 524.
2 Milburn, "Posthumanism," 524.
3 Milburn, "Posthumanism," 524.
4 Ye, "Buke de qiyu daodu."
5 My enumeration of Xiao's SF works before 1965 is based on the stories included in *Zhongguo kehuan xiaoshuo daquan* edited by Rao Zhonghua.
6 Ye, "Buke de qiyu daodu."

7 Krementsov, *Revolutionary Experiments*, 53.
8 The vernacular translations of these two accounts are included in *Zhongguo kehuan xiaoshuo Daquan* [A compendium of Chinese science fiction], edited by Rao Zhonghua, 1:5, 6, and 8.
9 Yan, "Xiao Jianheng he ta de kexue huanxiang xiaoshuo," 180.
10 Yan, "Xiao Jianheng he ta de kexue huanxiang xiaoshuo."
11 Li Yanli and Yan Shuchang, "Zhou Xiangeng yu Bapuluofu xueshuo 1950 niandai de yinjie," 332.
12 Li Yanli and Yan Shuchang, "Zhou Xiangeng yu Bapuluofu xueshuo 1950 niandai de yinjie."
13 Cao, "Jichu xueke de jianli: shengwu xue," 739.
14 Moore, *Give and Take*, 1–182.
15 Bolton and Bradley, "Mechanism of Immune Rejection of Stem Cell–Derived Tissue," 5–6.
16 Mao, "Lun renmin minzhu zhuanzheng," 1481.
17 Xiao, "Buke de qiyu," 81.
18 Xiao, "Buke de qiyu," 82.
19 Krementsov, *Revolutionary Experiments*, 55.
20 Xiao, "Buke de qiyu," 77.
21 See endnote 17 in Chapter 2.
22 Krementsov, *Revolutionary Experiments*, 58.
23 Xiao, "Buke de qiyu," 82.
24 Ye, "Lun kexue huanxiang xiaoshuo," 52.
25 Seed, *Science Fiction*, 59.
26 Seed, *Science Fiction*, 59.
27 Seed, *Science Fiction*, 62.
28 Wu Dingbo,"Looking Backward," xii.
29 For an English translation of Tong's story, see Tong Enzheng, "The Death of the World's First Robot."
30 Wu Dingbo,"Looking Backward," xii.
31 The vernacular version of this story is included in *Zhongguo kehuan xiaoshuo Daquan* [A compendium of Chinese science fiction], edited by Rao Zhonghua, 1:8–9.
32 Jin Wulun, "Zhongguo gao keji fazhan gaikuang," 1328–9.
33 Seed, *Science Fiction*, 60.
34 Seed, *Science Fiction*, 61.
35 Seed, *Science Fiction*, 63–4.
36 Xiao, "Shaluomu jiaoshou de miwu," 315.
37 Krementsov, *Revolutionary Experiments*, 62. This is the comment that Krementsov makes on Belyaev's *Professor Dowell's Head*. I believe Xiao's narrative shares commonality with Belyaev's story in its setting within a capitalist country.

38 Seed, *Science Fiction*, 64.
39 Xiao, "Qiao er huanbing ji," 101.
40 He, "Eight-Character Policies," 2.
41 Hayles, *How We Became Posthuman*, 283.
42 Hayles, *How We Became Posthuman*, 283.
43 Hayles, *How We Became Posthuman*, 283–4.
44 Jones, "Icons of Science Fiction," 167.
45 Jones, "Icons of Science Fiction," 167.
46 Xiao, "Shi tan wo guo kexue huanxiang xiaoshuo de fazhan," 21–41.

6. Tech-SF and the Four Modernizations

1 Liu Cixin, "Xiaoshi de xiliu."
2 Zhongguo zhongyang dangshi yanjiu shi, ed., "Zhongguo gongchandang dashi ji 1963," http://cpc.people.com.cn/GB/64162/64164/4416060.html.
3 Zhongguo zhongyang dangshi yanjiu shi, ed, "Zhongguo gongchandang dashi ji 1978."
4 Xiao, "Shi tan wo guo kexue huanxiang xiaoshuo de fazhan," 20.
5 Huang, "Kexue huanxiang xiaoshuo siti," 121.
6 Huang, "Kexue huanxiang xiaoshuo siti," 122.
7 Slonczewski and Levy, "Science Fiction and the Life Sciences."
8 Qian, Wang, and Qi, eds., *Ershi shiji Zhongguo xueshu dadian*, 443.
9 Xiong and Wang, "Kexue chubanshe shengwu xue xueke xueshu chuban gailan."
10 Zhang and Wei, *Shengming qu*, 1.
11 Lohmar et al., "China's Ongoing Agricultural Modernization."
12 Zhang and Wei, "Jin ditan pu shang le tian."
13 Scholes and Rabkin, *Science Fiction*, 144.
14 For details about this disaster in China's modern history, see Dikötter, *Mao's Great Famine*. The author consulted provincial, county, and city government archives to construct a detailed account of the famine.
15 Zhang and Wei, "Mo yuan," 33–48.
16 Scholes and Rabkin, *Science Fiction: History, Science, Vision*, 143–4.
17 Zhang and Wei, "Mo yuan," 44.
18 Zhang and Wei, "Mo yuan," 48.
19 Liu Cixin, "Xiaoshi de xiliu."
20 Xiao, "Zhang zai shushang de ya."
21 Zhang and Wei, "Lanse de baoweiquan"; Jin Tao, "Diyi zhi wang."
22 Ye, "Lun kexue huanxiang xiaoshuo," 51.
23 Yan, "Xiao Jianheng he ta de kexue huanxiang xiaoshuo," 181.
24 Xiao, "Shi tan wo guo kexue huanxiang xiaoshuo de fazhan," 34.

25 Rao and Lin, "Zhongguo kehuan xiaoshuo zai tansuo zhong qianjin," 1–20.
26 Wan, "Tu yanquan de nüyou."
27 Liu Cixn, "Xiaoshi de xiliu."
28 Lu Zhaowen, "Tiantian de shuilian."
29 Wu Dingbo, "Looking Backward," xxxvi.
30 Wu Dingbo, "Looking Backward," xxv.
31 Chen, *Qinli Zhongguo kehuan*, 185–6.
32 Zhou Jun, "Yao kexue huanxiang, buyao diji quwei."
33 Liu Cixin, "Xiaoshi de xiliu."
34 Tong, "Chuangzuo kexue huanxiang xiaoshuode tihui," 161–2.
35 Song, "Variations on Utopia in Contemporary Chinese Science Fiction," 86–96.
36 Liu Cixin, "Xiaoshi de xiliu."
37 Liu Cixin, "Xiaoshi de xiliu."
38 Li Hua, "The Political Imagination in Liu Cixin's Critical Utopia."

7. Fledgling Media Convergence: PRC SF from Print to Electronic Media

1 Zheng Jun, "Di er zhang: Zhongguo kehuan xiaoshuo jianzhi."
2 Li Yuan, "Kepu chatu yu tujie kepu xiaoyi," 240.
3 McLuhan, *Understanding Media*, 4.
4 McLuhan, *Understanding Media*, 24.
5 McLuhan, *Understanding Media*, 24.
6 McLuhan, *Understanding Media*, 24.
7 McLuhan, *Understanding Media*, 25.
8 Steinberg, *Anime's Media Mix*, 152.
9 Brown, *New Shorter Oxford English Dictionary*, 1:344.
10 Brown, *New Shorter Oxford English Dictionary*, 1:488.
11 Brown, *New Shorter Oxford English Dictionary*, 1:1132.
12 McCloud, *Understanding Comics*, 9.
13 Petersen, *Comic, Manga, and Graphic Novels*, 122.
14 Petersen, *Comic, Manga, and Graphic Novels*, 122.
15 "Zhongguo diyiben manhua qikan shi Shanghai Poke."
16 Petersen, *Comic, Manga, and Graphic Novels*, 120.
17 Petersen, *Comic, Manga, and Graphic Novels*, 120.
18 Petersen, *Comic, Manga, and Graphic Novels*, 120.
19 Li Yuan, "Kepu chatu yu tujie kepu xiaoyi," 236.
20 Li Yuan, "Kepu chatu yu tujie kepu xiaoyi," 237.
21 Li Yuan, "Kepu chatu yu tujie kepu xiaoyi," 237.
22 Li Yuan, "Kepu chatu yu tujie kepu xiaoyi," 240.
23 Miao, "Kexue manhua chuangzuo tan," 7.
24 Yao Di, "Mianhuai 'kepu manhua diyi ren.'"

25 Miao, "Kexue manhua chuangzuo tan," 5.
26 Ye, "Lun kexue manhua," 184.
27 Ye, "Lun kexue manhua," 184.
28 Petersen, *Comic, Manga, and Graphic Novels*, 117.
29 Petersen, *Comic, Manga, and Graphic Novels*, 123.
30 Petersen, *Comic, Manga, and Graphic Novels*,124.
31 Ye, "Heng zao pipan," 538.
32 Ye, "Guanyu kehuan lianhuanhua," 2.
33 Zhou Lin, "Xin Zhongguo gaochou zhidu," 122–7.
34 Ye, interviewed by author.
35 Ye, interviewed by author.
36 Ye, "Guanyu kehuan lianhuanhua," 2.
37 Ye, interviewed by author.
38 Ye, "Yuanqu de xiao zi bei," 3.
39 Ye, "Yuanqu de xiao zi bei," 3.
40 McLuhan, *Understanding Media*, 174.
41 McLuhan, *Understanding Media*, 174.
42 McLuhan, *Understanding Media*, 179.
43 McLuhan, *Understanding Media*, 174.
44 Petersen, *Comic, Manga, and Graphic Novels*, 124.
45 Xinjing Bao, "Liulang diqiu kaiqi zhongguo kehuan dianying yuannian."
46 Zheng Jun, "Di er zhang."
47 Xu and Wang, "Feiben ba! Kexue de hangchuan."
48 Ma, "1980 nian xin zhongguo diyibu kehuan pian."
49 Ma, "1980 nian xin zhongguo diyibu kehuan pian."
50 Ye, "Wo de kehuan dianying meng."
51 Ye Yonglie, "Wo de kehuan dianying meng."
52 Zheng Jun, "Di si zhang."
53 This section on PRC scientific animation during the post-Mao thaw was previously published in Li Hua, "Animating Science and Technology." See the article for a detailed analysis of these three early Chinese scientific animated movies.
54 Ye, "Kexue wenyi chuangzuo zhaji," 111.
55 Ye, "Kexue tonghua dianying de tedian," 168.
56 Pontieri, *Soviet Animation and the Thaw of the 1960s*, 57.
57 Wang and Cao, "Fusu yu congjian," 169.
58 The lyrics are quoted from the film *Dingding Fights the Monkey King*, directed by Hu Jinqing. Shanghai: Shanghai meishu dianying zhipianchang, 1980.
59 Wang and Liu, "Zhuanxing yu zhentong."
60 To be sure, Jenkins focuses mostly upon digital media in the United States, while Steinberg emphasizes TV in Japan, so contrasts with the

configuration of post-Mao thaw era PRC analogue media do qualify the comparisons I present.

61 Jenkins, *Convergence Culture*, 2.
62 Jenkins, *Convergence Culture*, 3.
63 Jenkins, *Convergence Culture*, 3.
64 Jenkins, *Convergence Culture*, 3.
65 Jenkins, *Convergence Culture*, 3.
66 Jenkins, *Convergence Culture*, 15.
67 Jenkins, *Convergence Culture*, 16.
68 Jenkins, *Convergence Culture*, 3.
69 Jenkins, *Convergence Culture*, 3.
70 Steinberg, *Anime's Media Mix*, vii.
71 Steinberg, *Anime's Media Mix*, viii.
72 Steinberg, *Anime's Media Mix*, viii.
73 Steinberg, *Anime's Media Mix*, 38.
74 Jenkins, *Convergence Culture*, 4.
75 Pool, *Technologies of Freedom*, 6.
76 Steinberg, *Anime's Media Mix*, 138.
77 Steinberg, *Anime's Media Mix*, 158.
78 Steinberg, *Anime's Media Mix*, 156.
79 Lee, *Consumer Culture Reborn*, 131.
80 Steinberg, *Anime's Media Mix*, 157.
81 Steinberg, *Anime's Media Mix*, 157.
82 Steinberg, *Anime's Media Mix*, 159–60.
83 Steinberg, *Anime's Media Mix*, 157.
84 "Zhangmuniang de yaoqiu yizhi douzai," 3 February 2018, https://kknews.cc/history/zgxklbq.html.
85 Lee, *Consumer Culture Reborn*, 131.
86 Steinberg, *Anime's Media Mix*, xiii.
87 Steinberg, *Anime's Media Mix*, ix.
88 Steinberg, *Anime's Media Mix*, xii.
89 Li Guijie, *Buhui chengfeng de jiyi*, 34–5.
90 Steinberg, *Anime's Media Mix*, 154.
91 Steinberg, *Anime's Media Mix*, 154.
92 Steinberg, *Anime's Media Mix*, 155.
93 Steinberg, *Anime's Media Mix*, 152.
94 Steinberg, *Anime's Media Mix*, 160.
95 Ellis, *Visible Fictions*, 112.
96 Steinberg, *Anime's Media Mix*, 162.
97 Steinberg, *Anime's Media Mix*, 163.
98 Steinberg, *Anime's Media Mix*, 160.

8. Blooming, Contending, and Boundary-Breaking Even in a Genre of Government-Backed Literature

1 Suvin, *Metamorphoses of Science Fiction*, 4; Wagner, "Lobby Literature," 43.
2 Kinkley, *After Mao*, 2.
3 Lee, "Politics of Technique," 161.
4 Lee, "Politics of Technique," 162.
5 Kinkley, *After Mao*, 2.
6 Kinkley, *After Mao*, 2.
7 Kinkley, *After Mao*, 3.
8 Kinkley, *After Mao*, 14.
9 The English translation is quoted in Wagner, "Lobby Literature," 31. For the original quotation, see Heller, *De la science fiction soviétique, par delà le dogme, un univers*, 251.
10 This English translation is quoted in Wagner, "Lobby Literature," 30. For the original quotation, see Britikov, *Russkij sovetskij nauchno fantasticeskii roman*, 361.
11 Gomel, "Gods like Men," 361.
12 Wu Yan made these comments at the International Conference on Utopian and Science Fiction Studies, Beijing, 3–4 December 2016.
13 Volland, "Soviet Spaceships in Socialist China," 194.
14 Volland, "Soviet Spaceships in Socialist China," 194.
15 Volland, "Soviet Spaceships in Socialist China," 195.
16 Volland, "Soviet Spaceships in Socialist China," 195.
17 Volland, "Soviet Spaceships in Socialist China," 195.
18 Wagner, "Lobby Literature," 29.
19 Wagner, "Lobby Literature," 26.
20 Wagner, "Lobby Literature," 35.
21 Wagner, "Lobby Literature," 24.
22 Lee, "Introduction," 3.
23 Wagner, "Lobby Literature," 20–1.
24 Wagner, "Lobby Literature," 30.
25 Wang, "Introduction," 2.
26 Louie, "Love Stories," 64.
27 Louie, "Love Stories," 65, 85.
28 Louie, "Love Stories," 70.
29 Louie, "Love Stories," 75, 67.
30 Louie, "Love Stories," 67.
31 Wagner, "Lobby Literature," 41–2.
32 I have used Wagner's English translation of Ye's statement in "Lobby Literature," 42. For the original Chinese sentences, see Ye, *Lun kexue wenyi*, 110–13.
33 *Guangming Daily* published "Shijian shi jianyan zhenli de weiyi biaozhun" (Practice is the sole criterion for arriving at truth) written by

the newspaper's "special commentator" on 11 May 1978. Soon after its publication, a heated debate about what constitutes "truth" spread across the PRC.

34 Kinkley, *After Mao*, 91.
35 Kinkley, *After Mao*, 111.
36 Kinkley, *After Mao*, 111–12.
37 Kinkley, *After Mao*, 112.
38 Kinkley, *After Mao*, 92.
39 Kinkley, *After Mao*, 92.
40 Wagner, "Lobby Literature," 45.
41 Wagner, "Lobby Literature," 45.
42 Wagner, "Lobby Literature," 59.
43 Wagner, "Lobby Literature," 59.
44 Wagner, "Lobby Literature," 59.
45 Wagner, "Lobby Literature," 59.
46 Wagner, "Lobby Literature," 59.
47 Kinkley, *After Mao*, 12.
48 Kinkley, *After Mao*, 11.
49 Wagner, "Lobby Literature," 43.
50 Louie, "Love Stories," 64.
51 Suvin, *Metamorphoses of Science Fiction*, 4.
52 Suvin, *Metamorphoses of Science Fiction*, 8.
53 Suvin, *Metamorphoses of Science Fiction*, 13.
54 Suvin, *Metamorphoses of Science Fiction*, 15.
55 Suvin, *Metamorphoses of Science Fiction*, 4.
56 Wagner, "Lobby Literature," 43.
57 Wagner, "Lobby Literature," 43.
58 Wagner, "Lobby Literature," 43.
59 Wagner, "Lobby Literature," 43–4.
60 Wagner, "Lobby Literature,"43.
61 Louie, "Love Stories," 68.
62 Wagner, "Lobby Literature," 25.
63 Wagner, "Lobby Literature," 25.
64 Wagner, "Lobby Literature," 23.
65 Wagner, "Lobby Literature," 23.
66 Csicsery-Ronay, "Science Fiction and the Thaw," 343.
67 Csicsery-Ronay, "Science Fiction and the Thaw," 341.
68 I have used Wagner's English translation in "Lobby Literature," 38. For the original, see Ye, *Lun kexue wenyi*, 86.
69 Wagner, "Lobby Literature," 59.
70 Duke, *Blooming and Contending*, x.
71 Tao, "Xu," ii.

Chinese Character Glossary

An Dou 暗斗
"β zhege mi" β这个谜
Bai Hua 白桦
Bai mao nü 白毛女
"Ban zhu ren" 班主任
Bingshan de mimi 冰山的秘密
"Bodou" 搏斗
Buguniao jiao chi le 布谷鸟叫迟了
Buke de qiyu 布克的奇遇
Bu yi er fei 不翼而飞
cengceng bosun 层层剥笋
chahua 插画
Chang Qu 常璩
"Chang xiang si" 长相思
Chaoye qianzai 朝野佥载
"Cheng huang se de toukui" 橙黄色的头盔
Chen Hanbiao 陈汉标
Chen Jiejun 陈杰军
Chen Ripeng 陈日朋
"Chongfan saichang" 重返赛场
"Chuangzuo kehuan xiaoshuo de tihui" 创作科幻小说的体会
Chu Fengge 褚凤阁
"Chuguo zhiqian" 出国之前

chun wenxue 纯文学
"Cong diqiu dao huoxing" 从地球到火星
Cuo wei 错位
"Dahai qiyu" 大海奇遇
"Dai guniang bian congming le" 呆姑娘变聪明了
Dai Houying 戴厚英
Dai Shan 戴山
"Dan" 蛋
Dangdai 当代
"Daojiao lingyan ji" 道教灵验记
Daqiceng xiaoshi 大气层消失
Deng Gangzhou 邓冈州
Deng Xiaoping 邓小平
Deng Xiaoqiu 邓小秋
Dianying chuangzuo 电影创作
"Dianzi danao de qiji" 电子大脑的奇迹
"Di er ge yueliang" 第二个月亮
Di huo 地火
Ding Binzeng 丁斌曾
Dingding zhan houwang 丁丁战猴王
Diqiu dapao 地球大炮
Diqiu de jingxiang 地球的镜像
"Di san ke niukou" 第三颗纽扣
"Di wu hao sishi" 第五号死尸
"Diyici shibai" 第一次失败
"Diyi zhi wang" 地衣之王
"DNA caise yang" DNA 彩色羊
Dongwu he renti qiguan de zaisheng 动物和人体器官的再生
Duan Chengshi 段成式
Du Guangting 杜光庭
"Er ling ling yi nian Tangshan da dizhen baogao" 二零零一年唐山大地震报告
"Ershiyi shiji tielu manyou" 二十一世纪铁路漫游
faming kehuan 发明科幻
Fang Weigong 方伟功

fansi 反思
fansi wenxue 反思文学
Feichu diqiu qu 飞出地球去
"Feicui dao" 翡翠岛
"Feitan de fengbo" 飞毯的风波
"Fei xiang mingwangxing de ren" 飞向冥王星的人
Fei xiang renmazuo 飞向人马座
"Feiyan zoubi de mimi" 飞檐走壁的秘密
Fengkuang de waixingren 疯狂的外星人
Feng Zikai 丰子凯
gaoji zhihui shengwu 高级智慧生物
Gao Juefu 高觉敷
Gao Weibin 高炜宾
gong'an 公案
"Guai niao" 怪鸟
"Guaishi lianpian" 怪事连篇
guangbo ju 广播剧
Guishan heiying 鬼山黑影
Guobao qi'an 国宝奇案
Guo Yicen 郭一岑
Guxia miwu 古峡迷雾
"Haidi mingzhu" 海底明珠
Hai guai zhi mi 海怪之谜
"Hai ma" 海马
"Halei huixing dailai de xinwen" 哈雷彗星带来的新闻
"Hangtian boyu" 航天播雨
Han Heping 韩和平
"Han liuxing xingshi zhanyan" 汉流星行事占验
Han shu 汉书
He Bin 何滨
Heiying 黑影
Heping de meng 和平的梦
Hong Mai 洪迈
"Hongye fei mantian" 红叶飞满天

Huacheng 花城
Huangchao 荒潮
Huang Tiange 黄天戈
Huangyang guo zhi 华阳国志
Hua Sanchuan 华三川
Huilai ba Luolan 回来吧，罗兰
"Huluobo di li de mimi" 胡萝卜地里的秘密
"Huoxing jianshe zhe" 火星建设者
Hu Yonghuai 胡永槐
jiandie xiaoshuo 间谍小说
Jiang Lai 江莱
Jia Wanchao 贾万超
Jia You 嘉尤
Ji Hong 嵇鸿
"Jin ditan pu shang le tian" 金地毯铺上了天
jingxian kexue huanxiang xiaoshuo 惊险科学幻想小说
jingxian xiaoshuo 惊险小说
Jin Tao 金涛
Jinxingren zhi mi 金星人之谜
jishu kehuan 技术科幻
"Jiujiu de shoubiao" 舅舅的手表
Kangde xingyun shuo de zhexue yiyi 康德星云说的哲学意义
Kehuan haiyang 科幻海洋
Kehuan shijie 科幻世界
"Keke dalang ji" 科科打狼记
Kepu chuangzuo 科普创作
kepu meishu 科普美术
Kepu xiaoyi 科普小议
kepu zuopin 科普作品
Kexue shenhua 科学神话
Kexue shidai 科学时代
kexue wenyi 科学文艺
kexue yiju 科学依据
"Kongque lanse de hudie" 孔雀蓝色的蝴蝶

kua meiti 跨媒体
Ku lian 苦恋
"Laili buming de bingren" 来历不明的病人
"Lanse de baowei quan" 蓝色的包围圈
"Laoshan daoshi" 崂山道士
Leng Zhaohe 冷兆和
Liang Baibo 梁白波
lianhuanhua 连环画
Liaozhai zhiyi 聊斋志异
Li Bo 李白
Lie zi 列子
lingguang zhaxian 灵光乍现
"Linghun chuqiao de wenxue" 灵魂出窍的文学
Liu Cixin 刘慈欣
Liu Husheng 刘沪生
Liulang diqiu 流浪地球
Liu Xinwu 刘心武
Liu Zhaogui 刘肇贵
Lu Ke 鲁克
Lun kexue huanxiang xiaoshuo 论科学幻想小说
Lüse kelong ma 绿色克隆马
Lu Xinhua 卢新华
Lu Zhaowen 鲁肇文
Lü Zhenhua 吕振华
Ma Guangfu 马光复
manhua 漫画
manhua shu 漫画书
Mao cheng ji 猫城记
"Meigui yu baojian" 玫瑰与宝剑
"Meiyou xinzang de ren" 没有心脏的人
"Meng" 梦
Mengxi bitan 梦溪笔谈
Miao Shi 缪士
Miao Yintang 缪印堂

"Milin huzong" 密林虎踪
"Milin shaobing" 密林哨兵
Mimi zongdui 秘密纵队
"Mingyun yezonghui" 命运夜总会
Mo biao 魔表
"Mo yuan" 魔园
"Mo zhen" 魔枕
Muji banjia 母鸡搬家
Mu ma ren 牧马人
"Mu yu" 牧鱼
"Nengfei de muyuan" 能飞的木鸢
nianhua 年画
niupeng 牛棚
Pan Shu 潘菽
pianmo jiemi 篇末揭秘
Pili Beibei 霹雳贝贝
pingfan 平反
Pu Songling 蒲松龄
"Qiangba de yanjing" 强巴的眼睛
Qian ying 潜影
"Qiao er huan bing ji" 乔二患病记
Qiguai de binghao 奇怪的病号
"Qiguai de dianbo" 奇怪的电波
Qiguai de qiusai 奇怪的球赛
"Qipao de gushi" 气泡的故事
Qi tan 奇谈
"Qiuchang wai de quwen" 球场外的趣闻
"Qiyi de jiqi gou" 奇异的机器狗
"Qiyi de lüke" 奇异的旅客
Qiyi de touming jiao 奇异的透明胶
Renmin wenxue 人民文学
Ru meng chu xing 如梦初醒
Sanguo yanyi 三国演义
Sanguo zhi 三国志

Sanmao 三毛
Sanmao ai kexue 三毛爱科学
Sanmao congjun 三毛从军
Sanmao jinxi 三毛今昔
Sanmao ying jiefang 三毛迎解放
Santi 三体
sanzhuan yixiang 三转一响
"Secai" 色彩
"Shaluomu jiaoshou de miwu" 沙洛姆教授的迷误
"Shamo zhuizong" 沙漠追踪
Shanghai baolei 上海堡垒
Shanghai manhua 上海漫画
Shanghai poke 上海泼克
"Shanghen" 伤痕
shangtu xiawen 上图下文
"Shanhu dao shang de jianzhushi" 珊瑚岛上的建筑师
"Shanhu dao shang de siguang" 珊瑚岛上的死光
Shanshan shuishui 山山水水
shaoshuo wei jia 少说为佳
"Shayu zhenchabing" 鲨鱼侦察兵
"Shejichang de mimi" 射击场的秘密
Shen Bochen 沈泊尘
Shengming qu: kexue huanxiang gushi ji 生命曲：科学幻想故事集
Shengsi bodou 生死搏斗
"Shengsi weibu" 生死未卜
"Sheng zhang shui" 生长水
"Shenhai yi an" 深海疑案
"Shenmi de bo" 神秘的波
"Shenmi de da shimu" 神秘的大石墓
"Shenmi de erhuan" 神秘的耳环
"Shenmi de xinhao" 神秘的信号
Shenmi yi 神秘衣
"Shenqi de deng" 神奇的灯
Shen Xueren 沈雪仁

Shen yi 神翼
Shiji 史记
"Shijie shang diyige jiqiren zhi si" 世界上第一个机器人之死
"Shijie zuigaofeng shang de qiji" 世界最高峰上的奇迹
Shi Lin 石霖
"Shiqu bizi yihou" 失去鼻子以后
"Shiqu de jiyi" 失去的记忆
"Shisun xing" 石笋行
"Shiyou danbai" 石油蛋白
Shiyue 十月
"Shizong de gege" 失踪的哥哥
"Shizong de jiqiren" 失踪的机器人
Shouhuo 收获
si da jian 四大件
Siwang de wen 死亡的吻
Taipingyang ren 太平洋人
"Taiyang tanxian ji" 太阳探险记
"Tang wen" 汤问
"Tantan wo dui kexue wenyi de renshi" 谈谈我对科学文艺的认识
"Tian guan shu" 天官书
"Tianmi de jijie" 甜蜜的季节
Tian qing xibei 天倾西北
"Tiantian de shuilian" 甜甜的睡莲
Tianyi Jushi 天一居士
tiaohe xinjiu, zhenbian mosu 调和新旧，针砭末俗
tichu xuannian 提出悬念
Tiedao youjidui 铁道游击队
Tong Enzheng 童恩正
tongsu wenxue 通俗文学
tongsu xiaoshuo 通俗小说
"Tuhua shang de qiji" 图画上的奇迹
tuili xiaoshuo 推理小说
tujie kepu 图解科普
"Tu yanquan de nüyou" 吐烟圈的女友

"T yinzi de beiju" T 因子的悲剧
Wang Bao'an 王宝安
Wangfu guaiying 王府怪影
Wang Jinhai 王金海
"Wanguo bolanhui shang de qie an" 万国博览会上的窃案
Wang Qi 王琦
Wang Xiaoda 王晓达
Wang Yafa 王亚法
Wan Huankui 万焕奎
"Wanneng fuwu gongsi de zuijia fang an" 万能服务公司的最佳方案
Wei Liao 未燎
weixing xiaoshuo 微型小说
Wei Yahua 魏雅华
Wenhui bao 文汇报
Wenyi bao 文艺报
Wen Yiduo 闻一多
Wo de pengyou xiao haitun 我的朋友小海豚
"Wo jueding he jiqiren qizi lihun" 我决定和机器人妻子离婚
Wu Boze 吴伯泽
"Wusongkou wai de jingbao" 吴淞口外的警报
"Wuwannian yiqian de keren" 五万年以前的客人
Wu za zu 五杂俎
"X-3 an jian" X-3案件
"Xiahe yizhi shu" 下颌移植术
Xialuoke qi'an kaichang 夏洛克奇案开场
Xiangyang she 向阳社
Xianhe yu ren 仙鹤与人
Xian wai zhi yin 弦外之音
"Xiaocheng fengbo" 小城风波
Xiao Erhei jiehun 小二黑结婚
Xiao faming jia 小发明家
Xiao honglian he xiao lanlian 小红脸和小蓝脸
Xiao Jianheng 肖建亨
Xiao kedou zhao mama 小蝌蚪找妈妈

xiaoren shu 小人书
Xiao Sun he Lao Sun 小孙和老孙
Xie Shijun 谢世俊
Xin Bao 忻趵
Xingxing ying 星星营
Xin Tianweng 信天翁
Xin xiyouji 新西游记
"Xinzang tingzhi tiaodong yihou" 心脏停止跳动以后
Xiongmei kaihuang 兄妹开荒
Xiongzhai meiren tou 凶宅美人头
"Xueshan modi" 雪山魔笛
Xu Jie 徐杰
xungen 寻根
yangge 秧歌
Yang Nan 杨楠
Yanshi 偃师
yansu wenxue 严肃文学
Yaoyuan de ai 遥远的爱
Ye Qianyu 叶浅予
Ye Yonglie 叶永烈
"Yiben donghua xiaorenshu" 一本动画小人书
"Yichang qiguai de yanchu" 一场奇怪的演出
"Yige mangren de shouji" 一个盲人的手记
Yi jian zhi 夷坚志
"Ying pai shoubiao de mimi" 鹰牌手表的秘密
Ying Wenhui 应文辉
Yinshen boshi 隐身博士
Yin xing ren 隐形人
Yi wen zhi 艺文志
Yixiang tiankai 异想天开
Yiyuan zhaohua 艺苑朝华
"Yizhi qiguai de mifeng" 一只奇怪的蜜蜂
Youyang zazu 酉阳杂俎
You Yi 尤异

Yuan Li 苑莉
yuannian 元年
"Yuantan shuijing shan" 远探水晶山
Yuanyuan de feizao pao 圆圆的肥皂泡
Yuanyuan he jiqi ren 圆圆和机器人
"Yuhangyuan de guilai" 宇航员的归来
Yuqin guzong 欲擒故纵
yuzhou kongjian 宇宙空间
Zaisheng yongshi 再生勇士
"Zai shijian de qian mu houmian" 在时间的铅幕后面
"Zhang chibang de mao" 长翅膀的猫
Zhang Fengjiang 张凤江
Zhang Leping 张乐平
Zhang Xiaotian 张笑天
Zhang Yiwu 章以武
Zhang Zhuo 张鷟
Zhanshen de houyi 战神的后裔
"Zhao Lan he ta de shuangqin" 赵岚和她的双亲
Zhao Yuqiu 赵玉秋
"Zhengfu yueliang de renmen" 征服月亮的人们
"Zhengui dongwu baojian yiyuan" 珍贵动物保健医院
Zheng Wenguang 郑文光
Zheng Yuanjie 郑渊洁
"Zhenqi dongwu de chuangzao zhe" 珍奇动物的创造者
zhentan xiaoshuo 侦探小说
Zhexuejia 哲学家
Zhihui shu 智慧树
Zhishi jiushi liliang 知识就是力量
zhishi yingkuai 知识硬块
Zhizui jinmi 纸醉金迷
"Zhong fangzi" 种房子
Zhongguo kehuan xiaoshuo bao 中国科幻小说报
Zhongguo lishi shang de yuzhou lilun 中国历史上的宇宙理论
Zhongguo tianwenxue yuanliu 中国天文学源流

Zhongguo 2185 中国2185
Zhou Baoqing 周保庆
Zhou Xiangeng 周先庚
Zhou yi wang 周懿王
Zhou Yongnian 周永年
"Zhuizong konglong de ren" 追踪恐龙的人
"Zuihou yige aizheng huanzhe" 最后一个癌症患者

Bibliography

Ashley, Mike. *Science Fiction Rebels: The Story of the Science Fiction Magazines from 1981 to 1990*. Liverpool: Liverpool University Press, 2016.

Baucom, Ian. "The Human Shore: Postcolonial Studies in an Age of Natural Science." *History of the Present* 2, no. 1 (2012): 1–23.

Bolton, Eleanor M., and J. Andrew Bradley. "Mechanism of Immune Rejection of Stem Cell–Derived Tissue: Insights from Organ Transplantation." In *The Immunological Barriers to Regenerative Medicine*, edited by Paul J. Fairchild, 3–36. New York: Humana, 2013.

Booker, M. Keith, and Anne-Marie Thomas. "The Alien Invasion Narrative." In *The Science Fiction Handbook*, 28–39. West Sussex: Wiley-Blackwell, 2009.

Bourdieu, Pierre. *The Field of Cultural Production*. Edited and introduced by Randal Johnson. New York: Columbia University Press, 1993.

– *The Rules of Art: Genesis and Structure of the Literary Field*. Translated by Susan Emanuel. Stanford: Stanford University Press, 1996.

Bradbury, Ray. *The Martian Chronicles*. Garden City: Doubleday, 1973.

Britikov, Anatoly. *Russkij sovetskij nauchno fantasticeskii roman* [Russian Soviet science phantasy fiction]. Leningrad: Izd. Nauka, 1971.

Brown, Lesley. *The New Shorter Oxford English Dictionary*. Vol. 1. Oxford: Oxford University Press, 1993.

Cao Yu 曹育. "Jichu xueke de jianli: shengwu xue" 基础学科的建立：生物学 [Founding of foundational disciplines: Biology]. In *Zhongguo jin xiandai kexue jishu shi* 中国近现代科学技术史 [A history of modern Chinese science and technology], edited by Dong Guangbi 董光璧, 688–739. Changsha: Hunan jiaoyu chubanshe, 1995.

Chakrabarty, Dipesh. "The Climate of History: Four Theses." *Critical Inquiry* 35, no. 2 (2009): 197–222.

Chen Jie 陈洁. *Qinli zhongguo kehuan: Zheng Wenguang pingzhuan* 亲历中国科幻：郑文光评传 [Experiencing Chinese science fiction: Zheng Wenguang's biography]. Fuzhou: Fujian shaonian ertong chubanshe, 2006.

Chu Qinghua 初清华. "Xin shiqi tongsu wenxue xingqi xianxiang chongxi" 新时期通俗文学兴起现象重析 [Re-evaluating the emergence of popular fiction in the new era]. *Nanjing shifan daxue wenxue yuan xuebao* 南京师范大学文学院学报 [Journal of the College of Literature in Nanjing Normal University] 4 (2012): 114–21.

Csicsery-Ronay, Istvan Jr. "Science Fiction and the Thaw." *Science Fiction Studies* 31, no. 3 (2004): 337–44.

Deng Xiaoping 邓小平. "Deng Xiaoping zai quanguo kexue dahui kaimushi shang de jianghua" 邓小平在全国科学大会开幕式上的讲话 [Deng Xiaoping's talk at the opening ceremony of the national science conference]. *Renminwang*, 18 March 1978. http://scitech.people.com.cn/GB/25509/56813/57267/57268/4001431.html.

– "Zai zhongguo wenxue yishu gongzuozhe disici daibiao dahui shang de zhuci" 在中国文学艺术工作者第四次代表大会上的祝辞 [Congratulatory speech at the Fourth National Conference of Chinese Writers and Artists]. *Xinhuawang*, 30 October 1979, accessed 25 March 2015, http://news.xinhuanet.com/ziliao/2005-02/04/content_2548288.htm (site discontinued).

Dikötter, Frank. *Mao's Great Famine: The History of China's Most Devastating Catastrophe, 1958–1962*. New York: Walker Publishing, 2011.

Dizhibao bianji bu 地质报编辑部, ed. *Kepu zuojia tan chuangzuo* 科普作家谈创作 [Popular science writers on writing]. Beijing: Dizhi chubanshe, 1980.

Dong Renwei 董仁威. "Liu Xingshi: kehuan xiaoshuo de laobing" 刘兴诗：科幻小说的老兵 [Liu Xingshi: A veteran science fiction writer]. *Renmin wang*, 19 September 2007, http://scitech.people.com.cn/GB/131715/131743/7791030.html.

– "Tong Enzheng zhuan" 童恩正传 [The biography of Tong Enzheng]. *Langman zhi lü: zhuming kehuan zuojia pingzhuan* 浪漫之旅：著名科幻作家评传 [The romantic journey: Biographies and evaluations of renowned Chinese science fiction writers], 4 January 2007, http://www.360doc.com/content/07/0513/18/21434_498170.shtml.

Dong Renwei and Yao Haijun 姚海军, eds. *Zhongguo kehuan mingjia mingzuo daxi: Tong Enzheng* 中国科幻名家名作大系：童恩正 [A grand collection of science fiction works of eminent Chinese writers: Tong Enzheng]. Beijing: Renmin youdian chubanshe, 2012.

Duke, Michael S. *Blooming and Contending: Chinese Literature in the Post-Mao Era*. Bloomington: Indiana University Press, 1985.

Ellis, John. *Visible Fictions: Cinema Television Video*. London: Routledge and Kegan Paul, 1982.

Engels, Frederick. "The Part Played by Labour in the Transition from Ape to Man." Translated by Clemens Dutt, 1876, https://www.marxists.org/archive/marx/works/1876/part-played-labour/.

"Ershi shiji bashi niandai: zhongguo wenxue zazhi fengbao" 二十世纪八十年代：中国文学杂志风暴 [The storm of Chinese literary magazines in the 1980s]. *Fenghuang wang dushu* 凤凰网读书 [Phoenix net: Reading], 21 April 2011. http://book.ifeng.com/gundong/detail_2011_04/21/5887250_0.shtml.

Fogg, Martyn J. *Terraforming: Engineering Planetary Environments*. Warrendale, PA: Society of Automotive Engineers, 1995.

Gelder, Ken. *Popular Fiction: The Logics and Practices of a Literary Field*. New York: Routledge, 2004.

Glover, David. "The Thriller." In Priestman, *Cambridge Companion to Crime Fiction*, 135–54.

Gold, Thomas B. "Just in Time! China Battles Spiritual Pollution on the Eve of 1983." *Asian Survey* 24, no. 9 (1984): 947–74.

Gomel, Elana. "Gods like Men: Soviet Science Fiction and the Utopian Self." *Science Fiction Studies* 31, no. 3 (November 2004): 358–77.

Gordon, Joan. "Literary Science Fiction." In *The Oxford Handbook of Science Fiction*, edited by Rob Latham, 104–14. Oxford: Oxford University Press, 2014.

Hayles, Katherine. *How We Became Posthuman: Virtual Bodies in Cybernetics, Literature, and Informatics*. Chicago: University of Chicago Press, 1999.

Heller, Leonid. *De la science fiction soviétique, par delà le dogme, un univers*. Geneva: L'Age d'homme, 1991.

He Qing. "Eight-Character Policies." In *Major Issues and Policies in China's Financial Reform*, edited by Chen Yulu and Guo Qingwang, 2:1–31. Hong Kong: Enrich Professional Publishing, 2013.

Hollinger, Veronica. "Science Fiction and Postmodernism." In *A Companion to Science Fiction*, edited by David Seed, 232–47. Malden, MA: Blackwell Publishing, 2005.

Huang Yi 黄伊. "Kexue huanxiang xiaoshuo siti 科学幻想小说四题 [The four questions about science fiction]. In Huang, *Lun kexue huanxiang xiaoshuo*, 120–9.

– ed. *Kexue huanxiang xiaoshuo xuan* 科学幻想小说选 [An anthology of science fiction]. Beijing: Zhongguo qingnian chubanshe, 1980.

– ed. *Lun kexue huanxiang xiaoshuo* 论科学幻想小说 [On science fiction]. Beijing: Kexue puji chubanshe, 1981.

– ed. *Zuojia lun kexue wenyi* 作家论科学文艺 [Writers on literature and art about science]. 2 vols. Nanjing: Jiangsu kexue jishu chubanshe, 1980.

Hulsewé, A.F.P. "Han shu." In *Early Chinese Texts: A Bibliographical Guide*, edited by Michael Loewe, 129–36. Berkeley: Society for the Study of Early China & Institute of East Asian Studies, University of California Berkeley, 1993.

Isaacson, Nathaniel. *Celestial Empire: The Emergence of Chinese Science Fiction*. Middletown, CT: Wesleyan University Press, 2017.

James, Edward, and Farah Mendlesohn, eds. *The Cambridge Companion to Science Fiction*. Cambridge: Cambridge University Press, 2003.

Jenkins, Henry. *Convergence Culture: Where Old and New Media Collide*. New York: New York University Press, 2006.

Jin Tao 金涛. "Diyi zhi wang" 地衣之王 [The king lichen]. In Rao, *Zhongguo kehuan xiaoshuo nianjian*, 208–25.

Jin Wulun 金吾伦. "Zhongguo gao keji fazhan gaikuang" 中国高科技发展概况 [A survey of the development of advanced technology in China]. In *Zhongguo jin xiandai kexue jishu shi* 中国近现代科学技术史 [A history of modern Chinese science and technology], edited by Dong Guangbi 董光璧, 1323–41. Changsha: Hunan jiaoyu chubanshe, 1995.

Johnson, Randal. "Editor's Introduction: Pierre Bourdieu on Art, Literature and Culture." In Bourdieu, *Field of Cultural Production*, 1–25.

Jones, Gwyneth. "The Icons of Science Fiction." In James and Mendlesohn, *Cambridge Companion to Science Fiction*, 163–73.

Jorgensen, Darren. "Postmodernism." In *The Routledge Companion to Science Fiction*, edited by Mark Bould, Andrew M. Butler, Adam Roberts, and Sherryl Vint, 279–87. New York: Routledge, 2009.

Kinkley, Jeffrey C., ed. *After Mao: Chinese Literature and Society 1978–1981*. Cambridge: The Council on East Asian Studies at Harvard University, 1985.

Krementsov, Nikolai. *Revolutionary Experiments: The Quest for Immortality in Bolshevik Science and Fiction*. Oxford: Oxford University Press, 2014.

Lee, Leo Ou-Fan. "The Politics of Technique: Perspectives of Literary Dissidence in Contemporary Chinese Fiction." In Kinkley, *After Mao*, 159–90.

Lee, Martyn J. *Consumer Culture Reborn: The Cultural Politics of Consumption*. London: Routledge, 1993.

Lee, Yee. "Introduction: A Reflection of Reality." In *The New Realism: Writing from China after the Cultural Revolution*, edited by Lee Yee, 3–16. New York: Hippocrene Books, 1983.

Li Guijie 李桂杰. *Buhui chengfeng de jiyi: baixing shenghuo sanshi nian* 不会尘封的记忆：百姓生活三十年 [Undusted memory: People's life during three decades 1978–2008]. Changsha: Hunan kexue jishu chubanshe, 2009.

Li Hua. "Animating Science and Technology: From Little Tadpoles to the Space Monkey (1950s–1980s)." *Association for Chinese Animation Studies*, 1 September 2017, http://acas.ust.hk/2017/09/01/animating-science-and-technology-from-little-tadpoles-to-the-space-monkey-1950s-1980s/.

– "'Are We, People from the Earth, so Terrible?': An Atmospheric Crisis in Zheng Wenguang's *Descendent of Mars*." *Science Fiction Studies* 43, no. 3 (November 2018): 545–59.

– "The Political Imagination in Liu Cixin's Critical Utopia: China 2185." *Science Fiction Studies* 42, no. 3 (November 2015): 519–41.

Li Jingze 李敬泽. "Wo buxiang tanlun bashi niandai" 我不想谈论八十年代 [I do not want to talk about the 1980s]. *Jiemian* 界面 [Interface], 5 May 2015. http://www.jiemian.com/article/274833.html.

Link, Perry. *The Uses of Literature: Life in the Socialist Chinese Literary System*. Princeton, NJ: Princeton University Press, 2000.

Li Qiang 李强. "Naoti daogua yu woguo shichang jingji fazhan de liangge jieduan" 脑体倒挂与我国市场经济发展的两个阶段 [Reverse wage disparities between white-collar and blue-collar employees, and the two stages of the development of China's market economy]. *Shehuixue yanjiu* 社会学研究 [Sociological research] 6 (1996): 5–12.

Liu Cixin 刘慈欣. "Shanhu dao shang de siguang" 珊瑚岛上的死光 [On "Death Ray on a Coral Island"]. *Kehuan Net*, 7 February 2011, http://www.kehuan.net.cn/article/25.html,

– "Xiaoshi de xiliu: Bashi niandai de zhongguo kehuan" 消失的溪流：八十年代的中国科幻 [A vanished creek: Chinese science fiction in the 1980s]. *Kehuan Net*, 7 February 2011, http://www.kehuan.net.cn/article/8.html.

Liu Jian 刘健. "Ershi shiji jiushi niandai zhongguo kehuan aihaozhe zazhi zongshu" 20世纪90年代中国科幻爱好者杂志综述 [A general review of Chinese fanzines in the 1990s]. *Dushu wenzhai* 读书文摘 [Reading excerpts] 2 (2015): 26–8.

Li Yang 李洋. "Kehuan shijie: 36 nian zhizhuo shouhu kehuan xiangxiang li" 科幻世界：36年执着守护科幻想象力 [*Science Fiction World*: A guardian of the SF imagination for thirty-six years]. *Beijing ribao* 北京日报 [Beijing daily], 24 September 2015, http://cul.qq.com/a/20150924/021653.htm.

Li Yanli 李艳丽 and Yan Shuchang 阎书昌. "Zhou Xiangeng yu Bapuluofu xueshuo 1950 niandai de yinjie" 周先庚与巴浦洛夫学说1950年代的引介 [Zhou Xiangeng and the 1950s popularization of Pavlov's theories]. *Zhongguo keji shi zazhi* 中国科技史杂志 [Journal of the history of Chinese science and technology] 35, no. 3 (2014): 332–45.

Li Yuan 李元. "Kepu chatu yu tujie kepu xiaoyi" 科普插图与图解科普小议 [Modest discussions on popular science illustrations and graphic popular science books]. In Dizhibao, *Kepu zuojia tan chuangzuo*, 236–43.

Lohmar, Bryan, Fred Gale, Francis Tuan, and Jim Hansen. "China's Ongoing Agricultural Modernization: Challenges Remain after 30 Years of Reform." *Economic Information Bulletin* 51 (April 2009). https://www.ers.usda.gov/webdocs/publications/44377/eib-51.pdf?v=0.

Louie, Kam. "Love Stories: The Meaning of Love and Marriage in China." In Kinkley, *After Mao*, 63–87.

Lu Bing 鲁兵. "Linghun chuqiao de wenxue" 灵魂出窍的文学 [Literature without a soul]. In *Kepu xiaoyi* 科普小议 [Modest discussions of popular science writing], edited by Zhongguo qingnianbao zhang zhishi fukan bianjibu, 23–5. Beijing: Kexue puji chubanshe, 1981.

Lu Xun. "Diary of a Madman." In *The Columbia Anthology of Modern Chinese Literature*, 2nd ed., edited by Joseph S.M. Lau and Howard Goldblatt, 8–16. New York: Columbia University Press, 2007.

Lu Zhaowen 鲁肇文. "Tiantian de shuilian" 甜甜的睡莲 [The sweet lily]. In Rao, *Zhongguo kehuan xiaoshuo nianjian*, 103–55.

Ma Li 马丽, ed. "1980 nian xin zhongguo diyibu kehuan pian: zai yi 'shanhu dao'" 1980年新中国第一部科幻片 再忆"珊瑚岛" [New China's first SF film in 1980: A recollection of *Coral Island*]. *Renmin wang*, 24 March 2005, http://scitech.people.com.cn/GB/1056/3267452.html.

Mao Zedong 毛泽东. "Lun renmin minzhu zhuanzheng" 论人民民主专政 [On the people's democratic dictatorship]. In *Mao Zedong xuanji* 毛泽东选集 [Selected works of Mao Zedong], 2nd ed., 4:1468–82. Beijing: Renmin chubanshe, 1991.

McCloud, Scott. *Understanding Comics: The Invisible Art*. New York: Harper Perennial, 1993.

McLuhan, Marshall. *Understanding Media: The Extensions of Man*. New York: Routledge, 2001.

Miao Yintang 缪印堂. "Kexue manhua chuangzuo tan" 科学漫画创作谈 [On Science Comics]. *Kepu chuangzuo* 科普创作 [Popular science writing] 3 (1993): 3–7.

Milburn, Colin. "Posthumanism." In *The Oxford Handbook of Science Fiction*, edited by Rob Latham, 524–36. Oxford: Oxford University Press, 2014.

Moore, Francis D. *Give and Take: The Development of Tissue Transplantation*. New York: Doubleday, 1964.

Otto, Eric C. "Kim Stanley Robinson's *Mars* Trilogy and the Leopoldian Land Ethic." *Utopian Studies* 14, no. 2 (2003): 118–35.

Pak, Chris. *Terraforming: Ecopolitical Transformations and Environmentalism in Science Fiction*. Liverpool: Liverpool University Press, 2016.

Petersen, Robert S. *Comic, Manga, and Graphic Novels: A History of Graphic Narratives*. Santa Barbara, CA: Praeger, 2011.

Pohl, Frederik, and Elizabeth Anne Hull, eds. *Tales from the Planet Earth*. New York: St. Martin's, 1986.

Pontieri, Laura. *Soviet Animation and the Thaw of the 1960s: Not Only for Children*. New Barnet, UK: John Libbey Publishing, 2012.

Pool, Ithiel de Sola. *Technologies of Freedom: On Free Speech in an Electronic Age*. Cambridge, MA: Harvard University Press, 1983.

Priestman, Martin, ed. *The Cambridge Companion to Crime Fiction*. Cambridge: Cambridge University Press, 2003.

Qian Yingqian 钱迎倩, Wang Yahui 王亚辉, and Qi Guorong 祁国荣, eds. *Ershi shiji Zhongguo xueshu dadian: shengwu xue* 二十世纪中国学术大典：生物学 [China's academic canons in the twentieth century: Biology]. Fuzhou: Fujian jiaoyu chubanshe, 2004.

Rao Zhonghua 饶忠华. "Yongjiu de meili: Zhongguo kehuan xiaoshuo fazhanshi chutan" 永久的魅力：中国科幻小说发展史初探 [Long-lasting charm: Exploration of the history of Chinese science fiction]. In Rao, *Zhongguo kehuan xiaoshuo daquan*, 1–26.

– ed. *Zhongguo kehuan xiaoshuo daquan* 中国科幻小说大全 [A compendium of Chinese science fiction]. 3 vols. Beijing: Haiyang chubanshe, 1982.

– ed. *Zhongguo kehuan xiaoshuo nianjian: kexue shenhua (san)* 中国科幻小说年鉴：科学神话 (三) [A yearbook of Chinese science fiction: Science fantasy (III)]. Beijing: Haiyang chubanshe, 1983.

Rao Zhonghua and Lin Yaochen 林耀琛. "Zhongguo kehuan xiaoshuo zai tansuo zhong qianjin" 中国科幻小说在探索中前进 [The development and exploration of Chinese science fiction]. In Rao, *Zhongguo kehuan xiaoshuo nianjian*, 2–22.

Scholes, Robert, and Eric S. Rabkin. *Science Fiction: History, Science, Vision*. New York: Oxford University Press, 1977.

Science Fiction World. Inaugural issue. January 1979, http://ishare.iask.sina.com.cn/f/17749646.html.

Seed, David. *Science Fiction: A Very Short Introduction*. Oxford: Oxford University Press, 2011.

– "Spy Fiction." In Priestman, *Cambridge Companion to Crime Fiction*, 115–34.

Shapiro, Judith. *Mao's War against Nature: Politics and the Environment in Revolutionary China*. Cambridge: Cambridge University Press, 2001.

Sima Qian. "Tianguan shu" 天官书 [Treatise on celestial offices]. In *Shiji* 史记 [*Records of the Grand Historian*], 91 BCE, https://ctext.org/shiji/tian-guan-shu/zhs.

Slonczewski, Joan, and Michael Levy. "Science Fiction and the Life Sciences." In James and Mendlesohn, *Cambridge Companion to Science Fiction*, 174–85.

Song, Mingwei. "Variations on Utopia in Contemporary Chinese Science Fiction." *Science Fiction Studies* 40, no. 1 (March 2013): 86–102.

Steinberg, Marc. *Anime's Media Mix: Franchising Toys and Characters in Japan*. Minneapolis: University of Minnesota Press, 2012.

Suvin, Darko. *Metamorphoses of Science Fiction*. New Haven, CT: Yale University Press, 1979.

Tang Shougen 汤寿根. "Wo yu kepu chuangzuo zazhi" 我与《科普创作》杂志 [The magazine *Popular Science Creative Writing* and me]. *360doc* (accessed 26 March 2015), http://www.360doc.com/content/09/0819/08/16239_5038313.shtml (site discontinued).

Tao Shilong 陶世龙. "Xu: Haishi yi yi yi hao" 序：还是议一议好 [Preface: It is better to talk about it]. In *Kepu xiaoyi* 科普小议 [Modest discussions of popular science writing], edited by Zhongguo qingnianbao zhang zhishi fukan bianjibu, i–iii. Beijing: Kexue puji chubanshe, 1981.

Tong Enzheng 童恩正. "Chuangzuo kexue huanxiang xiaoshuode tihui" 创作科学幻想小说体会 [My experiences of writing science ciction]. In Dizhibao, *Kepu zuojia tan chuangzuo*, 158–67.

– "The Death of the World's First Robot." In Wu and Murphy, *Science Fiction from China*, 3–8.

– "Diyici shibai" 第一次失败 [The first defeat]. In Dong and Yao, *Zhongguo kehuan mingjia mingzuo daxi*, 237–48.

– "Guanyu shanhudao shang de siguang" 关于《珊瑚岛上的死光》[About "Death Ray on a Coral Island"]. *Yuwen jiaoxue tongxue* [Chinese education newsletter] 3 (1980): 57–8.

– *Guxia miwu* 古峡迷雾 [Dense fog over the old gorge]. Shanghai: Shaonian ertong chubanshe, 1978.

– "Houji" 后记 [Afterword]. In *Xin xi you ji* 新西游记 [New journey to the West]. http://my285.com/kh/tez/xyxj/001.htm.

– "The Middle Kingdom." In *Tales from the Planet Earth*, translated by Dingbo Wu, edited by Frederik Pohl and Elizabeth Anne Hull, 193–207. New York: St. Martin's, 1986.

– "Shisun xing" 石笋行 [Song of the stalagmites]. In Dong and Yao, *Zhongguo kehuan mingjia mingzuo daxi*, 53–66.

– "Tantan wo dui kexue wenyi de renshi" 谈谈我对科学文艺的认识 [My understanding of literature and art about science]. In Huang, *Zuojia lun kexue wenyi*, 1:122–3.

– "Wode jingli" 我的经历 [My experience]. In *Wo yu ertong wenxue* 我与儿童文学 [Children's literature and me], 143–53. Hangzhou: Zhejiang shifan ertong wenxue yanjiushi, 1980.

– "Wuwan nian yiqian de keren" 五万年以前的客人 [The guest from fifty thousand years ago]. In Huang, *Kexue huanxiang xiaoshuo xuan*, 185–97.

– "Yaoyuan de ai" 遥远的爱 [Faraway love]. In Ye, *Zhongguo kexue huanxiang xiaoshuo xuan*, 283–311.

Verellen, Franciscus. "'Evidential Miracles in Support of Taoism': The Inversion of a Buddhist Apologetic Tradition in Late Tang China." *Toung Pao* 78, no. 4 (1992): 217–63.

Vermeulen, Pieter. "'The Sea, Not the Ocean': Anthropocene Fiction and the Memory of (Non)human Life." *Genre* 50, no. 2 (July 2017): 181–200.

Volland, Nicolai. "Comment on 'Let's Go to the Moon.'" *Journal of Asian Studies* 73, no. 2 (May 2014): 353–8.

– "Soviet Spaceships in Socialist China: Reading Soviet Popular Literature in the 1950s." *Modern China Studies* 22, no. 1 (2015): 192–213.

Wagner, Rudolph G. "Lobby Literature: The Archeology and Present Functions of Science Fiction in China." In Kinkley, *After Mao*, 17–62.

Wang, David Der-wei. "Introduction." In *From May Fourth to June Fourth: Fiction and Film in Twentieth-Century China*, edited by Ellen Widmer and

David Der-wei Wang, 1–15. Cambridge, MA: Harvard University Press, 1993.

Wang Dazhi 王大智 and Cao Ying 曹莹. "Fusu yu chongjian: Zhongguo donghua de di er ci fanrong 1977–1983" 复苏与重建：中国动画的第二次繁荣 1977–1983 [Recovery and reconstruction: The second boom of Chinese animation 1977–1983]. In *Zhongguo donghua shi* 中国动画史 [The history of Chinese animation], edited by Gong Chengbo 宫承波, 139–202. Beijing: Zhongguo guangbo yingshi chubanshe, 2015.

Wang Dazhi and Liu Xiaowei 刘小玮. "Zhuanxing yu zhentong: Zhongguo Xuepai de shiluo yu xiaoyin 1984–1994" 转型与阵痛：中国学派的失落与消隐 1984–1994 [Transition and pain: the Decline of the "Chinese school" 1984–1994]. In *Zhongguo donghua shi* 中国动画史 [The history of Chinese animation], edited by Gong Chengbo 宫承波, 204–46. Beijing: Zhongguo guangbo yingshi chubanshe, 2015.

Wang Defeng 王德风. "Wo suo jieshi de Ye Yonglie" 我所结识的叶永烈 [Ye Yonglie as I have known]. In *Fengzheng bu duanxian* 风筝不断线 [The kite with an unbroken string], edited by Shi Xinrong and Hao Gefei, 18–20. Beijing: Xianzhuang shuju, 2003.

Wang Qi 王琦. "Meigui yu baojian" 玫瑰与宝剑 [Rose and sword]. *Kexue shidai* 科学时代 [Science era] 1 (1978): 54–8.

Wang Yafa 王亚法. "Huiyi Tong Enzheng" 回忆童恩正 [In memory of Tong Enzheng]. *Xuexi bolan* 学习博览 [Expansive study] 12 (2010): 22–3.

Wan Huankui. "Tu yanquan de nüyou" 吐烟圈的女友 [The girlfriend who blows smoke rings]. *Kexue wenyi* 3 (1982): 39, 53.

World Bank Data. "Urban Population: China." *United Nations, World Urbanization Prospects*, http://data.worldbank.org/indicator/SP.URB.TOTL.IN.ZS?end=2015&locations=CN-MO&start=1960&view=chart&year=1982&year_low_desc=false.

Wu Bin 武斌. "Xin Zhongguo chengli chuqi gaochou zhidu de zhiding yu xiugai" 新中国成立初期稿酬制度的制定与修改 [Drafting and revising remuneration systems in the early years after the founding of New China]. *Chuban faxing yanjiu* 出版发行研究 [Publication and circulation research] 4 (2014): 96–100.

Wu Dingbo. "Chinese Science Fiction." In *Handbook of Chinese Popular Culture*, edited by Dingbo Wu and Patrick D. Murphy, 257–78. London: Greenwood, 1994.

– "Fandom in China." In *Science Fiction Fandom*, edited by Joseph L. Sanders, 133–6. Westport, CT: Greenwood, 1994.

– "Looking Backward: An Introduction to Chinese Science Fiction." In Wu and Murphy, *Science Fiction from China*, xi–xli.

Wu Dingbo and Patrick D. Murphy, eds. *Science Fiction from China*. New York: Praeger, 1989.

Wu Yan 吴岩. "Lun Zheng Wenguang de kehuan wenxue chaungzuo" 论郑文光的科幻文学创作 [On Zheng Wenguang's science fiction]. *Journal of Daqing College* 22, no. 2 (April 2002): 111–18.

Xiao Jianheng 肖建亨. "Buke de qiyu" 布克的奇遇 [Buke's adventure]. In Ye, *Zhongguo kexue huanxiang xiaoshuo xuan*, 71–84.

– "Jinxing ren zhi mi" 金星人之谜 [Mystery of the Venusian]. In Huang, *Kexue huanxiang xiaoshuo xuan*, 154–85.

– "Qiao er huanbing ji" 乔二患病记 [Qiao the Younger fell ill]. *Renmin wenxue* 人民文学 [People's literature] 12 (1982): 97–102.

– "Shaluomu jiaoshou de miwu" 沙洛姆教授的迷误 [Professor Shalom's confusion]. In Ye, *Zhongguo kexue huanxiang xiaoshuo xuan*, 312–35.

– "Shi tan wo guo kexue huanxiang xiaoshuo de fazhan" 试谈我国科学幻想小说的发展 [On the development of Chinese science fiction]. In Huang, *Lun kexue huanxiang xiaoshuo*, 8–47.

– "Zhang zai shushang de ya: xiaoyi women weishenme huanxiang" 长在树上的鸭：小议我们为什么幻想 [A duck growing on a tree: A discussion of imagination]. In, *Kepu xiaoyi* 科普小议 [Modest discussions of popular science writing], edited by Zhongguo qingnianbao zhang zhishi fukan bianjibu, 9–10. Beijing: Kexue puji chubanshe, 1981.

Xinjing Bao 新京报. "Liulang diqiu kaiqi zhongguo kehuan dianying yuannian" 流浪地球开启中国科幻电影元年 [*Wandering Earth* marks Year One of Chinese science fiction movie]. *Xinhua wang* 新华网 [New China net], 10 February 2019, http://www.xinhuanet.com/tech/2019-02/10/c_1124095946.htm.

Xiong Weimin 熊卫民 and Wang Jing 王静. "Kexue chubanshe shengwu xue xueke xueshu chuban gailan" 科学出版社生物学学科学术出版概览 [A general review of books on biology published by Science Press]. *Zhongguo kexueyuan yuanyou fuwu wang* 中国科学院院友服务网 [Chinese Academy of Sciences Alumni Net:], 28 November 2014, http://alumni.cas.cn/kyws/201411/t20141128_4264396.html.

Xu Hong 徐宏 and Wang Liping 王立平. "Feiben ba! Kexue de hangchuan" 飞奔吧！科学的航船 [Fly! Spaceship of science], 1980, http://m.zhaogepu.com/qita/400186.html.

Yang Yang 杨洋. "Bashi niandai de Ye Yonglie: Zenyang cong xing ke zhuandao xing wen" 八十年代的叶永烈：怎样从姓科转到姓文 [Ye Yonglie in the 1980s: From science fiction to reportage literature]. *Xin zhou kan* 新周刊 [News weekly] vol. 400 (accessed 14 March 2015), http://www.neweekly.com.cn/newsview.php?id=5251 (site discontinued).

Yan Hui 严慧. "Xiao Jianheng he ta de kexue huanxiang xiaoshuo" 肖建亨和他的科学幻想小说 [Xiao Jianheng and his science fiction]. In Huang, *Lun kexue huanxiang xiaoshuo*, 178–87.

Yao Di 姚迪. "Mianhuai 'kepu manhua diyi ren' Miao Yintang xiansheng, zhuiyi qi sanshiba zai 'zhili yuan'" 缅怀"科普漫画第一人"缪印堂先生，追忆其三十八载"知力缘" [In memory of the top Chinese popular science *manhua* artist Miao Yintang, and the recollection of his thirty-eight-year connection with *Knowledge Is Power*]. *Wei wenku* 微文库 [Micro library], 2 August 2017, https://www.weiwenku.org/d/101783893.

Yao Haijun 姚海军 and Yang Feng 杨枫. "Kehuan Shijie sanshi nian" 《科幻世界》三十年 [Thirty years of *Science Fiction World*], *Kehuan shijie sanshi zhounian tebie jinian* 《科幻世界》三十周年特别纪念 [Special commemoration of *Science Fiction World* on its thirtieth anniversary], 26 March 2010, https://www.douban.com/group/topic/10498882/.

Ye Yonglie 叶永烈. "Buke de qiyu daodu"《布克的奇遇》导读 [Preface to Buke's adventure]. *Zhongguo kehuan xiaoshuo jingdian* 中国科幻小说经典 [Classics of Chinese science fiction], https://www.xstt5.com/kehuan/9338/526945.html.

– "Guanyu kehuan lianhuanhua" 关于科幻连环画 [About SF graphic novels]. Unpublished essay in an email attachment to author, 14 July 2019.

– *Heiying* 黑影 [Black shadow]. Beijing: Dizhi chubanshe, 1981.

– *Hei ying* 黑影 [Black shadow]. Zhongguo kehuan huangjin shidai kehuan dashi zuopin xuan 中国科幻黄金时代科幻大师作品选 [Selective works of Chinese SF writers during the golden age of Chinese science fiction]. Guiyang: Guizhou daxue chubanshe, 2010.

– "Heng zao pipan" 横遭批判 [Unwarranted animadversion]. In Ye, *Zhuixun lishi zhenxiang*, 2:531–80.

– "Jingxian kehuan xiaoshuo dayi" 惊险科幻小说答疑 [Responses to questions about SF thrillers]. *Dushu* 读书 [Reading] 46, no. 1 (1983): 63–9.

– *Kexue fu er mo si* 科学福尔摩斯 [A scientific Holmes]. In Ye, *Zhongguo jingxian kexue huanxiang xiaoshuo xuan*, 528–641.

– "Kexue tonghua dianying de tedian" 科学童话电影的特点 [The characteristics of scientific fairy-tale films]. In Ye, *Lun kexue wenyi*, 167–8.

– "Kexue wenyi chuangzuo zhaji" 科学文艺创作札记 [Notes on the creation of literature and art about science]. In Huang, *Zuojia lun kexue wenyi*, 1:96–121.

– "Lun kexue huanxiang xiaoshuo" 论科学幻想小说 [On science fiction]. In Huang, *Lun Kexue huanxiang xiaoshuo*, 48–60.

– "Lun kexue manhua" 论科学漫画 [On science *manhua*]. In Ye, *Lun Kexue wenyi*, 184–5.

– *Lun kexue wenyi* 论科学文艺 [On literature and art about science]. Beijing: Kexue puji chubanshe, 1980.

– "Rongyu fenzhi" 荣誉纷至 [Awards and fame flooded in]. In Ye, *Zhuixun lishi zhenxiang*, 1:421–530.

– "Wo de kehuan dianying meng" 我的科幻电影梦 [My dream of making SF film]. *Yeguang bei* 夜光杯 [Night luminous cup], 30 July 2019, https://mp.weixin.qq.com/s/1gG59BqF60XEFZUrZLYxRA.
– "Wo de kehuan qimeng" 我的科幻启蒙 [My early education in science fiction]. *Ye Yonglie's Sina Blog*, 5 May 2011, http://blog.sina.com.cn/s/blog_470bc6dd01017jwn.html.
– "Xu" 序 [Preface]. In Ye, *Zhongguo jingxian kexue huanxiang xiaoshuo xuan*, 1–4.
– "Yuanqu de xiao zi bei" 远去的小字辈 [Young generation has gone far]. Unpublished essay in an email attachment to author, 16 July 2019.
– ed. *Zhongguo jingxian kexue huanxiang xiaoshuo xuan* 中国惊险科学幻想小说选 [An anthology of Chinese SF thrillers]. Nanjing: Jiangsu kexue jishu chubanshe, 1981.
– ed. *Zhongguo kexue huanxiang xiaoshuo xuan* 中国科学幻想小说选 [An anthology of Chinese science fiction]. Shenyang: Liaoning renmin chubanshe, 1982.
– *Zhuixun lishi zhenxiang* 追寻历史的真相 [Pursuing historical truth: My writing career]. 2 vols. Shanghai: Shanghai wenyi chubanshe, 2001.
Zhang Feng 张峰. "Shei shi xia yige Yao Haijun: zhongguo huanxiang lei Fanzine huigu" 谁是下一个姚海军：中国幻想类 Fanzine 回顾 [Who will be the next Yao Haijun: A review of Chinese speculative fiction fanzines]. *Xin huan jie* [World of new fantasy] 1 (2009): 37–40.
– "Zhongguo kehuan zazhi jijian shi" 中国科幻杂志极简史 [A very brief history of Chinese science fiction magazines]. *Douban xiaozu SF* 豆瓣小组 SF [Douban SF forum], https://www.douban.com/group/topic/48611985/.
Zhang Xiyu 张希玉. "Zhongguo diyi jia kehuan xiaoshuobao yaozhe shimo" 中国第一家科幻小说报夭折始末 [How China's first science fiction newspaper came to a premature end]. *Chuban shiliao* [Historical sources about publishers] 2 (2008): 27–30.
Zhang Yiwu 章以武 and Wei Liao 未燎. "Jin ditan pu shang le tian" 金地毯铺上了天 [A golden carpet extending to the horizon]. In Zhang and Wei, *Shengming qu*, 97–111.
– "Lanse de baoweiquan" 蓝色的包围圈 [The blue encirclement]. In Zhang and Wei, *Shengming qu*, 82–96.
– "Mo yuan" 魔园 [The magic orchard]. In Zhang and Wei, *Shengming qu*, 33–48.
– *Shengming qu: kexue huanxiang gushi ji* 生命曲：科学幻想故事集 [Songs of life: A collection of science fiction stories]. Guangzhou: Guangdong keji chubanshe, 1979.
Zhao Shizhou 赵世洲. "Jingxian kehuan xiaoshuo zhiyi" 惊险科幻小说质疑 [Questions about SF thrillers]. *Dushu* 读书 [Reading] 41, no. 8 (1982): 60–5.

Zhao Yao 赵瑶. "Peiyang shehui zhuyi xinren yu dang de jiaoyu fangzhen de lishi tansuo" 培养社会主义新人与党的教育方针的历史探索 [A historical exploration of cultivating socialist new men and the Party's educational agenda]. *Qianxian* 前线 [Frontline] 101, no. 11 (2003) (accessed 17 February 2017), http://www.bjqx.org.cn/qxweb/n3448c177.aspx (site discontinued).

Zheng Jun 郑军. "Di er zhang: Zhongguo kehuan xiaoshuo jianshi" 第二章：中国科幻小说简史 [Concise history of Chinese science fiction]. In Zheng, *Zhongguo kehuan zhi lu*, http://www.51flying.com/say/the2.htm.

– "Di si zhang: Kehuan dianying fazhan jianshi xia" 第四章：科幻电影发展简史 下 [Concise history of Chinese science fiction film, part two]. In Zheng, *Zhongguo kehuan zhi lu*, http://www.51flying.com/say/the4.htm.

– *Zhongguo kehuan zhi lu* 中国科幻之路 [The odyssey of Chinese science fiction]. December 1999, http://www.51flying.com/say/theory.htm.

Zheng Wenguang 郑文光. "Bian hou ji" 编后记 [Postscript]. In Zheng, *Zheng Wenguang zuopin xuan*, 341–3.

– "Cong diqiu dao huoxing" 从地球到火星 [From Earth to Mars]. In *Zheng Wenguang 70 shouchen ji congshi wenxue chuangzuo 59 zhounian jinian wenji* 郑文光70寿辰及从事文学创作59周年纪念文集 [A Festschrift for Zheng Wenguang: A celebration of his 70th birthday and the 59th anniversary of his engagement in creative writing], edited by Wu Yan, 1–7. Privately published. Beijing, 1999.

– "Da Xianggang Kaijuan yuekan jizhe Lü Chen xiansheng wen" 答香港《开卷月刊》记者吕辰先生问 [Response to Mr. Lü Chen, the Hong Kong journalist from *Open the Book Monthly*]. In Huang, *Lun kexue huanxiang xiaoshuo*, 139–48.

– "Di er ge yueliang" 第二个月亮 [The second moon]. Serialized for four installations on *China Youth Daily* on 23, 25, 27 and 30 November 1954.

– *Fei xiang Renmazuo* 飞向人马座 [Flying toward Sagittarius]. Beijing: Renmin wenxue chubanshe, 1979.

– "Hou ji" 后记 [Postscript]. In *Dayang shenchu* 大洋深处 [In the deep ocean], 159–61. Beijing: Renmin wenxue chubanshe, 1981.

– "Huoxing jianshe zhe Shang" 火星建设者 上 [The Mars Pioneers I]. *Chinese Youth* 22 (1957): 25–7.

– "Huoxing jianshe zhe Xia" 火星建设者 下 [The Mars Pioneers II]. *Chinese Youth* 23 (1957): 17–19.

– "Kexue wenyi zatan" 科学文艺杂谈 [A miscellany on literature and art about science]. In Huang, *Zuojia lun kexue wenyi*, 1:80–95.

– "Mingyun yezonghui" 命运夜总会 [Destiny nightclub]. In Zheng, *Zhanshen de houyi*, 17–86.

– "The Mirror Image of the Earth." In Wu and Murphy, *Science Fiction from China*, 125–33.

– "Qian yan" 前言 [Foreword]. In *Shayu zhencha bing* 鲨鱼侦察兵 [The shark scouts], 1–2. Beijing: Zhongguo shaonian ertong chubanshe, 1979.
– "Tantan kexue huanxiang xiaoshuo" 谈谈科学幻想小说 [On science fiction]. *Dushu yuebao* 读书月报 [Reading monthly] 3 (1956): 21–2.
– "Xingxing ying" 星星营 [Star Labour Camp]. In Zheng, *Zheng Wenguang xinzuo xuan*, 1–44.
– "Xu" 序 [Preface]. In Zheng, *Zhengwenguang xinzuo xuan*, 1–2.
– *Zhanshen de houyi* 战神的后裔 [Descendant of Mars]. Guangzhou: Huacheng chubanshe, 1984.
– *Zheng Wenguang xinzuo xuan* 郑文光新作选 [An anthology of Zheng Wenguang's recent works]. Changsha: Hunan shaoer chubanshe, 1981.
– *Zheng Wenguang zuopin xuan* 郑文光作品选 [An anthology of Zheng Wenguang]. Guangzhou: Guangdong renmin chubanshe, 1982.
– "Zhexuejia" 哲学家 [Philosopher]. In Zheng, *Zhanshen de houyi*, 1–16.
Zheng Wenguang and Gao Shiqi 高士其. "Kexue wenyi xuan xu" 科学文艺选序 [Preface to selected works of literature and art about science]. In Huang, *Zuojia lun kexue wenyi*, 1:124–32.
"Zhongguo diyiben manhua qikan shi Shanghai Poke" 中国第一本漫画期刊是《上海泼克》[The first Chinese cartoon magazine is *Shanghai Puck*]. *Zhongguo zhizui* 中国之最 [World records in China], 29 November 2012, https://www.do1do2.com/chinasmost/complement/6443-1.
Zhongguo zhongyang dangshi yanjiu shi 中共中央党史研究室, ed. "Zhongguo gongchandang dashi ji 1963" 中国共产党大事记 1963 [Chronology of major events of the Chinese Communist Party: 1963]. *Zhongguo gongchandang xinwen* 中国共产党新闻 [News about the Chinese Communist Party], http://cpc.people.com.cn/GB/64162/64164/4416060.html.
– "Zhongguo gongchandang dashi ji 1978" 中国共产党大事记 1978 [Chronology of major events of the Chinese Communist Party: 1978]. *Zhongguo gongchandang xinwen* [News about the Chinese Communist Party], http://cpc.people.com.cn/BIG5/64162/64164/4416109.html (accessed October 11, 2017).
Zhou Jun 周筠. "Yao kexue huanxiang, buyao diji quwei" 要科学幻想，不要低级趣味 [We want science fiction, but we do not want it in poor taste]. In Zhongguo qingnianbao, *Kepu xiaoyi*, 51–2.
Zhou Lin 周林. "Xin Zhongguo gaochou zhidu yanbian yu zuozhe diwei de bianhua" 新中国稿酬制度演变与作者地位的变化 [Fluctuations in remuneration for Chinese writers and changes in the status of writers in New China]. *Shaoguan xuebao* [Shaoguan journal] 23, no. 8 (2002): 122–7.

Index